Why We Dance

Why We Dance

A Philosophy of Bodily Becoming

Kimerer L. LaMothe

 COLUMBIA UNIVERSITY PRESS   *NEW YORK*

Columbia University Press
Publishers Since 1893
New York   Chichester, West Sussex
cup.columbia.edu
Copyright © 2015 Columbia University Press
All rights reserved

Library of Congress Cataloging-in-Publication Data

LaMothe, Kimerer L.
  Why we dance : a philosophy of bodily becoming / Kimerer L. LaMothe.
      pages   cm
  Includes bibliographical references and index.
    ISBN 978-0-231-17104-5 (cloth : alk. paper)—ISBN 978-0-231-17105-2 (pbk.)—
  ISBN 978-0-231-53888-6 (e-book)
    1. Dance—Philosophy.   2. Dance—Social aspects.   I. Title.

  GV1588.3.L36 2015
  793.301—dc23   2014034072

Columbia University Press books are printed on permanent and durable acid-free paper.
This book is printed on paper with recycled content.
Printed in the United States of America
c 10 9 8 7 6 5 4 3 2 1
p 10 9 8 7 6 5 4 3 2 1

COVER PHOTOS: Kimerer LaMothe and Geoffrey Gee
COVER DESIGN: Evan Gaffney

References to Webs ites (URLs) were accurate at the time of writing. Neither the author nor Columbia
University Press is responsible for URLs that may have expired or changed since the manuscript
was prepared.

published with a grant from

Figure Foundation

for the alphabet of dance

For Geoffrey

Though there are swamps and thick melancholy on earth, whoever has light feet runs even over mud and dances as on swept ice.

—FRIEDRICH NIETZSCHE, *THUS SPOKE ZARATHUSTRA*

Contents

Acknowledgments

We have a saying here at home that has proven true again and again: the farm will provide. Our family moved to this retired dairy operation eight years ago, as Geoffrey and I pursued our dream to move out to the country and create a center for arts and ideas. We bought ninety-six acres of glorious fields, trees, ponds, and a stream, as well as an 1840s farmhouse and a jumble of barns in various states of disarray. Yet whenever we need something, or need to fix something, we inevitably end up finding just the right piece or resource lurking in a corner we had not yet explored, whether board or baling twine, stovepipe or hay pile.

The saying holds true for this book as well. *The farm will provide.* As I come to the conclusion of the writing process, I realize that I could not have written it anywhere else. This corner of our green planet has consistently provided me with the experiences and opportunities that I have needed in order to learn how to make a case for dance as a vital art. Here I am regularly, repeatedly, moved to move by the movements of the natural world. Walking, running, and dancing; digging, sowing, weeding, mowing, and harvesting; and caring for animals of varied shapes and sizes, including human ones, I am daily impressed with the value and benefits of moving in ways that align our bodily becoming with the rhythms of earth in us and around us.

Life on a farm is not all rosy and romantic. It is riddled with sadness, frustration, and disappointment. Birds eat our corn seed. Foxes eat our hens.

Acknowledgments

Rabbits eat our strawberries. Deer eat our kale. A promising tomato harvest gets the blight. Squash beetles devastate our zucchini crop. A favorite cow dies as we gather around to help. The oxen break the new sled that my son has worked on making them for weeks. On the road that slithers by in front of our house, cars and trucks race at fifty miles an hour, killing cats and chickens. Our electricity flickers. Our computers crash. Our satellite stops working. We try. We fail. Sometimes we succeed. Sometimes we don't.

Nevertheless, and regardless of what happens, I am most able to make something out of whatever is given when I align my movements with life's creative, healing energies and dance along. As a result, I am incessantly grateful to *this land and this life*—with all its beauty, challenge, and generosity—for the inspiration it provides on an ongoing basis.

The cast of human creatures to whom I am indebted begins with the youngest, my fifth child, Leif, born in June 2009. The experiences of carrying him, birthing him, and watching him unfold to greet his world not only catalyzed ideas that appear in this work, they provided the structure and rhythm that made writing both impossible and necessary. For a while, when he was very young, all I could do was read, and that reading ended up providing me with a raft of new resources for thinking through the issues I knew I wanted to explore.

An opportunity to teach for Dr. Gay Lynch and her students in the LINES BFA program at Dominican University catalyzed my vision for the shape and scope of the work. A residency at St. Johnsbury Academy, teaching dance to the students of Marianne Hraibi, opened new perspectives for me on dance as knowledge. Speaking engagements at Syracuse University, Williams College, Columbia University, and Long Trail School helped push the project along. Ongoing conversations with many individuals helped tease forth perspectives on the work, including Bill Throop, Sharron Rose, and Erica Dankmeyer.

I am exceedingly grateful to readers who agreed to read the entire first draft and then offered both counsel and encouragement, especially longtime mentor and colleague, Mark C. Taylor, Colby Devitt, and my parents, Cynthia and Jack LaMothe, who read the manuscript aloud to one another while driving from Massachusetts to Florida. I am also grateful to Kathleen Skerrett, Gail Hamner, and Miranda Shaw for reading portions of the manuscript and spurring some critical redirecting.

Acknowledgments

Finally, I am ever grateful to my family—residents of the farm—for their ongoing presence in my life. Each one of my five children is an absolute blessing, enriching me beyond what I could imagine. Singly and together, they have an uncanny knack for prodding me along the path toward my dreams even as I help them find and live their own.

My life partner, Geoffrey, has read more drafts than anyone, and has consistently responded with blasts of optimism. So too his music continues to provide me with one of my primary inspirations. I have learned as much about dance from the experience of moving to—and being moved by—his piano playing as I have from anyone or anything else.

May the dance continue.

Why Dance?

One has to become what one is.

—MARTHA GRAHAM

I want to dance. I have always wanted to dance. Ever since I can remember wanting to do anything, I have reveled in the free feeling of moving through space—skipping and leaping, limbs lunging and reaching for an experience of joy that I know is waiting there just for me.

More often than not, I have felt this desire when I am in nature—atop a mountain, on a seashore, shaded by forest, or buffeted by fronds of a grassy field. Nature is movement—nature is moving—every twig, worm, rock, and cloud. The movement that nature is gathers my eyes, catches my ears, tickles my nose, and impresses my skin. All I smell and hear and see and touch evokes in me an impulse to *connect* with what is appearing—to take in, move with, and dissolve into. *I want to dance.* In the response of my spiraling cells, I know: I too am movement; movement is what I am. As I dance, regardless of whether I am feeling happy, sad, angry, or somewhere in between, my heart overflows in love for the life that moves in me, as me, through me—for the nature that I am.

Nevertheless, despite the clarity with which I know this truth, I have spent most of my life struggling to give myself permission to live it. In nearly every respect, my desire to study and practice dance has rammed into ideals fostered in me by society, family, and my own compulsive drive to succeed. For years I have wanted *and* not wanted to dance—ever convinced that there is something more worthwhile, more productive, and more meaningful that I should be doing with my time to help others, the earth, or myself. Dancing, it seems, I have nothing. I do nothing. I am nothing. *Why dance?*

Even those who practice dance assiduously often do not have an answer that reaches beyond personal preference: they do it because they like to do it. Those of us raised in the culture of the modern West are not generally taught how or why or that bodily movement matters. We most often dance "for fun" at a party, a family gathering, or perhaps in a class, convinced that our gyrating, whirling exploits are mere exercise or entertainment. As a result, when we dance, or watch others dance, we lack conceptual resources to appreciate what is occurring. Without such resources, we are unable to invest our ample minds in our experiences of dancing. When our dancing pleasure pales, we convince ourselves that we were right. Dancing is just for fun.

How could we know otherwise? How could I have known otherwise?

• • • • •

I am writing this book for the younger person I was when I first admitted to myself that, regardless of what anyone else said or thought or wanted for me, *I am a dancer.* It was not easy to admit. I was a junior in college, immersed in the study of political economics, intent on becoming an investment banker. I was too old for ballet. I had lost interest in Broadway. I had no mentors in dance, no teachers in dance, no technique of note, and no friends who danced. I knew I always *wanted* to dance, but I had no way to *think* about this shock of insight. What was I to do?

I am writing the book I wish I could have read then—a book with a vision of dance broad enough to match my ardor for it, and deep enough to back effective responses to the wide range of internal and external critics that writhed within me in response to this realization. I am writing a book that could have met me at the level of personal, practical experience while illuminating the significance of that experience in relation to rigorous philosophical, theological, and scientific discussions concerning the nature of human life.

While the vision of dance evoked in these pages is plump enough to nourish a young heart, it is one only an adult could conjure. It stems from the subsequent decades of my own intellectual and emotional wrestling with a seemingly endless parade of Western cultural habits and ideals that deny dance recognition as an artistic, intellectual, or religious endeavor. Yet this vision also expresses a jubilant affirmation of what this engagement has helped me to appreciate about dance as an integral, necessary part of human life, my own included. Dance, as an activity that animates every dimension of our bodily selves, is one whose secrets we discover slowly as we allow our dancing to guide us deep into the vortex of our endlessly creative bodily selves and back out again.

Over the years, through this work, I have come to believe that dance is a vital art. It is vital not only for the health and well-being of our physical selves. It is vital for the health and well-being of our emotional, intellectual, and spiritual selves; for our families, our communities, and our relationship with the earth in us and around us. It is vital for our *humanity*. Dance is so, I propose, because dancing exercises a fundamental sensory creativity whose nuance and range distinguishes humans from other living organisms. This creativity is one that finds expression in an ability to notice and recreate patterns of movement and so nurture mutually life-enabling relationships with whomever or whatever sustains our ongoing human living. For this reason, dancing, as the chapters to come will tell, is for humans a biological, ethical, spiritual, and ecological necessity.

In short, this vision of dance as a vital art is for those desperate to affirm their desire for dance—as I was—as well as for those who do not yet know they want it. It is for those who know they are dancers, and those who do not; those who study or practice dance and those who wish they had or could. It is for dancers and scholars, philosophers and theologians, as well as anyone else who needs or wants to know: Why study it? Why do it? Why care about it? *Why dance?*

• • • • •

What do I mean when I use the word *dance?* This book does not offer a comprehensive definition or philosophy of what dance, in essence, "is." It does not offer a history of the dancing that humans have done. Nor does it survey dance traditions from around the world extant today. Instead, *Why We Dance* offers a visionary account of what dance has the potential to become for us in the twenty-first century that is based on but not determined by what "it" has been. This vision is one that finds inspiration in the knowledge we are currently acquiring across disciplines about ourselves and our world, as well as in the ecological and health concerns with which we are at present occupied.[1] It is as much a vision *for* dance as a vision *of* dance, informed by equal parts empirical evidence, scholarly research, kinetic imagination, and personal experience.

As such, the three elements of this account work together to compose a formal yet flexible understanding that is designed to illuminate existing dance phenomena while catalyzing the creation of new ones. Here I briefly introduce the vocabulary I will be using to elaborate this account of dance in the chapters to come. As the argument of the book unfolds, the significance of these terms will further appear as the tenets comprising a dance-enabled, dance-friendly philosophy of bodily becoming.[2]

1. First, to dance is to *create and become patterns of sensation and response*. Dance is movement, bodily movement, and every bodily movement that happens appears as a *pattern* that unfolds in time and space. There is no dance without a pattern. Yet these patterns are neither static nor simply visual; they are rhythmic and figurative, in a word, kinetic. They exist only within the multidimensional sensory space of a bodily self as a potential to move. They appear only as "images" in the moment of mobilization.

So too, every movement pattern made by a bodily self involves both sensing and responding. Not only does every movement made register within as a sensation, it also provides the occasion for sensory experiences. Every movement animates and orients our sensory surfaces in varying degrees and directions. Further, this action of sensing is itself always already occurring in response to whatever is appearing to us based on the movements we are and have been making. Any kinetic image, intentional or not, repeated or unique, is thus a pattern of sensing and responding.

As we dance, however, we not only *create* movement patterns with our bodily selves, we *become* the patterns we create. As we animate patterns of sensation and response, these patterns lodge in our bodily selves as possibilities for further action. We remember them; they become who "we" are. Once these kinetic images exist in us, as us, we are able to sense and respond quickly, without thinking, along trajectories of movements they represent. Given the option, we are more likely to deploy these patterns in response to new circumstances rather than create new ones. We grow more graceful, responsive, and adept in ranges of motion we have rehearsed; more bound by habit and reflex. In a word: *the movements we make make us*.

To dance, then, at a most basic level, whether improvising in silence or disciplining oneself to a codified form, is to exercise this capacity of a human bodily self in *creating and becoming patterns of sensation and response*. It is to participate in what I call a *rhythm of bodily becoming*. Whether a dancer is practicing hip-hop or fox-trot, contact improvisation or folk dancing, he is making the movements that make him able to do what he can do and become who he has the potential to be.

2. To dance, second, is not only to create and become patterns of sensation and response. At some level humans are always already participating in this rhythm of bodily becoming. To dance is to do so in ways that *cultivate a sensory awareness* of our participation in it.

As we become new patterns of sensation and response, these movements gather in us not only as habit and ability but also as forms of emerging self-consciousness. The kinetic images we create and become influence what we can perceive and how we choose to respond to the world around us as well as to sensations arising within ourselves. As we create and become patterns of sensation and response, we begin to notice how we move, why we move, and, more basically, that we move. So too, we can begin to realize, at a sensory level, not only *that* but *how* the movements we make in a given moment are making us who we are.[3] As this sensory awareness of our movement making grows, we have within ourselves an instrument of discernment that is capable of guiding us to assess the value and benefits, the pain and pleasure, of making one movement rather than another.

Further, as we create and become movement patterns, we also become more aware of the fact that at any moment in time there are an infinite array of impulses to move that come to us along the trajectories of movements we have already made. We can and may grow a lived sense of how actively to invite impulses to move by attuning ourselves to the sensations occurring within us and around us. Our experience of our (selves as) bodily selves shifts.

This awareness is, again, *sensory*. It is not *conceptual*. It is not that, as we dance, we are increasingly able to *think* about our bodily selves as movement makers, at least not initially. Rather, this awareness hums within us as an ability to receive and follow through with impulses to move. It opens within us as a vulnerability to being moved by the movements we perceive. And, as we shall see, it forms within us as a sense of having or being a "self"—that is, one who dances.

To dance, then, is to cultivate this sensory awareness of ourselves as move-ment-in-the-making. To dance is to yield to this development as it happens in us and to us by virtue of the movements we are making. To dance, whether one is on a brightly lit stage in a modern dance performance or alone in the desert on a dark night, is to allow oneself to become a living stream of sen-sory, kinetic creativity—a continuous flow of erupting impulses—banked by the movement patterns one is making. This *experience shift*, while always pos-sible, is never inevitable.

3. Third, to dance is not only to exercise the rhythm of bodily becoming, nor even grow (into) a sensory awareness of it. To dance is *to participate con-sciously* in this rhythm of bodily becoming by using this sensory awareness as a *guide* in creating and becoming patterns of sensation and response that *realize* our potential to move. Said otherwise, to dance is not only to invite movement impulses, it is to play with the movements that appear so as to discern the best moves to make. To dance is to attend consciously to the sen-sations that our movements are making—of pain, pleasure, and possibility— and allow our bodily selves to find ways to move in response that align our health and well-being with the challenges of the moment.

Certainly, this dynamic happens spontaneously, without thinking, when the felt sense of pressure on a tendon prompts a knee to adjust or when the tight feeling of a hamstring stretch shifts us sideways to improve the release. At one level we humans are always already playing with movement possibili-ties and finding ways to move that align with our ability to do so. We are al-ways already creating and becoming patterns of sensation and response that represent a sensory awareness of how to move in movement-enabling ways.

Nevertheless, humans can also *practice* and *develop* this ability to play with our movement potential. The opportunity to do so arises when we apply our energies to creating and becoming specific movement patterns that appear to us (as a result of movements we have made). Whether we strive to imitate the kinetic images made by an accomplished elder, a flying eagle, or the raging wind, or clear a space and time to improvise movements specific to our bodily selves; whether we intentionally practice a set progression of move-ments or prepare to lose our sense of self in a communal ritual, we are *partici-pating consciously* in the *rhythms of bodily becoming*. We are engaging our *sen-sory awareness* as a guide to finding movements that ex-press and evolve our health and well-being. We are dancing.

· · · · ·

While the stakes and implications of this three-part account of dancing will appear as the following chapters put it to work, I offer three brief comments here.

First, admittedly, this visionary account solves some problems and raises others. Most notably, it recasts the binary oppositions that scholars frequently deploy to distinguish "dance" from "bodily movement," i.e., by asking whether the movement in question is intentional or not, functional or not, formal or not, expressive or not, rehearsed or not.[4] Dancing, in the vision offered here, is an *emergent phenomenon*. It emerges out of bodily movement as a form and expression of bodily movement that is also a sensory self-consciousness of that bodily movement. As such, dancing is inherently dynamic. In every moment dance is a continual coming-into-consciousness as well as a dissolving of consciousness. It is a becoming-form and a breaking-from-form. It is an expression of emotion that is also an occasion for discerning and feeling emotion. Dance engages a rhythm of bodily becoming that occurs regardless of intention, but can nevertheless give rise to intentions that exercise and deepen the experience of it. Dancing is bodily movement that, whether or not it accomplishes any practical task, always accomplishes the all-important task of exercising the medium through which humans live: their sensory, kinetic creativity.

Nevertheless, in embracing dance as an emergent phenomenon it may seem that this account runs the risk of implying that every bodily movement humans make is "dance." Does it? Yes and no. As I shall argue, there are good reasons for affirming that all humans are dancing, to some degree, from the moment of conception to the moment of death: we cannot not participate in the rhythms of bodily becoming. We cannot not be made by the movements we make. However, by describing dance as *emergent*, this account also makes it possible to ask questions about *how* the movements we are making are making us. It makes it possible to perceive and evaluate any patterns of bodily movement based on whether or not they encourage a conscious participation in the ongoing rhythms of bodily becoming. It thus enables us to acknowledge and examine the ways in which how we dance impacts—and is inseparable from—all aspects of human living.

Whether we are considering the performance of trained dancers, the rituals of an indigenous tribe, or our own ecstatic experiences, this account of dance enables us to identify movement patterns, discern the sensory education those movements provide, and evaluate what possibilities for human thinking, feeling, and acting are becoming real by way of those movements—especially in relation to the ongoing action of dancing itself.

In short, given this vision for dance, any movement or activity—whether sport or chore or ordinary action—*can* be dance. Any movement opportunity can offer a chance (1) to create and become our bodily selves, (2) shift our sensory experience, and (3) do so attentive to what we are creating and becoming. We can dance while folding laundry or while whirling in a waltz, while hiking up a mountain or circling an altar, while alone or with others. What I am calling "dance" happens when we consciously engage our sensory awareness as a guide to participating in the rhythm of bodily becoming.

At the same time, not every movement equally fulfills its potential as dance, not even every movement we might describe as "dance." Movements that are imposed upon our bodily selves (by us or others) without regard to the pain involved, movements that serve to deaden our sensory awareness, or movements that otherwise impede our ability to participate consciously in our own bodily becoming do not, by this account, realize their potential as dance. They represent moments in which we dance poorly—moments in which we are neglecting and narrowing our sensory creativity and thus undermining our ability to create and become ourselves.

When the three criteria listed previously are met, the dancing that happens—whether erupting from feelings of despair or carefully calibrated to a complicated musical score, whether rehearsed for years or invented in the moment, whether trance, performance, or play—grows in humans who do it (as well as those who bear witness to it) a knowledge that they cannot secure any other way. It is knowledge about how to create and become patterns of movement that *enable ongoing* participation in the rhythms of bodily becoming—that are, in other words, *life enabling*. It is a knowledge I call *ecokinetic*. It is knowledge, as we shall see, about how to move in ways that grow healthy bodily selves, establish loving connections, heal pain, resist forces of oppression, discrimination, corruption, and ecological destruction and, in all, cultivate mutually nurturing relationships with the earth in us and around us.

Dancing makes us human. It is an expression of life energy whose potential human beings evolved to exploit. Dancing is an enabling source of our human consciousness, compassion, and cooperative natures. It is the reason we can be born so helpless and why we take so long to mature. It lies at the root of our spiritual striving and its nearly infinite adaptability. This capacity to dance even explains why humans can train themselves to imagine that dancing is not vital to their ongoing existence, even though it is.

• • • • •

The time is ripe for this visionary account of dance as a vital art. It is possible now, as it has never been before, to appreciate the constitutive role that dancing has played to date in the evolution of human nature and culture. It is also more possible than ever to appreciate how dancing can help us advance our thinking and acting in relation to problems that concern us. The data, the tools, the interest, the inclination, and the need are all present.

For one, scholars and scientists continue to amass vast repositories of bones and fossils, artifacts and texts, from cultures around the world and throughout time, revealing ever more about the lineage of Homo sapiens, the emergence of human civilization, and the varied articulations of human culture. As this information accumulates, it is increasingly impossible to ignore the fact that dancing is a human universal, present in every known society from the earliest imprints of human living to its latest signs and wonders.[5]

In rock art from the Late Paleolithic found at the cave of the Trois Frères in France (18–12,000 BCE), we find an image of a human wearing a deer mask, with limbs posed.[6] In images of the earliest known ritual—the Eland Dance of the San people from South Africa—we find humans surrounding a young girl, dressed as eland, limbs arranged in particular shapes.[7] On material artifacts dating from the earliest agricultural civilizations, found in an arc ranging from the Near East and Egypt through Southern Europe, we find repeated, stylized dancing figures.[8] Examples of dance imagery continue into the present and do so among people who are actively moving their bodily selves. Greek vases to Hindu temples, Dante to Picasso, Slavic to Maori, folk dancing to classical ballet, disco to hip-hop, the wealth of visual and now video materials documenting endlessly creative practices of bodily movement is overwhelming and undeniable.

Meanwhile, at least since the 1990s, scholars in the humanities have demonstrated a marked interest in reviving and reconfiguring the materialist traditions of the Western philosophical canon so as to honor the bodily conditions of knowledge. Scholars in a range of fields are paying renewed attention to living bodies, social relations, disciplinary practices of power, and the performance of movement itself, keen on discerning the material mechanisms by which both meaning and matter are produced. In the midst of this activity, the study of dance and movement is thriving, with new branches of scholarship extending in anthropology, philosophy, performance studies, feminist theory, and the study of religion.

So too, in science and data-driven social science fields, researchers are developing elaborate mechanisms for mapping the mysteries of our neurological, biochemical, and kinetic bodily selves. We have tools for tracking and recording movement patterns at varying scales, cellular to systemic. Scholars and scientists are developing theories and methods of analysis capable of making sense of the resulting deluge of information. Here too it is increasingly impossible to deny the instrumental role that bodily movement plays in the development of a distinctively human self, capable of intersubjectivity, self-consciousness, and symbolic thinking. Traces of our dance heritage are as present in our bodily systems as they are in our cultural artifacts and traditions.

We are also finally beginning to realize that our survival as a species on this planet is at risk. We have been squandering, polluting, and otherwise destroying the ability of the earth to support human life and putting in jeopardy the ability of our bodily selves to support "us." The complex formed by industrial capitalism, digitization, consumerism, and globalization is transforming the earth, including our bodily selves, into an assortment of commodities. "Nature" as we once knew it, if we ever knew it, no longer exists.[9] Some already know and many are beginning to realize that, if we want to survive as a species, we must learn to *move* our bodily selves differently than we have been doing. As individuals and cultures, communities and nations, we need to move in ways that create mutually enabling relationships with the bodily self of the earth and our bodily selves of earth.[10]

For all of these reasons, the stage is set to welcome a visionary account of dance that enables us to acknowledge dancing's integral, enabling, and vital role in the past, present, and future existence of human beings.

• • • • •

Nevertheless, despite these favorable conditions, the challenge of introducing a visionary account of dance remains daunting. Making a case for dance as a vital art in the context of contemporary culture still faces nearly insurmountable obstacles in the realm of Western cultural ideals and values. Nearly every element in the account of dance I have offered bumps up against a limiting idea that is foundational to the thought-world in whose ongoing life I, as a philosopher, dancer, and scholar of religion, participate.

Specifically, the attempt to acknowledge dancing as essential for humanity—as my account does—pushes against an edifice of values built upon the idea that *matter is real*. It challenges what I call a materialist paradigm that sustains most theories and practices of contemporary art, science, religion, politics, and economics, permeating all levels and in all dimensions our relationships to our selves, others, and the natural and social worlds in which we live.[11] It is a "paradigm" that this book unmasks as a collection of *movement patterns*—ways of thinking, feeling, and acting—that reinforce (even if by refuting) the idea that a human mind, sufficiently trained, can analyze data about the material world gathered through the senses to arrive at true and certain knowledge about what is.[12] Mind over body.

This materialist paradigm dominates modern Western culture. It gained ascendance during the interval of time when "science" emerged alongside "religion" as an approach to knowing nature, and when many religions reformed their traditions to privilege models and methods of spirituality that identify the essence of human being as soul, spirit, or mind over and against an earthen, material body.[13] During this era, the meaning of "nature" changed. It dropped rank and became "matter," an object available for human analysis, consumption, and enterprise. God retreated to the highest heavens, and most dancing taking place in religious contexts lost favor.[14] The best way to know and understand matter, people came to believe, was via the scientific method; the best explanation of why matter is the way it is, they supposed, lay in theories of evolution; and the best way to know God or Truth was through His Word. In all spheres of life—scientific to religious, cosmic to familial—material bodies were called to submit to verbal, rational forms of authority.

This era was also one in which capitalism and its markets emerged as a preferred solution for organizing the means of production; when the locus of that production moved from household to factory; when women's roles were circumscribed within the family; when nation states took shape as arbiters of political power, and when colonial empires sought to impose their dualistic, verbal, often Christian cultures on the rest of the world, appropriating natural resources and devastating dance traditions as they went.

Of course, since the materialist paradigm's inception, and at every point of its application, there have been critics denouncing its assumptions, rejecting its political and aesthetic implications, and calling for an appreciation of the movement, the intelligence, the vital principle, or Spirit of what is—from Spinoza, Hegel, Kierkegaard, and Nietzsche to the early American modern dancers, ecofeminists, and "new materialists" today. To make a case for dance as a vital art, then, is to collaborate with these dissenting voices in an attempt to shift Western culture beyond its fixation on matter as a measure of the real.[15]

Given this reach and range of the materialist paradigm, any attempt to introduce a new account of dance must do more than call attention to dancing that has occurred, or to dances that already exist. Nor is it enough simply to roll out a new definition and assume that it will stick. Rather, in order to advance the cause of dance as a vital art, we need to dismantle the ideological structures of scientific materialism. We must re-myth the narratives of human nature and culture that remain dear to Western society—from the perspective of dance. We must challenge habitual perceptions of what is, what matters, who we are, and how we become—from the perspective of dance. And we must recreate our relationships with bodily others of all kinds, human and beyond, including our own selves. In short, we must find in the experience of dancing itself what American dance pioneer Ruth St. Denis once called the "seeds of a new order."[16] It is a personal act; a political act; even a theological act. Ultimately, it is an ecological act.

· · · · ·

In taking on this admittedly unwieldy task, this book adopts an original approach. It mobilizes the vision for dance I have described in this introduction to catalyze a critical reappraisal of the materialist paradigm at those moments that discourage attention to dance as a vital art. To this end, every chapter, from 1 to 7, spirals through a common set of critical and constructive moves performed in relation to primary strands of thinking and valuing that comprise the materialist paradigm. In this way, over the course of the book, an account of dancing as vital art emerges as a critical lever in a thoroughgoing revaluation of modern Western culture.

Specifically, every chapter revisits a foundational tenet of the materialist paradigm that has proven hostile or at least indifferent to the consideration of dance as a vital art. With the help of allies, I identify contradictions in this tenet that point toward a new idea—one that overcomes those contradictions by privileging *bodily movement* as the source and telos of human life.[17] I then demonstrate how this overcoming opens the way for conceiving dance as conscious participation in the act of creating and becoming life-enabling patterns of sensation and response.

In chapters 1 through 3 I lay the groundwork for arguments I will make in chapters 4 through 7 concerning dance as a vital art. Chapter 1 takes on the idea that matter is real; chapter 2 takes on the idea that matter evolves; chapter 3 takes on the idea that knowledge about matter that matters can be written down. After exposing the contradictions implicit in these claims, I explore the directions of thought these contradictions open—namely, the ideas that *movement* matters; that *movement* evolves, and that a *rhythm of bodily movement* is the primary and ultimate medium of human knowledge. Here I trace an emerging philosophy, capable of supporting a vision of dance as conscious participation in the rhythms of bodily becoming and a uniquely human expression of the ongoing evolution of life.

In chapters 4 through 7 I explore the implications of this movement-enabled perspective on dance for our understanding of what it means to be human. Each of these four chapters, following the set of moves common to the first three, engages a matter-based dance-hostile idea about human beings, reveals its shortcomings, and then casts a new narrative—one that shifts the locus of agency from matter (or mind) to bodily movement.

Specifically, I challenge the materialist ideas—all inclined against dancing—that we humans are minds living in bodies (chapter 4), individuals first who choose to enter into relationships (chapter 5), bodies whose diseases and injuries can be fixed (chapter 6), and creators of culture whose humanity consists in living over and against the natural world (chapter 7). These ideas, though criticized for centuries, continue to dominate Western culture and scholarship. Finding new points of leverage in a movement paradigm, I propose that dancing—as a conscious participation in rhythms of bodily becoming—is the activity humans evolved to do in order to *become* the bodily selves that we are, *connect* with other humans who sustain our life, *heal* ourselves and others, and cultivate mutually enabling relationships with the *earth* in us and around us. Together, these four chapters make the case for dance, respectively, as a biological, ethical, spiritual, and ecological necessity and thus a vital art.

Throughout the book, I not only write about dance; I use words to evoke the living experience of dancing on earth that funds my own writing.[18] Each chapter has an experiential frame that enacts the emergence of the ideas about dance found within the chapter. As such these experiential accounts are not merely personal; they are "exemplary."[19] By attending to concrete examples of singular moments in time, these accounts invite readers to move not only into new spaces of thinking but also into new spaces of sensing and respond-ing to the movement in and of their own bodily selves. In this way these pas-sages seek to catalyze the sensory reeducation that the project of overcoming a materialist paradigm requires, and highlight the particular kind of sensory education that dancing can provide.[20] I not only hold what I write account-able to the dancing I claim it represents, I do what I hope readers will as well: play with these ideas, put them to the test in practices of creative bodily move-ment, and find ways to move that enable the best becoming of their own rela-tional bodily selves. By the end, I hope that readers will have answers to the question "why dance" that propel them to experiment for themselves.

Of necessity, the argument in this book draws from a range of disciplines through which it quickly moves—including theoretical physics and neuro-science, evolutionary biology, anthropology, feminist theory, philosophy, and the study of religion. It knits a connective tissue among discourses that are often far apart, and so reveals the extent to which dance is a resource for recrafting the myths that form the philosophical and theological mesh of Western culture. As such, it may seem at every turn that more is needed. More explanation. More research. More substantiation. More engagement with referenced material. Yes. More is needed. Much more. Every chapter raises as many questions as it answers. Each could be its own book.

My hope is that *Why We Dance* will prove an energizing jolt, inspiring readers to move in new directions, conceive new projects, and advance the case for dance along its myriad branches. Many moving hearts, hands, and heads, of dancers, philosophers, theologians, scholars, and scientists of all stripes, will be needed to birth movement-oriented ways of knowing capable of affirming dancing as vital art.

In order to reach this rainbow of potential readers, I have kept the narra-tive as free of jargon as possible. For those who are interested in tracking sources and tracing ideas, I have provided ample notes. These notes serve as a gateway to a realm of scholarly and scientific projects whose findings shed light on the significance of dance for human life.

As much as I have tried to capture the evolution of my thinking, however, I often receive my best ideas while dancing. As I cross a threshold into a sensory awareness of movement making; ideas thread forward. When I try to map their origins and influences, I find a bewildering tangle. Once an idea occurs to me, I see it everywhere. Thus I am humbly aware that this book is a continuation of work that many before me—cited and not—have already begun.

· · · · ·

If movement is what matters, then we humans are essentially movement too. And if humans are movement, then we are—in every dimension of our bodily selves—a constant process of bodily becoming. Every movement that we make, every movement that we are impelled or compelled to make, consciously or not, participates in the making of who we are. And every movement that participates in the making of who we are also participates in the making of what is.

From this perspective, humans are who we are by virtue of how we participate in the rhythms of bodily becoming. We become who we are as we learn to move effectively and efficiently, consciously and creatively, in support of our own ongoing movement in human form.

Within such a paradigm, as we shall see, dancing appears as the kind of human movement that helps us learn how. Humans, as we dance, participate consciously in making the movements that make matter matter, reality real, and humans human.

Humans can learn to ignore the dancing we do. We can learn to restrict our sensory awareness to the barest minimum. We can repress our impulses to move, bind our kinetic imagination, and deny that our bodily selves have any role to play in determining who we are. We do so at our peril.

There is a dancer in each of us and a dance in everything we do. Our task at this moment in time is to find it, nurture it, and so let the dance continue.

1

To Dance Is to Matter

The principal defect of all materialism up to now—including that of Feuerbach—
is that the external object, reality, the sensible world, is grasped in the form of *an object or
an intuition*; but not as a *concrete human activity*, as *practice*, in a subjective way. That is
why the active aspect was developed by idealism, in opposition to materialism—but
only in an abstract way, since idealism naturally does not know real concrete activity as
such.

—KARL MARX, *THESES ON FEUERBACH*

. . . . .

If one considers . . . that a man's every action, not only his books, in some way becomes
the occasion for other actions, decisions, and thoughts; that everything which is happening is inextricably tied to everything which will happen; then one understands the
real *immortality*, that of movement: what once has moved others is like an insect in
amber, enclosed and immortalized in the general intertwining of all that exists.

—FRIEDRICH NIETZSCHE, *HUMAN ALL TOO HUMAN*

I begin as I always do—on the floor, on my back, knees pulled up to my chest,
palms wrapped around my shins. Breathing in, I sink my inner belly down,
push my ribs out, and then let go. Air escapes. Tension escapes. Patterns of
held energy escape. The buzzing of my brain comes into view. I am ready for
it to yield. There are other movements I want to make.

I pull another breath deep into my torso and let go. The rushing air sets off
a cascade of awakening sensory cells. New shapes of inner awareness appear.
A foot. A lung. A shoulder. My mind finds these forms fascinating and dives
down to take a closer look.

All of a sudden I feel the shift I have been waiting to feel. My awareness
drops over some internal edge and rushes along paths traced in time and space

by my physical form. I am no longer mired in mental muck. No longer circulating old thoughts. Consciousness floats and spreads through my bodily self. I become a field of waves where new impulses arise—new thoughts, feelings, shapes of action. I am this stream streaming through me.[1]

I want to be this current right now, for I want to think about movement—my movement, your movement, and the movement of all that is. I want to think about *life* from the perspective of movement while I myself am feeling it and then I want to write it down.

From years of practice, I already know that dancing makes a difference in who I am. It makes a difference in what I know, how I know, and what I care to know how to do. And it is these differences and their importance for human being that I want my writing to convey. I want to communicate participation in the experience shift that happens as I dance—the shift that enables me to perceive and know myself as essentially movement.[2] I want to dance chapter and book into being, rooting every word I write in this lived, living experience. How else will I know that what I write is true?

I press my heels toward the ceiling, root my tailbone into the ground, and exhale in search of an inner vibration that will hold these legs aloft. Today, in particular, I want to think anew about one of the primary obstacles in Western culture to acknowledging dance as a vital art: the idea that *matter is real*. It is an idea that is so common, so matter of fact, that we barely even register the degree to which we believe in it. Regardless of how sophisticated our philosophical or theological thinking, regardless of how abstract or intellectual our spiritual pursuits, most of us still operate minute to minute, day to day, week to week as if matter is real, objects exist, and my body is a thing I call mine.

It is an idea, I know, that the lived experience of dancing proves false, repeatedly. Every time I lie down on a dance studio floor and begin my practice in earnest, the materiality of my bodily self stands revealed as the movement that is making me.

So here I am here, rolling and reaching, scribbling and editing, moving to think, thinking as I move, and hoping that, if I can use my words to communicate participation in the action of dancing, then, you, even if you have never danced or never recall having danced, will remember what at some level I believe you already know: *movement matters*.

The Matter with Matter

What is *matter*? How and why is the idea of it an obstacle to acknowledging dance as vital art? In short, if we give matter priority as a cipher for "the real," then movement is forever its attribute, never itself a subject, and so is dance.

The materialist paradigm that has undergirded modern science, dominated scholarship, and infiltrated all aspects of cultural, social, and personal life for at least the past four hundred years revolves around the idea that matter exists.[3] According to this paradigm, matter is a substance. Matter has mass; it has being. Matter resists change.[4] Matter is atoms and their parts; electrons, protons, neutrons, and their orbital paths; chemical elements and their variations. Matter is solid, liquid, or gas. Matter appears in a variety of shapes or bodies. It appears in tools and toys, ferns and fir; in tigers and tortoises and the toes and tissues of our own human anatomy. Matter, we assume, forms the basis of what is. It is the ground beneath us, the currents enswirling us, and the bodies beside us.

Further, within this paradigm, "matter" is (what is) accessible to our senses and thus to our thinking minds. It abides by universal laws pertaining to bodies in motion and at rest. Matter can be seen and heard, smelled, tasted, and touched. It can be measured, isolated, taken apart, and put back together. It can be amputated, confiscated, polluted, and surgically altered. Matter is something we believe we can shape and bend and move according to our will, for it has no will of its own. Matter is something that our rational, objective minds can theoretically, practically, and perhaps eventually comprehend and control.[5] Matter, in short, *is* what is *real*.[6]

From a perspective for which matter is real, *movement* is something that happens to matter or something that matter does in response to another material thing.[7] Movement is what happens as some force, whether internal or external to it, propels matter to change coordinates of space and time. It moves, as Newton imagined, until some opposing materiality slows it down. This movement that matter makes, then, is largely incidental to the essence of what "it" is.[8] While the location of a raindrop, acorn, or ape may change, its substance does not. While its movements may express its reality, they do not alter *it*. "It" has an established identity. It is real. In effect, in a materialist paradigm, to claim that some material entity moves—or to claim to make it move—is to admit that *it* doesn't move. *It* stays the same. It simply is. We can move matter and it may move us, but either way, it remains what it is. So do we.

Of course, ever since Newton formulated the mechanical models within which matter functions as a cipher for the real, there have been those resisting both the reduction of matter to mere substance and the dualistic thinking that results from such an assertion. Critics affirm that matter is dynamic, in process, ever becoming.[9] Over the years and to this day, thinkers have argued that matter *appears* to be real due to some Presence or process that animates and engenders material forms. Many affirm a monistic worldview in which matter appears as a degree or manifestation or even an idea of the more active "mind." Yet in most of these accounts, even when reversed, displaced, and embraced, "matter" still stands as a cipher for "concrete reality"; its features still shape the most basic patterns of perception that characterize modern Western thinking, feeling, and acting.[10] "It" remains as what must be explained, or explained away.

Furthermore, this cultural belief in matter as real does not just underlie basic assumptions and perceptions concerning reality. It subtends the scientific and scholarly methods that researchers use to frame problems, gather information, and establish knowledge.[11] Presuming that matter is real, we outline procedures for acquiring knowledge about what *it* is, how *it* works, and how best to improve upon *it*. Insofar as matter is real, *it* can be subjected to experiments that yield converging results, providing us with a ground as stable as matter itself for establishing certain truth. We seek a truth that is constant and repeatable—a truth that will, like matter, remain what it is. Belief in the value and validity of such matter-based methods forms the bedrock on which modern science has been built, including quantum physics.[12]

Following this matter-paved path to knowledge, practitioners of scientific methods identify measurable things and chart relationships among them. We isolate variables that we can manage and define the terms of a causality that we can stage and repeat. We ask: what is the effect of x on y? We set up a control case. We induce the relationship to occur again and again, making adjustments until our results converge—because they must. Because we believe they will. Because matter is real. Because reality abides by laws that we can apprehend—even if we have no idea of what "it" is. So we crunch the data and make generalizations that we presume will hold for similar instances across time and space.

Within a materialist paradigm, in short, matter is a problem to explain that also offers the solutions we seek. We strive to explain its complexity and seeming intractability, its chaotic emergences and processes of becoming, by manipulating it (or what we think "it" is) in various ways to get desired or desirable, understandable results. Using uniform units, we gauge, clock, and predict what matter will do, and our measurements form the basis of the laws and principles whose veracity our experiments confirm. We measure movement as a way to arrest the matter we assume is making it.[13]

While rooted in the sciences, this materialist paradigm organizes the modern university, its fields, disciplines, theories, and methods as well. Abiding by its logic, scholars and scientists have made incredible advances in technology, medicine, and philosophy. We have gathered unprecedented amounts of information about processes and relationships occurring in nature and culture, in our bodily and spiritual selves. Nevertheless, the limitations of this paradigm are becoming increasingly clear. Chief among them, for the purposes of this book, is that this paradigm lacks the conceptual resources needed to appreciate one of the earliest, oldest, and most universal human actions—dancing—as a vital art.[14]

Within a materialist paradigm, a human body is a material entity, and dancing appears as a subset of possible movements that "it" can make in response to external or internal stimuli. This general understanding of dance is widespread and common sense. As further chapters reveal, dance scholars who draw on matter-based methods to study particular dance traditions and techniques tend to operate with the assumption that humans are creatures who can choose to move their "bodies" in symbolic patterns that warrant interpretation like any other cultural text. How a person dances may thus perform her culture or race, her gender or age, but it does not matter to her fundamental humanity. She is a human whether or not she dances.

When dancing does appear in contemporary scholarship, it most often does so, across the board from the sciences to the humanities, as a *metaphor* used to describe the movement of material bodies or material-like entities in relation to one another. Atoms, waves, and dead leaves dance. Ideas, words, principals of logic dance, as do subatomic particles and political parties engaged in conflict or diplomacy. *Dance* functions ubiquitously as a word whose meaning we assume we already know, referring to material realities we assume we understand. The term rarely appears in an index; it need not be explained.[15]

Even while we admit that movement is necessary for human life—a heart must beat, a diaphragm contract, neurons network, and blood vessels squeeze—we assume that dance is different, a matter of personal choice. Humans need not *dance* in order to exist. So mostly, in Western culture anyway, they don't, and, given our training in materialist models, scholars do not wonder why.

Movement That Matters

As I breathe and release, my bodily self heaves and shudders into life. Lines of limbs, surfaces of skin, a mesh of muscles and bones all ease into sensory view as an endless inner galaxy. Every spot of awareness is a point of light with the potential to emerge as one star in a constellation of attention, a pattern of action, a potential for coming alive.

I ease into a set of exercises that are as familiar as friends and pay attention to the range of changes that are occurring as my experience continues to shift. It is not just that "my body" is appearing to me as movement. "I" am not the same either. Our relationship is no longer the same. "I" no longer exist over and against "it." "I" melt into something more akin to a sensory awareness—a lived, felt experience of being a bodily self. I dissolve into a wide-open receptivity. Response-ability.

Suddenly, impulses to move arise in me, coursing through me, enticing me to move. Whether or not they were there before, I do not know. I did not feel them, but I do now. And not only do I feel them, I feel a desire to follow them. I do so before thinking about what I am doing, because that is who I am. I am no longer a material mass of flesh and blood, muscle and bone. I am movement expressing the energy of life.

As my sense of self melts into this sensory awareness of myself as movement, additional impressions come to mind—thoughts and feelings. I am aware that every movement I make is affecting me, effecting me. I feel how every movement tugs and stretches, grips and releases, opening me to some new range of responsivity. Every movement is its own sensory organ. Sure I have made some of these movements before and I will undoubtedly make them again, but neither me nor my movements are ever the same. Whoever I am now is the result of every movement I have made since the moment I was conceived. Every movement makes me anew, and sets the stage for its own overcoming.

I am dazzled again by the thought: *every movement matters*. Whether I am asleep or awake, conscious or not, every movement I make makes me who I am. *I am the movement that is making me.*

An impulse to stretch out through my toes pulls me long, and I ponder this phrase so familiar to me. I know that I can think this thought, and even write it down, but I also know that "it" is not just a thought. This idea is both a memory of a movement made and a potential for movement to be made. It dwells in me as a subtle murmur that at any moment could burst forth into a flourish of kinetic sound. It marks the experience shift that happens every time I dance and never the same way twice.

I am not sure how I first discovered this shift, or formed a thought around it, but I have not forgotten. The idea stuck as a reminder to dance again.

• • • • •

Despite its longevity and persistence, the materialist paradigm is breaking apart. The balance is tipping from matter to movement as the locus of the real, and, as it does, a movement perspective—a philosophy of bodily becoming—is emerging with the potential to appreciate dancing and what dancers know. In relation to dance, by way of dance, the materialist paradigm is overcoming itself.[16]

The seeds of such a paradigm shift are implicit in the scientific definition of matter noted earlier. If matter is that which "resists change," then "change" is the norm. Change is changing, and matter changes that change by resisting it. Matter exists as a variation of movement.[17]

This idea that movement is the defining character of matter is currently popping up across disciplines in research and scholarship that materialist methods are themselves yielding. In biology, psychology, and physics, in astronomy, philosophy, and phenomenology, the search for the smallest unit, the firmest ground, the most stable point around which, from which, and into which all bigger and smaller things flow has produced similar results. Across disciplines, practitioners have been finding that there is no such object on which to base their studies.[18] No atom. No individual. No self. No God. As small as our sensory extensions can probe, and as far out as they can reach, there are only probabilities, conditions of appearance, and the relationships within which things appear. There are fields and fluctuations, structures and systems, processes and potentials, waves and/of energy. There is, in other words, *movement*.

While the guiding assumption has been that this movement proves that some thing exists, many contemporary thinkers are venturing toward a conclusion that has been reached by shamans, mystics, dancers, and some others throughout time: movement is all there is. Before the beginning and after the end, all the way up and down, deep within us and all around us, movement is what is. Movement, complex and multisensory, is the medium of which all is made, within which every thing appears.[19]

For example, evidence of how the materialist paradigm is overcoming itself appears in the work of philosophers and theologians concerned with its pernicious political, cultural, and environmental effects. New materialists, affect theorists, process theologians, feminist theorists, and others are drawing from forgotten streams of the philosophical canon to evolve conceptions of materiality that grant matter a kind of agency or vitality or plurality. They do so, eager to kindle a new appreciation of human others, as well as of the more-than-human community.[20] In promoting this justice-oriented, ecological consciousness, a range of postmodern and post-postmodern philosophers are calling our attention to movements of becoming and relating, differing and deferring, as forces that constitute matter and subjectivity in relation to one another, allowing "us" to experience any "it" as real.[21] In many of these accounts matter exists as its own cause in relation to human will in ways that humans can neither control nor predict.[22] And dance often appears as a metaphor for this kind of animate materiality.[23]

Biologists, neuroscientists, and philosophers as well, are admitting that there is a fundamental problem with a materialist paradigm. The *idea* that matter is real cannot explain itself. It cannot explain how humans *know* that matter is real. It cannot explain how consciousness emerges out of material processes to reflect upon them.[24] Consciousness has no mass or substance that can be broken into analyzable pieces. Its movements are ferociously difficult to measure. Scientists can document the effects that a thought or sensation has on blood flow to certain areas of the brain, but have yet to catch the thought or explain why or how it emerges.

Until recently, in the effort to solve this problem, scientists have redoubled their commitment to materialist methods, treating the brain as a biological system. Such approaches focus on electrical and chemical activity in the brain—the firing and wiring of neural connections and the floods of hormones that help them along. Notably, however, some of the latest entries strive to overcome a matter/mind dualism by focusing on *movement* as the enabling condition of both. As one scientist argues, mind emerges from the constraints on movement that any material form represents. These "absential" influences force movement along paths of reflexivity.[25] Another scientist holds that a mind exists as the "internalization" of bodily movement. Here the need to make effective, efficient bodily movements is what pulls the brain and its "mindness state" into shape.[26] The purpose of a brain is to help us move.[27]

In these cultural moments, and others like them, the materialist paradigm is overcoming itself along the trajectories of its own development. Theorists are attending to the *movement* of matter as a way to advance our understanding of processes that can no longer be subsumed within a time-space grid. Whether seeking the Higgs Boson, charting the parameters of a black hole, mapping chemical markers of depression, or tracking the psychological implications of industrial capitalism, thinkers pursuing knowledge are privileging *movement* as a causative, indicative agent.[28]

Nevertheless, more work is needed in order to craft an alternative to a materialist paradigm. It is no longer enough to say that matter is movement, however dynamic, complex, and emergent. Such an assertion still gives primacy to matter as the site of the "real"—as that in relation to which any claim for an idea or Ideal, spirit or God, must defend itself.[29] Inevitably, dance remains a metaphor.[30]

Instead, once we are able to appreciate the range of ways in which matter moves, we are poised to make the leap that the experience of dancing regularly confirms for me: movement is the locus of the real. Movement is not only what matter expresses; movement is what matter exists to do. Movement is the source, medium, and telos of all matter—of life. *Movement matters.*[31]

Once again, to make this shift is not simply to grant primacy to movement over substance as the distinguishing character of matter. To make this shift is to assert that matter itself *is* movement. At the same time, matter is not simply movement. It is movement that emerges in the shape that it does as a result of other movements, resisting, yes, and also enabling, boosting, and redirecting. It is not just amorphous energy, but formed energy.[32] Again, it is not that matter exists as some thing that would move if not for resistance; but rather, matter would not appear at all if the movement that it expresses did not interact with other movements, crossing, canceling, funding, and fusing with itself. The form in which matter appears is relative to the kinds of resistance and change in play. Its shape is determined by the forces and currents of which it is composed and to which it conforms. Nor is its form simply relative in space; it is also relative in time. It resists the passage of time, at least for a while. Eventually, however, the movements that make matter yield to the movements whose resistance enabled them to be. A shape of matter gives way in patterns of dissolution specific to its own movement. Bones break. Glass shatters. Rivers flood. Tomatoes rot. Matter exists relative to a movement matrix from which it emerges and into which it disappears.

Yet, even when a shape of matter succeeds in remaining itself for a while it still does not simply resist movement. Any "thing" that "matters" exists as an opportunity for movement in another dimension—movement en masse—along trajectories its form represents. When some granularities of freedom close, others open. The cells that bond together as an organism move farther and faster together than they would on their own. The fallen branch hurtles downstream, pushing away plants, getting stuck on rocks, and changing the water's course. The boulder that breaks from a mountaintop smashes trees and bushes along its path. Matter that resists change at one scale (by remaining branch or boulder) exploits a potential to move at another. In fact, shapes of matter *create* movement opportunities—allowing them to come into reality as an expression of the movement of life.

In a movement paradigm, then, movement is the medium out of which matter is made. Movement is what matter represents, and what it exists to enable. While any material form represents a reduction in possible movement along some scale, it nevertheless promotes movement on another. Matter thus not only conceals movement; it reveals movement. Matter is an opportunity for movement to make more of itself.

A world in which movement matters is a world in which everything at every scale in every dimension exists as movement—as *patterns* of movement made, remembered, and recreated. These patterns are not visual. We cannot form them in our minds.[33] They are *kinetic*. They are accessible to us only as a multidimensional transformation of our sensory experience of time and space. They are accessible to us only through the sensory awareness of movement that we have cultivated in our lives. They represent potentials for moving in ways that grant us an appearance of a material reality when there isn't one.

A world in which movement matters is a world in which every body and bay, every cell and canyon, every sensation and thought, appears as a result of movements made, as an expression of movements being made, in anticipation of movements that could be made. Every apparent thing is what it is only as it exploits the potential for making movement that the movements around it and within it afford. From the perspective of a movement paradigm, matter is nothing more or less than a potential for making movement along the trajectories its form and dimension imply. "It" is what it is by virtue of the movement that it makes possible—even in the case of a human body.

Moving with Movement

I wind my legs in large arcs, to the left and to the right, uncurling like a sun-kissed fern and contracting again. Rolling to my side, I open and close as I learned to do before I was born, when I pressed my heels and fists against the walls of my mother's womb, using the resistance to grow muscles whose twitching fibers would sustain the weight of limbs balancing on earth.

As I open and twist again, a new vitality pulses through me. More impulses to move pop into my sensory awareness, feeling like an itch that longs for a scratch or a tickle seeking touch.

This leg is not (just) a thing! It is an urge to point and flex, bend and straighten, jump, skip and leap. This arm is not (merely) an object! It is a longing to reach and curl, swing and swat. This torso is not (simply) a congealed mass! It is a desire to explode in sheets of effort that ripple through my abdominal wall as I pull myself off the ground, together in a ball, and rocket upward. This brain is not a mass of neurons! It is a collection of kinetic images, ready to sense and respond, create and remember.

As I move, my experience of myself continues to shift. Every cell is storing and making. Every system processing and gathering. Every limb remembering and refining. Dancing, I am a spring ready to be sprung. A pod ready to burst. A bird about to take flight.

· · · · ·

What is *movement*?[34]

Movement is what I am doing, in the woods, across the fields, on my studio floor, as I move and breathe and breathe and move and participate in the becoming of my bodily self. It is what I am. It is who I am. Movement is what my senses do and what my feelings do to me. It is what happens to me and what I make happen through me. It is what arises in me, entrances me, and guides me as I give myself to it.

What is *movement*?

Movement is a word, a verbal noun, a part of speech that takes an action and resists it, creating a form we can handle as if it were a thing. But the moving that "movement" arrests or represents is not a thing. "It" is only in passing, in relationship to other movements, evident by virtue of differences in time and space.

Movement as a word is itself a *pattern* of movement. It appears as a word in the movement of a hand or eye across a page. It appears as an articulation of sound and script, an application of thought and attention. "It" is what it is only when read and received as a potential for moving our consciousness in new directions along trajectories of sensing and responding its patterns make possible.

What is *movement*?

Movement is what is and has always been. Movement is the universe. The all. The One. The Many. Quivering, rippling, folding; giving rise to a swell, an arc, a difference, a dance. Movement is creating, becoming, relating. Movement stirs in every story of how it all begins, whether that tale is religious or scientific, political or mythic. At the limits of human knowledge, there is no one nor thing that moves. There is breathing, blowing, spitting, laughing, weaving, or banging about. There is no mass, no entity, no being that exists prior to the moving that begins it all. There is only that which gives rise to some "thing." That which comes. Before. And after.

Movement is what is—appearing, erupting, becoming present and disappearing again—in and through every possible scale and scope of existence. Movement is the medium of life—its manner of existence. Regardless of obstacles—and even by way of them—movement always finds a way to continue.[35]

Movement is what cannot be separated into parts and remain what it is. Movement is energy, but not just energy. It is energy with a form that is not material. The patterns that are movement have no presence or constancy. They are *patterns of sensing and responding* where that *of* is critical. To sense is to move. To respond is to move. And any movement is both a sensing and a responding—a feeling and a feeling of a feeling—and not just in relation to itself.[36] There is no vacuum within which movement occurs—only a matrix of more movement. Any singular movement, as a result, is itself a sensing and responding to other movements, its particular "pattern" of becoming given in the moment of its unfolding. These patterns of sensation and response that movement makes do not appear as matter; they are what enable matter to appear as some thing. For any "thing" or "body" there are multiple movements, giving, receiving, receding.[37]

The pattern of sensation and response that any movement is is always a product, a process, and a potential—always past, present, and future—with an ever undetermined end. For movement is always becoming something other than it is, even as it always is. It appears only in relation to itself, by virtue of itself, as a function of what it is.

What is *movement*?

Movement is transformation. What moves is never the same. Every shape of movement is always productive, generative of its next shape.[38] Each movement occurs in a uniquely new space and time, opening up possibilities for further movement that have not yet existed. Every movement is itself a becoming whose rhythm is given by the patterns of sensation and response it is. With each pattern released, that rhythm skips a beat, marking a difference, whose specificity—though not in a determined or directive way—is given from the moment it made before. The patterns of potential that make some apparent thing what it is evolve with each release. Every thing that matters *is* enmeshed in a rhythm of bodily becoming.

What is *movement*?

Most important for this book is the acknowledgment that we as human bodies are. As members of the human species, "we" humans are not owners or inhabitants of material bodies. We *are* bodies, but not even. For the bodies that we are are not things. They/we are *movement*. In the curves and contours of our bodily selves, in every scale and dimension, we are patterns of movement—patterns of sensing and responding—that are always already making us able to think and feel and act at all.

Every aspect of our bodily selves exists to move, and to do so in ways that keep us moving as human bodily selves. The contractions of iris, small intestine, blood vessels, or heart; the wag of arms, legs, heads, and tongues; the torque of knee and ankle joints, big toe and hip, all exist to move and to enable further movements. It is not just that muscles move our passive bones or that firing neurons move our limbs. Every moment in the hardest and softest tissues of our bodily selves is moving so that we, as mind and muscle, can also move some more. Every move begets and is begotten by another—many others. We are *bodily selves*. We are *rhythms of bodily becoming*, ever creating and becoming patterns of sensation and response with every move we make.[39]

This idea of our bodily selves as movement is not easy to bring to mind. Trained as we are in materialist modes of being, a bodily self seems to us really to be a material thing: it looks and feels like an object existing in the world. When it moves, it does not (usually) fall apart. It remains what it is, fragile but firm, with heft and height. It stands as an entity occupying time and space that wants food and warrants control. I can stub my toe, cut my finger with a kitchen knife, or dash around in a thunderstorm. "My body" seems to exist as that thing to which "I" am attached. It persists. It can also be torn and ravaged, invaded and infected, or broken beyond repair, while "I" continue to think. The difference seems real. Like Descartes, I can even imagine that "it" does not exist.

Then again, it is almost too obvious to say that this sense of my body as a material thing depends on movements that that bodily self is making with and without "my" help.[40] A bodily self never sleeps. Without its constant ongoing rhythms, without its heartbeat pulse and metered breathing, without its neural crackling, "I" would not think or feel or act or sleep at all. Beyond these basic metabolic functions, however, movement is what enables me to think about "my body" as an "it." Only when "it" moves in relation to itself and other objects can "I" gather a sense of "it" as some thing. It is only as I hit hand against hand, scratch an itch, rub a muscle in my leg, or chew my food that I come to know my bodily self as that which resists change.[41] My sense of myself as "I" emerges in between movement-enabled perceptions of "it."

So too, this apparent stability actually precedes and enables the reception of movement impulses that would not otherwise exist. The ways in which a bodily self seems stubbornly stable represent enabling conditions for further movement. The knee that cannot bend sideways can leverage an explosive upward leap. The fist that cannot pass through a door can knock it ajar. The thumb that cannot bend backward can grip and hurl a rock or a stick. A bodily self is an infinite matrix of such movement patterns that exist as capacities to exploit resources and challenges, pains and pleasures, as catalysts and occasions for moving anew.

Moreover, the movement patterns that we humans are are not just those made and remembered by ourselves. We are an extensive choreography that extends far beyond our sensory reach. Our bodily selves are home to more microscopic living creatures than we have cells. Without swarms of bacteria that dwell only in our singular selves, we could not digest our food, metabolize its energy, prime our immune systems, or fight illness. So too, our bodily selves exist as members of social matrices whose reach extends to the edges of the earth. We are born and bred, raised and routed, moving in and among and because of the families, communities, cultures, and countries whose economic and political maneuverings sustain our own.

Nor is our movement repertoire bound by the time and space of our life span. The potentials for movement that we are represent movements made and remembered by myriad creatures since the beginning we assume began. The shape of our limbs has been perfected over millions of years by many other swimming, crawling, walking, and running creatures.[42] Our systems of ingestion and respiration, circulation and motivation have been tried and tested and evolved to exploit the potentials for large-body movement present in the flow of oxygen, nitrogen, and carbon; air, water, and earth; gravity, electricity, and electromagnetic forces.[43] We are, in every strength and skill we call "ours," equally amoeba, fish, amphibian, and mammal; we are potentials for moving in relation to other creatures and concrescences that have been recreated in us, as us, from a time far before we were born.[44] As a result, every movement we make, even when made consciously and intentionally, opens and forecloses trajectories of life that extend far beyond what we can know. Movements of ours that seem most basic to our survival—beating and breathing, consuming and digesting—not only work for us, but for others as well. Every move we make lets others live. Or not.

Electrical impulses contract a diaphragm, pulling air into lungs along a path charted by lobes and vessels and capillaries. Smaller puffs of air, diffusing into cells, find release in coordinated patterns of action—tilling, planting, weeding, harvesting—that cross the paths of vegetable, animal, and mineral. Carbon dioxide exhaling feeds the plants and trees whose leaves, roots, stems, and seeds feed other animals who all feed us.

Movements of a hand heading toward a mouth pull fruits sprung from the ground into an undulating tube that is neither in nor out but exists as a possibility of moving through. Jaws chomp and saliva oozes, bacteria ingest and enzymes dissolve, until plant pieces mashed so small squeeze into cells where they burn as energy that throttles thighs up a hill, clears a building site, or drives a well-digging shovel into the earth.

In short, humans are bodily selves for whom the movements we are making—that are making us—are not properly "ours," but rather enabled and supported by the movements of others moving around us, within us, passing through us, and preexisting us. Any movement we make that makes us expresses our interdependence with an infinite, eternal web of creatures and elements without which it would not occur.

Finally, as a choreography of movement patterns, our bodily selves are not only not properly ours, they are inherently creative. This creativity is not about our ability to paint pictures or design mosques. It is a question of every human being's basic sensory relationship to what is.[45] In every moment the movements we make in relation to what is bring "it" to life as what it is for us. We humans, based on how we move, participate in the creation not only of poems or plows, nor even of our own bodily selves. As we move, we participate in the cocreation of the reality in which we live.

Take our five external senses as an example. Every sense organ exists as a capacity to move in a certain pattern that is vulnerable to being moved by patterns of movement occurring within a certain range or medium.[46] To sense some thing is to register a change in an ongoing pattern of movement. Eyes scan, cilia wave, hairs vibrate, and that which resists these movements gets noticed. A hand will not feel a table unless the table moves against it, interrupting the movements it is always already making. What moves the movement of our sensory selves is what appears to us to (or as) matter.

Yet, the movement patterns that our senses are are not simply given. The movement of our senses is enabled by the movements of bodily selves that support those senses in moving and being moved. Our eyes and ears rely on the swivel of our head for orientation. Our skin, nose, and taste buds depend on our ability to move them close to whatever has the potential to move us. So too, each sensory capacity—sight, hearing, smell, taste, touch—represents a configuration of movement possibilities brought into being by the matrix of movements in which a person is conceived, born, and educated; aerated, warmed, fed, and encouraged (or not) to participate in the rhythms of her own becoming.

Further, even though human bodily senses may seem to share a common human physiological structure, that regularity is not a function of matter. It is not a function of a reproductive process in which genes are passed on and realized. A nose that looks and functions like a nose does so because of movements made along trajectories of possibility that allow it to develop as it has: the movements of embryo, air, and odor; of mucous, cilia, electric sparks, and neural axons; of place and time and of the nose itself. All these movements— and more—combine in a complex choreography that allows a nose to be what it is: a potential for being moved by the movement of an airborne scent.

Given this thoroughgoing presence of movement, what we perceive is never simply a function of material relationships. There is no material "thing" anywhere to perceive and there is no bodily "thing" to which "it" exists in relationship. What appears to us always already expresses patterns of interactive sensing and responding—a configuration of movement over time that gives rise to a unique pattern of perception. These "patterns," again, are not visual; they are kinetic. They exist as a *mobilization* of sensory awareness—as coordinated pattern of moving into the world, being moved by whatever one's movements enable, moving in relation to what appears, and in the process, becoming "one" who has moved and been moved in this way.

Our senses, then, as movement-generating patterns of movement, are far from doorways conveying external information to an internal processing center. Our capacity for sensing is not determined in advance by nature or nurture. Our bodily selves are not created once and for all. As sensory selves we are *rhythms of bodily becoming*, ever engaged in an entangled development that exceeds our bodily selves and ends only when we die. Asleep or awake, conscious or not, enrapt in a project or bored out of our wits, *we are creating and becoming patterns of sensation and response* that dwell within us as guides to further movements—further perceptions and responses, thoughts, feelings, and actions—we can/not make. With every movement we make, at every level, in a constant unending rhythm, we create and become ourselves.

At the same time, this inherent bodily creativity present in our capacity for sensory perception is not only restricted to the shape and form of our bodily selves in their immediate relationship to their surroundings. What we create in and through the movement of our sensory selves is reality itself—the reality that is real for us. The matter we perceive as real is fluid or emergent by virtue of our participation in it. The implication is not that there is "no reality" or that what we perceive is an "illusion." Rather, the point is that we perceive matter as real because we are moving in ways that enable it to be so for us.[47] What seems still and stable to us, even infinite in duration, *is* still and stable—but only relative to the movement of our sensory selves. The foot I place on the ground will feel resistance. That resistance is real. That reality is not, however, a function of matter as a constant, inert substance. That reality is a function of movement—its movement, my movement, past, present, and potential, and the movements of the universe moving in relation to one another.[48]

We, as moving bodily selves, make matter what it is for us. "It" will not exist as it does without our reaching, grasping, registering of it. We perceive only that by which we are capable of being moved. The movements we make at all levels determine what can and does appear to as real—as concrete or ideal, material or abstract. Otherwise, it does not exist for us. "It" is simply part of the infinite flux, as am "I."[49]

When movements around us or in us are too small or too big to effect the movements of our seeing, hearing, smelling, tasting, or touching, we assume that there is nothing there—no things, nothing that matters. Just to be sure, we create machines to replicate our senses at smaller and larger scales so as to extend their reach. To our extended senses, other forms of "matter" appear, as they will always do, when our senses move and are moved. But, even extended to an infinite degree, our senses remain *our* senses, enabled and limited by the unique patterns of movement potential that they are.

In sum, the movements that make matter real are not just those operating at quantum, celestial, interpersonal, economic, or political levels. The movements that make matter real are operating in the specific sensory movements of a singular human bodily self, without being properly ours and, much of the time, without our conscious awareness at all.[50] Even so, with some effort and attention, human beings can learn to participate consciously in the rhythm of bodily becoming that every moment of our individual lives expresses. As seen in chapters to come, we can train ourselves to notice impulses arising within us that respond to the pain and pleasure we experience more and more precisely, thereby cultivating a source of wisdom that exists only in the rhythms of bodily movement making that we are.

Movement never lies.[51] Nor does it tell the truth. Our senses are never wrong. Nor are they ever right. To claim either would be to assert that there is some real material thing out there against which those sensations may be judged. There are no such things. There are no such bodies. What we imagine is "there" are the kinds of movement patterns by which our own movement patterns—both embodied and learned—are capable of being moved.

Moving Toward Dance

If we consider movement as the source, medium, and telos of all matter and reality, including our human bodily selves, much changes, specifically, our sense and experience of what it means to dance as well as our approach to studying it.

In a world where movement matters, nothing is constant, and even change changes; truth evolves right along with everything else, including the truth of what dance is and does. Whatever can continue, by whatever means it can continue, will, including the shape and form and meaning of *dance*. We can never know what dance definitively is. There is no "there" there. New shapes and potentials of dance are being born every moment, with the potential to revalue our sense of what dancing is. As a result, we can only participate as consciously as possible in the evolution of this idea, this practice, moving along the trajectories of possibility that open out of our current cultural moment and our current patterns of thinking, feeling, and acting.

So too, in a world where movement matters, any schema or method of study that attempts to isolate one segment of movement from the rest—including and especially dancing—will fail. Any technique or technology that assumes that a given process of life is constant will find itself quickly surpassed. The very nexus of relations within which a tool is effective will evolve in response to its use, even with our best sciences. As such, any vision of dancing we care to hymn must appear fully contextualized in our sense of what it means to be human, to be an earthling.

Furthermore, in a world where movement matters, there is no seemingly material thing whose movement—whether impelled from within or without, across or through—does not make it what it is on an ongoing basis, including dance. What appears to me as dance, as a technique or meaning or reason for being, does not do so because "it" is "there." It appears to me because of the dance forms I have studied—modern and ballet, Graham and Duncan, Haitian and Indian, yoga and improvisation; because of the dancing I have experienced in rituals and when performing; because of the dances I have created, formally and in the moment, as well as the thoughts about dance I have read and pondered. As I write about dance and as I practice dance the potential range of what "it" can be for me and in the world changes.

Thus, in a world where movement matters, the path to making a case for dance as a vital art must proceed *indirectly*, as I am doing, through a reconsideration of our most basic assumptions about who we humans are. To take this path is to unearth the resistance to acknowledging dance as a vital art in places where we do not even notice that it exists, including and especially in our most intimate relationship with our bodily selves. For the materialist paradigm does not just exist in the realm of ideas. Or rather, it exists in the realm of ideas because it persists in and through the movements of our bodily selves. The movements that matter to how we perceive and value dance are bodily movements we make every day as we sense and respond to our own perceptions of pleasure and pain and as we relate to ourselves, to other people, and to the natural, social, and cultural worlds in which we live.[52]

Chapters to come retell the stories of evolution and knowledge, of birthing, connecting, healing, and grounding from the perspective of bodily becoming. In so doing, these chapters reeducate our sensory selves to the bodily movements we are making—consciously or not, willingly or not, freely or under duress—within a materialist paradigm. They guide us to examine how these movements are giving rise to others that promise to overcome materialist models. I ask: what is becoming possible in ourselves, in our relationships, and in the world?[53] What capacities for understanding and practicing dance itself are we creating? Through this revaluation of our movement making, *dance* will appear as the best description for a kind of bodily movement that is vital to our human future in a range of identifiable ways—biological, ethical, spiritual, and ecological.

Humans dance to exercise a fundamental kinetic creativity that we carry with us in every moment of our lives. Humans dance because we are primed to feel the pleasure of doing so as a guide to our best becoming as persons living on this planet. The techniques and traditions of dance that persist are expressions of this kinetic creativity; they are patterns of movement that humans have created and become so as to help awaken the dance in themselves for the benefit of everything they do.

· · · · ·

Movement is everywhere. It is what we know and how we learn. It is how we sense and how we respond. It is what we do without thinking and what we do when we are thinking. It is the source of who we are and the agent of who we are becoming.

We are making movements and we are registering movements. And in the relationship between how we move and what we register we find all the information, all the material that we ever have for knowing, thinking, feeling, or doing anything.

We are pattern perceivers, pattern creators, and pattern performers, but not because we are driven by a need to control, master, and understand matter. We are so because we exist to move with greater facility and precision. Because we are rhythms of bodily becoming, participating in a kinetic creativity that exceeds us and sustains us.

Because we are, first and foremost, dancers.

· · · · ·

I rock back and forth along my spine, until the momentum carries me onto the soles of my feet. Reaching forward, fingers to earth, I touch gently, send my hips to the sky, and breathe my weight down into the ground. I roll slowly upward, knees bent, head hanging, until I come to a stand. My head is last to arrive.

I am no longer the same. I have made and become a whole sequence of new movement patterns that have come alive in me. As I sink my feet into the floor, the earth holds me up, granting me the resistance I need to unfold, to roll up, to reach for the stars. Beginning with my fingertips, I roll back down to the floor, imagining myself as a cascading waterfall, a curling beetle, an avalanche.[54]

As energy flows through my moving bodily self, so do ideas. Among them is this. *If I were doing something else, I wouldn't be thinking these thoughts. These thoughts I am thinking bear some relationship to what I am doing; they express the sensory awareness I am cultivating. It is not that I am just thinking about danc-ing. I am not. I am also thinking about how to be more patient with my son than I was this morning. I am considering the plan for my next blog post. I am remember-ing a friend who could use a supportive message. I am writing this chapter. Still, there is a difference. These thoughts are dance enabled.*

It happens every time. As I dance, my breathing opens me up to feel what I am feeling. Issues that matter to me come alive in me. They become real for me, compelling me to move in response. I move with them, and, as I do, my movement opens up new perspectives on them—perspectives enabled by the care and attention I am paying to my bodily self. Voices of judgment yield to voices of affirmation and encouragement. I find degrees of freedom I hadn't before. I participate in a flow of conceptual, kinetic shapes that seems endless and endlessly creative, responsive in the moment and for the moment through me. I have no idea how or why it continues, but it does.

When I move in these ways, what I feel more strongly than any pain is joy. The joy of being alive. The joy at being this moving plane where movement moves. It is not an intellectual idea. There is no argument that makes it so. It is not mediated to me by a higher authority. It is what happens when the move-ments I make are movements that align with the movement-making potential remembered in the form of my human body. I am in touch with the freedom and power of a bodily self. Dancing, "I" yield to an imagination far greater than my own that wants nothing more than to move me, move through me, along the trajectories of constraint and possibility that my particular human form allows.

As I wind up my session, my bodily self is humming. Thoughts stir and settle. I feel gratitude and love. I feel a desire to live in this outwardly moving inward space regardless of where I am or what I'm doing. With whomever I am interacting, I want to think and feel and move in ways that express this sense of being human. I want to make this love real, in all moments, as the truth of what is and who I am.

Dancing, I know: my bodily self exists to move. It is why I matter.

2

To Dance Is to Evolve

The dance of the future will be a new movement, a consequence of the entire evolution which mankind has passed through.

—ISADORA DUNCAN, *ART OF THE DANCE*

. . . . .

Evolution . . . a wheeling motion in dance.

—*AMERICAN HERITAGE DICTIONARY*

I need to walk. Alone. On the land. I can feel it.

For the past few days I have spent my movement time running along the road. Often before a busy day, striding along a hard, straight, narrow band of tar helps me organize my thoughts, calm my fears, and prepare for the challenges to come. I breathe hard. I sweat. I relax.

In between running days I have been dancing in my studio, which, at the moment, feels too small. While usually good for helping me focus on the small spans of sensation that strong movements require, today the walls and ceiling feel too confined, too confining. I need to get out. I need to uncurl myself in the infinite softness of meadows and trees and open skies. To unwind in air that pulses with the rhythms of living things. I need, most of all, to get out of my mind. It is scrambled with anxiety, always surrounding dance. I want to do more of it, but how? What am I supposed to be doing? There are issues to ponder while circling the pond.

I say good-bye to my family and head out from the house. I will meet them all in an hour at the wood's edge where we are planning to harvest firewood from fallen trees. I start upward, past the withered, snow-strewn garden with its bent and broken stalks. I turn right, as I often do, and hug the top of the pasture we made for our quarter horse, Marvin, which he refuses to inhabit. He prefers the pasture that connects him with his sun-filled stall, his grain and water buckets, his view. He wants to feel at home. Me too.

As I prepare for my usual 180 degree turn to backtrack up the hill, an invisible pulse pulls me sideways. *Come this way!* Why?! I ignore the sensation and take a few steps. The pull persists. I give in and reverse my steps. Why not? I am on my way to a new place.

I cross our property line onto a neighbor's hillside and begin ascending steeply. I notice that I am not noticing anything. It is amazing that I even was able to feel that pull.

I breathe down into the earth, surrendering to a fate woven through my genes. The ground crunches beneath my feet. A cold breeze sweeps my cheeks. Bright sunshine closes my eyes. I am so wrapped in the stress of my own yearning. I need to get out. I breathe deeply into my chest and send the oxygen down my revving thighs and through my feet into the earth. As I mount, toe after toe imprints itself on the dirt.

Suddenly, a flare of feeling lights my sensory self. I see something. It is not much, but I am relieved to have an experience of being moved. Paths appear before me, stretching side to side across the hill. I cross one. Five feet later, I find another, rimming the headwall. Ten feet later, I cross another. I see scat and tracks—deer, fox, rabbit, mouse. And me. We are all walking this face of the earth, all picking through the briars, all looking for a way through.

Yet I am the only animal who is striding straight up the hill, perpendicular to the lines of elevation. Only I, the human, feel the need to force my way up against gravity, against the shape of the mountain, against the muscles in my legs, against the stress-mortared walls ringing my heart. I am blazing my own trail. I love it.

My chest softens. The pressures ease—the pressure of wanting to know, wanting to succeed, wanting to support my five beautiful children, wanting to nurture the art of my beloved spouse, wanting myself. I am increasingly vulnerable to being impressed by the world through which I walk. A dusting of grounded snow mirrors the swirling of clouds in the sky. Mostly brown, mostly blue, both flecked with white, below and above, with me in the middle. I swim in this space between. Moving through it, I am moved by it. And I know: there is no other way to be . . . here.

A wisp of pure desire wafts through my awareness. *I want to dance.*
I smile and keep walking. I am.

Evolving Views

In science and beyond, when mapping the material phenomena of nature, whether human, herbal, fungal, or otherwise, scholars consistently rely on theories of *evolution* variously understood to provide them with a conceptual paradigm. At least since Charles Darwin published *The Origin of Species*, "evolution" has served as the best scientific explanation of why matter is what it is and why it has taken shape in the way it has. What is, according to evolutionary theories, has evolved. "It" has evolved into its current materiality through a process of natural selection in which those traits that allow it to survive and reproduce define it as what it is. For researchers in pursuit of knowledge, whether social, psychological, or scientific, the idea of evolution plots questions, organizes data, and frames the terms of subsequent debates. It ranks as the primary alternative in Western culture to the Jewish and Christian idea that God said "Let there be light" to create it all.

So too, theories of evolution are not only called upon to explain why matter is what it is, their use most often perpetuates and reinforces a materialist worldview. Typically understood, theories of evolution *presume* that matter is real and that matter is what evolves. Scientists and scholars plot the course of evolution in terms of entities—whether individual, species, colony, population, or gene—that resist change unless forced to change by the challenges and opportunities of their environments.[1] Material units are the coin of evolutionary theory.[2]

Moreover, the idea that matter is that which resists change finds expression in the notion, central to evolutionary theories, that material entities survive in order to *reproduce themselves*. Discernible units of matter, in this view, are essentially and fundamentally selfish.[3] They exist to make more of them. They act, it follows, in ways that replicate their current material state—or at least, in ways that ensure the enduring legacy of their genetic matter. Either way, it is *matter* and its reproduction that must be explained. Even sexual selection, while encouraging diversity within the gene pool, is described as a strategy for finding mates that maximizes the chances that the species will remain more or less the same.

Further, once it is assumed that matter exists to reproduce itself, evolutionary models surmise that differences that emerge in the process of reproduction do so as a result of *mistakes*. These differences are random genetic *mutations* in the replicating process. Scientists assume that such errors are inevitable because the process is material. There is no intelligence involved to ensure correct outcomes.[4] Evolution cannot plan forward. It cannot perceive need and respond. When a random error proves helpful to a given organism in exploiting available resources, then evolutionary theories predict that those organisms will do what they would ever always do and reproduce their new selves. In doing so, they will be more likely than others to survive.

Suspended as it is by this net of assumptions, much research into biological forms pivots on issues of reproductive fitness. Scientists identify a particular scale and shape of matter and ask: how does this limb or organ, tooth or nail, membrane or mitochondria, leaf shape or root system improve the ability of the material entity to which it belongs to reproduce itself? How does this material configuration aid an organism in finding food, mixing seed, escaping predators, and spawning and protecting able young?

In pursuit of these questions, researchers evoke the scientific method described in chapter 1. They isolate the material item under scrutiny from its context. They analyze its physiology, its uses, and its DNA. They identify a relationship between it and some prey, predator, or plant in the environment and look for evidence of a resulting reproductive advantage. They test their hypotheses by devising ways to restage that relationship, holding other variables constant, until results converge.

What do researchers find? They find knowledge that falls into patterns that their questions predict. Scientists debate whether a material node evolved (i.e., was found useful) for a precise purpose, or whether it was appropriated for that use after evolving for something else.[5] They argue over whether a given unit of matter acts selfishly (as one would expect given the definition of matter) or altruistically (which usually resolves to selfishness on a larger scale, "the group").[6] They argue whether evolution occurred gradually (by accident) or in punctuated bursts (by accident).[7] The terms and findings of these debates, as interesting, far-reaching, and even contradictory as they are, reinforce the beliefs that matter is real, that matter exists to reproduce itself, and that matter evolves by random mutations in order to do so more effectively given the circumstances.

In buttressing these beliefs, theories of evolution also reinforce perspectives on *bodily movement* that accompany a matter-based paradigm. Movement is the function of a material form that an organism evolves via genetic mutations in order to reproduce itself. The speed spurt of a cheetah, the long leap of a gazelle, the wiggle of a worm, or the turning of a flower to the sun all represent physical characteristics that enhance the organism's ability to find food and support its seed. This movement, in this view, is not itself agential. If the bear grows stronger or the bird more agile, the initiating cause is random changes in the material substance of its bodily self. It is these material features—able as they are to produce movement—that remain the focus and medium of evolution. As matter evolves, new movements become possible. But, in the end, it is matter and not movement that evolves.

Given this implication for bodily movement, the idea that matter evolves, like the idea that matter is real, proves an obstacle when it comes to considering dance as a vital human art. Insofar as dance is bodily movement, it appears in an evolutionary framework as something that a material human body does. The questions scholars ask fall into categories noted above. Did humans evolve to dance, or is dancing a manifestation of material characteristics that evolved for other purposes? What are the physical characteristics that make humans able to dance? Does dancing enhance survival and reproductive fitness and, if so, how? Does it enable humans better to secure food, shelter, mates, or protection for their young? Did it emerge gradually or in a sudden leap?

In pursuing these questions about dancing, researchers tend to rely on material artifacts for evidence identifying the earliest form of human dancing: community dancing.[8] Comparing these artifacts with the oldest extant traditions of dancing in existing hunter-gatherer populations, scholars in dance, religion, and anthropology look for measurable materialities to isolate, relate, and recreate. Most often, scholars focus on the prolonged rhythmic repetition of bodily movements such as stepping and stamping or spinning, hopping, jumping, and clapping. Such dancing, many agree, induces chemical changes associated with pleasure that are so strong as to promote feelings of euphoria, alter human consciousness, and even induce trance.[9] According to what contemporary machines can measure, dancing triggers responses in the parasympathetic nervous system, thereby releasing the restorative powers of a bodily self.[10]

These observations lead researchers to conclude that humans did evolve the capacity to move in time together—that is, to dance. The material effects it generates—and the pleasures they afford—are too pronounced to ignore. But the question remains why did humans evolve (as) this physiological capacity to be moved by movement?

An evolutionary framework, as commonly invoked, tilts responses toward group survival. Of the reasons offered, most are pegged to the communal function of feeling pleasure together with other humans.[11] Sensations of joy felt at the same time, in the same space, are contagious. They amplify one another. This enhanced joy creates emotional bonds between members. People come to rely on one another to help them access these pleasurable states and so come to appreciate one another as enabling their well-being. This sense of mutual need, it is thought, exerts a cohesive force in group activities, smoothing the way for cooperative ventures in distinctively human projects from hunting to cooking to caregiving to pair-bonding to ritual performance and intertribal warfare.[12]

A matter-based evolutionary approach to dancing, then, interprets dancing as a communal activity that promotes collective action among humans who, as material entities, would otherwise privilege their own interests above those of the group.[13] Dancing, by expanding our sense of self rhythmically, viscerally, to include persons and forces larger than ourselves, provides us with an evolutionary advantage. This advantage, scholars conclude, must have been strong enough that it served as a node of natural selection. Humans evolved the genetic, neural, cognitive, physiological apparatus they needed in order to dance often and dance well.[14] And in this engineering of social relations, dancing laid the genetic, neurological, cognitive ground for later developments in language, religion, ethics, law, and science.[15]

While this account of dance provides a robust defense of dancing when evoked in discussions of early human history, it is less able to defend the ongoing practice of dancing as human civilization takes hold. These answers for why humans dance affix that dancing to a function that can and eventually will be served by other cultural means that humans go on to create. Human beings evolve into material makers of material artifacts. They evolve the neural and muscular facility to manipulate symbols, invent languages, and devise implements of writing for recording those languages. As a result, scholars conclude, dance as communal adhesive is no longer needed to foster communal bonding or cultivate social cohesion.[16] We have more effective means and memes.[17]

From a matter-based, evolutionary perspective, dancing is at best instrumental to the process of becoming human. It is an activity that humans can do to facilitate social solidarity, but it is not something that they must do in order to be or become human. Dance can be left out, left behind, and, according to some, it *should* be. It should be left behind because it is an activity that humans do with their material bodies, and, as the story continues, humans distinguish themselves from the plants and animals of nature by evolving and exercising *intelligent, self-conscious minds*.[18]

When we begin to appreciate that movement is what matters, however, an idea emerges with the potential to reinterpret existing theories of communal dancing in such a way that we can appreciate the ongoing value of dance as vital art here and now. If we privilege *bodily movement* rather than matter as the currency of evolution, if we insist upon seeing any and all bodily forms as potentials for movement making, then we can begin to perceive dancing, then and now, as a practice in which humans exercise a distinctive human potential to participate in the ongoing evolution of the universe in human-enabling ways.

Here the task of this chapter comes into view. By exploring the idea that movement (and not matter) evolves, this chapter clears the ground for envisioning dance not just as an activity that human beings evolved to do but as the bodily capacity whose potential for creating life the human species exists to maximize.

Movement That Evolves

I break through the hedgerow into the hay fields. The hill's pitch tips horizontal here. My stride eases. I turn my left side to the open air and walk the field's perimeter. Someone else walked here. Something else. This time I follow the path. Its path. Its moves were wise ones, flanking the hedgerow, hanging out in shadows, while keeping one eye on the wide sideways space.

I slip into a corner of the field and veer to the left, skirting the briars that guard the edge. My thoughts drift back in time. How many humans have walked as I am doing now—feet padding on matted earth? Yes, this ground has been mowed and its grasses gathered; its rocks dug and stacked into dividing walls. But still, these forms of frond, bush, and tree would have been familiar to the earliest humans.

It occurs to me. We all evolved together, in one ungainly mass of mutually enabling movements. The movements I make in sensing evolved in collusion with the movements of other bodily selves who were capable of being sensed. I can see this tree and hear this bird and feel this earth because the movement patterns made by my senses are tuned to theirs. The movement my senses are is keyed to the scope and scale of movement patterns that serve as food, that threaten danger, that block my way, or that offer pliable substances for my hands to work. Lung and air, hand and branch, foot and field all evolved together.

The flash of experience yields a thought both severe and comforting: my sensory self *needs* the infinite dimensions and depth of the natural world in order to exercise and develop its range of movement potential. My senses need these particular patterns of stimuli in order to unfold, even as this pulsing web needs my movements in order to be what it is in relation to me.[19]

I don't want to go anywhere else. The thought ignites my bodily self. I feel its bolt as a clearing, broad as the field along which I walk. In this moment I know: I want to live a life that enables me to be here, on this gorgeous piece of ground, free to live with it, be moved by it, and express it in the thoughts it enables. I like to walk like this, to feel and think like this—with a swelling sense of earth within.[20]

I am at home. I do not want to leave. I want to be free to stay here. To dance here. To become human here.

I take one last look at the field and duck through the hedgerow into a favorite patch of forest. The trees welcome me. I don't know their names. My son Jordan does. Although he tells me, I can't seem to remember. I can't relate to them as oak, hickory, maple, and elm. To me they are friends. Though far taller than I, they meet my eyes as slender and round. I can throw my arms around each one.

Walking past their stillness, I feel the shapes of their movement—energy flowing down into the earth, up toward the sun, out along the branches, swirling through twigs, emptying into a few dying leaves, and returning again. These trees are alive. They are animate columns of life, teaching me how to move as they do. How to stand as an open conduit between earth and sky;

how to make matter from the movements of dirt, air, water, and light. I linger with the kinetic image of living trees as it forms in me. Earth within.

Do other animals have similar experiences of awe? I wonder. Do they see a tree as a symbol and metaphor of themselves? Do they feel an impulse to hug it? Do they learn about themselves by feasting their eyes on its shape? Do other animals see in themselves a pattern of tree-movement that gives them permission to be that pattern? Do they need permission to be?

· · · · ·

The notion that matter evolves, just like the idea that matter is real (chapter 1), carries within it the seeds of its own overcoming. It too harbors a contradiction that cannot be resolved within the terms of a materialist paradigm: *matter evolves to reproduce itself*. Herein lies the contradiction. The motivation that propels matter to *change* is a desire to stay the *same*—to achieve a stable state that can be re-produced. As noted, in order to resolve this contradiction, scientists propose a theory of random genetic mutations. A given individual (or species) reproduces itself until some error in its process of replication proves beneficial to the twin goals of survival and reproduction.

Yet this explanation does not explain how genetic mutations can be so well-adapted to the challenges of the environment, nor how they erupt with such diversity and spread so quickly. It does not explain why, of all possible mutations, these ones emerged.[21] Nor does it explain (as seen in chapter 1) how something as complicated and seemingly immaterial as human consciousness could emerge out of a merely material process.

The nascent field of epigenetics attempts to reduce the random element in evolutionary theory by studying the effects of the environment on the ability of genes to express themselves. While still holding that genes are matter, that matter exists, and that matter evolves, scientists in this line of inquiry go far in admitting that genetic development is context sensitive. Genes are not the equivalent of a blueprint that makes use of whatever resources are present. Genes have options. Genes "decide" to unfold one way or another based on available, ingested food; environmental factors, and even its organism's traumatic experiences. A recent study revealed that as much as 98 percent of our genetic matter—so-called junk DNA, which scientists previously assumed had no purpose—actually consists of switches capable of turning genes on or off in response to a yet uncharted range of stimuli.[22]

Still, once we acknowledge that genetic expression is context sensitive, we are a short step from admitting that the ability of a gene to express itself depends on relationships that it (or its organism) creates with others—that is, on patterns of movement. From this perspective, the ability of any gene to express itself depends upon the movements of its bodily entity, of the elemental streams that comprise it, of the environmental forces that surround it, and, most important, of the gene itself. The findings of epigenetics support the idea that genes are movement memories, representing complex choreographies of cause and effect that may or may not release in response to other proximate movements. Genes, in other words, represent potentials for *movement itself* to find other outlets. Genetic development may be *movement dependent* to an extent not yet appreciated, carrying implications not yet explored.[23]

New questions arise. What difference would it make to think about *bodily movement* as the medium, the motivation, and the goal of changes that occur within and among species over time? What if all material forms, humans in particular, exist for the purpose of giving rise to new movements and thus *overcoming* rather than reproducing themselves?[24] What if every shape of matter is simply an occasion for the movement of life to know and express more of itself, that is, for more movement?

What if evolution itself is best described as a rhythmic process of bodily becoming—even as a dance? And what if humans, when they dance, participate in the process of evolution in such a way that they grow better able to discern how and when and where to move *humanly*?

To Evolve Is to Dance

I get to our neighbor's motorbike track, a serpentine scar on the hillside where local residents periodically blast the peace with their deafening, engine-driven machines. I deliberately walk into the path and follow it upward, wanting to heal this wound. Another human made it, with human-made landmovers, for fun.

In some ways, walking along, I feel closer to the ground. There is no stubble on this motorbike track to block my way, only smooth dirt to beckon me forth. I feel every pebble. Yet in another way I feel farther from the earth, for

I have lost it. I feel as if I am walking on a dead strip, looking out on somewhat richer land, just to the left and right of my falling feet.

I glance up to my right. The pond appears, frozen flat and round and white. I feel its pull and leave the bike track to move toward it. Its icy surface is soft with snow, twinkling like stars in the sunlight. As I walk onto it, into it, an unexpected surge of happiness releases my heart. I am in a place I have never been before, inhabiting a span of stability the cold has made, where I can stand and see what I have never seen before. This view. This angle. This opening.

I move quickly across the dusted glass, leaving traces that call me back to play with them. I twist my left arm up into the air and use it to propel my right toe in a circle around me. I leave a circle in the snow and then another and another, as if some round-footed creature had padded by.

I am dancing. Before I think it, I am doing it. I am playing with shapes and patterns of movement—those that my bodily self is making with itself as it passes. While walking along, without even knowing it, I had opened my sensory awareness and was now receiving impulses to move up and down, left and right, around and through. Dancing with the air. The snow. The light.

Where are these movements coming from? I have no idea. Each one is both familiar and strange. As a particular sequence unfolds, so does a shiver of pleasure. I could stop the flow, but I choose not to. I choose to follow. To surrender. To give way. I allow myself to enjoy this capacity of a human body to be moved, anywhere, anytime, by whatever appears to it, by virtue of its own movements, as moving. This capacity to make new movements for the pleasure of it. The beauty of it. The heart-opening thrill of it.

I dance to the center where a herd of four-wheelers has spun out, scraping the surface clean. I breathe the tension of what must have been a screaming noise away. I weave curlicues right through the center. *This is what I do. This is who I am.*

I am dancing, yes. I am dancing because I was in pain. Because I had to walk. Because the land moved me. Because dancing is the best way I know to open to the depth and reach of my creativity—my fundamental human ability to find new ways to move. New thoughts. New feelings. New habits. New patterns of sensing and responding that better honor my relatedness to all that is. To all that sustains me. To all that I love. Here, at home, on earth.

Dancing, I evolve. I become a response to whatever anxiety and confusion have gathered in me. I overcome myself along trajectories of the movements I am making, in line with my own well-being. Dancing, I am life, ever finding in the rocky field of the present, occasions to move some more.

· · · · ·

At its etymological root, *evolution* is a rolling out, an opening up. In the *American Heritage Dictionary* evolution is "a wheeling motion in a dance." Evolution is the movement by which all forms are rolled out and opened up within a world so that they become occasions for the movement of life to spiral on. *Evolution* does not refer to some thing that moves; it evokes the actual moving in and of all those forms as they spin out, open up, and empty into others.

To evolve is to move. To move is to evolve. No movement ever repeats. Evolution never stops. Any movement becomes something different than it was as a result of what it effects. Every movement participates in an ever evolving process of evolution by taking shape, assuming a new pattern of sensing and responding, and then, in the next moment, overcoming it again. Movement is constantly creating kinetic images of itself that appear to resist change—movement makes some "thing" that can and did make that shape, take this shape, and thus can make and take another.

Every form of life, minuscule to gargantuan, is not only a pattern of movement, but it is one in a series of patterns, erupting out of one another, building onto one another, over time. Every leg or fin or wing represents a trajectory of movement that not only represents a given set of possibilities, but opens onto further possibilities. Every rivulet is a possible canyon. Every mass is a snapshot—a kinetic image—that nonetheless allows us to grasp, in some limited way, the flow that is enabling it to be. To evolve is to be always searching, reaching, running along given shapes of repeated movement, looking for new outlets, new patterns of sensation and response.

The movement that is evolution is like a stream running downhill. It spills and pools, flooding cracks and crevices, finding fractures and fissures through which it can squeeze. It follows along the shapes it has carved and banked and molded in the past, looking for every new channel available to it, creating and becoming new patterns of movement with every gurgle, indifferent to how and when and where it flows.

The implications of thinking about movement as the medium of evolution carry us farther along the path opened by thinking about matter as movement (chapter 1), a lot farther. For one, if movement is what evolves, then no form of life, not even a human, exists solely to reproduce itself. Every form, including the human, is a pattern made and remembered that exists as stepping stone and spur to the creation of *new* forms. Forms are flexible conduits through which movement finds additional possibilities for maximizing its form-creating flow. Their *only* purpose is to move in ways that give rise to more.

Further, this more to which movement gives rise is not simply more of the same. From a movement perspective, every form is always becoming *different* than it was, giving rise to movements that change it further, creating (it into) something else. Every form—animal, vegetable, fungal, or human—participates in a rhythm of bodily becoming, overcoming itself along the trajectories plotted by its own patterns of sensation and response.[25] Every form, as movement, invites novelty as it seeks the enabling conditions for releasing the movement potential of its own life situation. Pro-creating is one way in which that creation can happen; it is one means by which organisms express their desire to *move* with one another. But it is not the only way, or even the most important. Any form—any pattern of potential movement—succeeds insofar as it provides life with opportunities to move beyond itself.

Second, once we identify movement as the locus of evolution, then we realize it is impossible to isolate the evolution of any bundle of kinetic potential, including a human, from the contexts in which it exists. Evolution is not what one "individual" does in response to its environment. There is no "one" apart from any context. There is no context that holds constant while evolution occurs. Evolution is what all movement patterns at every level of existence are doing all the time—bumping, jostling, interleafing, entwining, flowing into and through—with each movement exploiting whatever resources exist for funding more movement. More life.

Evolution is taking place all at once on the smallest and largest scales, and every degree in between, with every moment in relation to everything else. Each individual—whether gene, cell, body, or colony—is nothing more or less than the patterns of relating it creates with whatever supports it in making those moves. Every unit of matter that we pretend to identify and isolate actually blends into the next. There are no spaces between. The shape of the intestine, its colonies of bacteria, the nutrients in the soil, the flavor of the foliage, and a cow's ability to sense it all evolve at once. Every particular movement potential is dispensable; yet no one can live without the others. No unit of material organization has more inherent importance than any other. Every movement we make that makes us derives from and empties into the webs of relationships on which we depend and to which we give life. Any lines we draw are a function of our perceiving, not its reality.[26]

Third, when we embrace the ubiquity of movement evolving, we can also perceive in evolution a drive toward diversity and variability—toward ever larger and ever smaller patterns of interdependent coordination. Evolution is inherently creative; it proceeds through the creation of new relationships among patterns of movement within and across scales. Every new movement is thus a new branch, capable of sprouting further branches. Each individual is a new point in the history of evolution, a potential beginning of an entirely new species.

Once we embrace movement as the source, medium, and telos of evolution, then we realize that changes expressed in material forms over time are not necessarily or completely random. Genetic differences that arise through processes of reproduction represent possibilities for movement that open at a given moment along the branch of the reproductive process in response to movements that are being made. They arise as a play and exploration of movement possibilities that past movements have made possible.[27] At every point in that process there are options that track along trajectories of past movement patterns. While they arise within an organism, they may or may not support the life of that organism. Their emergence may support life in other possible degrees and dimensions. While we may name these vectors as disease, dysfunction, or disaster, movement wields no such judgment over the forms it takes. It has no other purpose than to continue in whatever shapes by whatever means it can.

Humans are not exempt from this evolutionary indifference. We too are patterns and possibilities for movements that may or may not sustain the health and well-being of our own bodily selves. We are potentials for supporting life at myriad scales, not just a human one. The movement manifest in us, as us, is as much for us and against us as it is for and against any other constellation of movement images, from virus and bacteria to ecosystem or atmosphere. Life in our size and shape enjoys no privilege and no preference. We are the movement of nature, and we are nothing without it. The movement that we are is indifferent to us, but not indifferent to itself. This movement *loves* itself; and so loves us as parts of it. In so far as we acknowledge our participation in it, we love (ourselves as) it too—as the source and telos of our living.[28]

From the perspective of movement, then, the kinds of activities we humans take for granted as the goals of (human) life are not. Our surviving and reproducing are mere means by which the ongoing movement of life finds more freedom for itself—more capacity for expressing or even enjoying itself. We move so that life can keep moving in us, through us, as us, and we do so because doing so is what gives us the greatest pleasure we are capable of feeling. There is no end or goal, no purpose outside of our ongoing participation in the eternal rhythms of bodily becoming.

Once we embrace these ideas that movement matters and movement evolves, we are in a position to approach dance differently. We can now perceive that human bodies are not material entities whose minds may choose to dance or not, but rather ever evolving patterns of movement made and remembered. We are poised to reconsider, as chapters 4 through 7 do in detail, that humans are creatures in whom life exploits the advantages accrued to those who can learn to participate consciously in the rhythms of their own bodily becoming.

From this perspective, dancing is not one human activity among many. It is not just a means for cohering community, though it may be used as such. Rather, more fundamentally, it is the bodily practice that pulls humans into reality as animals who, through such bodily practice, can engage and transform their circumstances in *human*-enabling ways.[29] Dancing is a distinctively human action that is constitutive of our very being and becoming in the world.

Evolved to Dance

As I make my way across the pond, spinning and swirling, through sparkling air and snow sprinkles, I see Geoff and Jordan on the hillside in the hedgerow working on the fallen elms I had told them about. I see their coated shapes as small bits of color moving about. They do not see me.

I move toward them, imagining people of all times and places and the movements they have made toward one another. We humans are driven by an *impulse to connect* with whatever will nourish and support our well-being, human and not. Compared to other animals our size, we are weak. Our senses are dull. Our eyes do not see like the hawk; our nose pales in strength to that of the sniffing fox; our ears miss mice that the cat does not. Our skin is soft and pliable, tender to the touch. It is easily bruised, broken, and torn. But it does register small vibrations, nuances of movement, as calls to connect, to touch, to move with.[30] By moving with others, we adapt, we make ourselves at home, and we keep the movement of the earth alive in us.

Humans move with and toward each other as they do because we too have been moved—moved by the bird to fly, by the fish to swim, by predators to gather, by storms to circle round, by the touch of a parent to smile back. Everything we imagine, everything we desire, comes to us because we move as a movement arising in us that moves us further along the trajectories of movement we have already made. It is how we think. How we know. How we learn. How we find answers to problems. How we imagine ways to ease our sorrows. How we decide who we are, what we should do, and which way to walk. How we heal.

As I leave the pond, making my way up across the field toward Geoff and Jordan, I marvel at how little I know about what is going on in the world right here. Jessica has been reading us stories written by a tracker. To one who learns to notice, every ripple and every bump is a sign of something or someone's movement. We humans used to be able to read these signs as pulses of life— as movements we ourselves could learn to make. Now we read them as if they were static marks on a white page—representations of a material form that exists somewhere else.[31] We spend our hours reading about the travels and travails of models and gurus, sports stars and movie stars, and wonder why we feel so alienated and alone.

Dancing, I muse, is the movement that brings me home.

· · · · ·

Working with a matter-based paradigm, accounts of human evolution tend to focus on the material forms of human physiology—the big toe, thumb, larynx, or skull—and then proceed to assess the how those forms function relative to a human's ability to survive and reproduce.[32] Such accounts identify the opportunities that arose for making new movements with each anatomical change and then assess the impact on the development of Homo sapiens. As noted in chapter 1, scientists working in these veins alternately trace the lineage of human organs, limbs, and systems back through time, revealing our inner fish, amphibian, worm, and virus. In their studies they compare our use of such forms to those of creatures sharing similar genealogies or environmental challenges. Such studies map the inevitable glitches that result from repurposing physical forms for different movement patterns, as when humans use legs—originally formed to swim—to support an upright stance. Suddenly getting blood back up to our hearts is a problem as it never was for a fish.[33]

This kind of matter-based evolutionary analysis holds for human behaviors as well. Books appear regularly pointing to a particular behavior that humans evolved that gave them a competitive advantage over other primates and earlier hominids. Recent candidates include running,[34] cooking,[35] speaking,[36] and cooperative breeding.[37] Debates ensue over which activity was more likely to give humans the biggest boost in their journey toward our current hegemony over other species.

Yet if you list all the anatomical forms, metabolic features, or behavioral functions that are said to distinguish human animals from other animals, a curious pattern appears. Nearly all these qualities are distinguished by their *adaptability*. A thumb can allow us to grasp and hold and sew and throw; running takes us away from predators and closer to prey. Using fire we are able to warm our bodies, sleep on the ground, process skins, and eat any manner of vegetable, fruit, and meat. In every case, the traits that humans have perfected as human are rarely if ever keyed to one particular function.[38] Language, consciousness, or empathy; a hand, a big toe, and a head are all multipurpose instruments. And sometimes their functions conflict. Words can signal love or hate; empathy can be used to comfort or deceive. Cooperative breeding can bind adults in a common project or pit them against one another as competitors. This fact poses a problem for scientists trying to identify the evolutionary pressures guiding the development of these qualities, for no one end easily outweighs others in usefulness.

However, if movement and not matter evolves, and if the goal of evolution is that movement continue not that matter reproduce, then the problem of understanding human evolution shifts. Rather than ask about the function of a given material formation, we can ask about the capacity for movement making that enables that trait or tool to function over time and across generations as it does.

In many ways humans are born more vulnerable and less secure in the world than most other animals. We are born not knowing who we are or where home is. We are born not knowing what we should eat, wear, or build around us. We have to learn who and how to be, and we do so in a specific place and time, in relation to particular humans, in a given community, culture, and ecosystem. While we are not at home anywhere, we can learn to be at home everywhere, and we do so by moving and being moved in a place, by a place, such that it exists in us as much as we exist in it. Earth within.

What is it that enables humans to move and be moved in response to novel situations and so create a guiding sense of earth within? It is the capacity I have been describing as dance: the ability to create and become patterns of sensation and response that relate us to ourselves, each other, and the earth in pain-transforming, life-enabling ways.

Of the many organisms on the planet, humans can and do learn to make patterns of movement from just about anything—whether tree trunk, waterfall, or crow; the predators they fear; the prey they seek; the materials they handle; or the persons with whom they cook, fight, share, and mate. Humans evolve not simply by adapting themselves to what is; they learn from what appears to them (where that appearing occurs as a result of movements they are making), whether berry or boulder, how to move in ways that release "its" potential to support human life. And they do so for the *pleasure* of it.

In this account humans need to move and be moved in ways that open us up to our own ability to create and become new movements. We need to move and be moved in ways that encourage us to cultivate a receptivity and responsiveness to the impulses arising in us as a result of the movements we are making. We need to be experiencing, on an ongoing basis, the pleasure of learning to make movements that unfold and release the ever evolving movement potentials of our bodily selves. Our health and well-being, as well as the health and well-being of our relationships and communities, depends upon it.

· · · · ·

Historically speaking, across time and place, humans have learned how to make movements that relate them to their natural and social contexts in life-enabling ways by learning to dance the dances that the people in their communities are and have been dancing.

To dance is human. All cultures and all toddlers exhibit some kind of dancing; the range of forms is as nearly as diverse as the number of living humans. From tightly crafted to invented on the spot; from honed through years of training to performed once in the moment; from complicated gestures to the simplest of walks, shuffles, and hops, dancing moves bodily selves in ways that exercise their capacity to create and become patterns of sensation and response.

While scholars working within a materialist paradigm, have, as we have seen, done excellent work in pegging human dances to their social functions, the shift to a movement-oriented theory of evolution suggests a broader perspective. Just as the thumb did not evolve in order to hold a hammerstone, nor segments of the brain evolve solely to use language, dance did not evolve for one use either. Dance, as with other human qualities, evolved for its nearly infinite applicability. In this view, the varied uses of dancing illustrate how humans can and do engage dance as a primary resource for helping them confront nearly every challenge and opportunity they face.

From a movement perspective, humans evolved with a basic ability to participate consciously in the rhythms of their own bodily becoming. In order to survive, they need to be *creating* where the medium and the end is not necessarily a freestanding work of art but one's own sensory-kinetic palette of possibilities. And they have done so constantly, consistently, in all realms of their living, as guided and energized by the cultural forms of their dancing.

Here, the efforts by scholars to embrace dancing as a paradigmatic—but expendable—stage of human evolution find a complementary interpretation. Dancing may indeed have generated the neuromuscular matrix out of which communal forms of language, art, technology, science, and religion evolve. However, it may also be true that any human creation is useful if and only if another human has the ability to move toward it, with it, or because of it and make the mental, emotional, bodily movements that using it requires. In this sense, in order for humanity to *continue* to exist and persist, individual persons must be able to perceive, practice, and remember movement patterns and then recreate them spontaneously in novel but similar situations. They must, in other words, be able to *dance*.

Without the capacity to create and become patterns of sensation and response, humans would not only *not* have the ability to create forms of knowledge that stand apart from a human bodily self; we would not have the ability to do anything with them once there. In this view, dance is something we do *because* we are caring, cooking, running, speaking creatures, and it is also something we do that *enables us to become* the caring, cooking, running, speaking creatures we are on an ongoing basis.

This shifted perspective on evolution thus yields the thesis that chapters 4 through 7 will explore in depth. In these chapters, I argue that humans have evolved into the creatures we are by exploiting a bodily capacity, evolved in multiple species over millions of years, to cultivate a sensory awareness of ourselves as movement that allows us to participate consciously in an ongoing bodily process of creating and becoming relational, life-enabling patterns of sensation and response. Perhaps humans are human because they dance.

First, however, there is one additional tenet of the materialist paradigm to dismantle--one that reinforces the notions that matter is real and that matter evolves: namely, the idea that objective knowledge of the material world is possible. Chapter 3 takes on this task.

· · · · ·

When I arrive at the hedgerow, I see that Kai and Leif, ages six and two, are there as well. Their bodily selves were too small to appear to my eyes until I was close. They are blinking in the sunshine, not sure what to do with themselves. Geoff, Jordan, and I go to work clearing the brush from the trees that we want Jordan's steers to pull home.

Leif drops his glove and starts to cry. I put it back on. Kai is restless and bored. He starts to complain. "I want to go home!" he cries. I realize that it would be best for all involved if I took the small boys down to the pond.

Kai, Leif, and I trudge through the snow back down to the ring I recently left. The boys approach the edge, tentatively.

"Is it safe" Kai asks, his words brimming with trepidation.

"Yes," I reply.

We venture out into the center. I start making my circles in the snow. At first the boys watch. They are entranced. Then, as if something within them suddenly releases, they start running, sliding, and rolling along, following in my tracks. There is no need to tell them what to do. They feel the pulse in me and around us and cannot not respond.

Together, we dance, as the sun dips blue behind the trees.

3

To Dance Is to Know

We do not belong to those who have ideas only among books, when stimulated by books. It is our habit to think outdoors—walking, leaping, climbing, dancing, preferably on lonely mountains or near the sea where even the trails become thoughtful. Our first questions about the value of a book, of a human being, or a musical composition are: Can they walk? Even more, can they dance?

—NIETZSCHE, *THE GAY SCIENCE*

· · · · ·

Dance is an absolute. It is not knowledge about something, but is knowledge itself. . . . It is independent of service to an idea, but is of such highly organized activity that it can produce idea.

—MARTHA GRAHAM

"Why do you dance?" I ask. I am in the dance studio of a private New England high school. The students, all girls but one, are sitting on the floor. I look around the circle of faces. It is the third day of my residency here and my last class with these students. I have been talking a lot to them—about Martha Graham, about human evolution, about dance as a vital art. We have been dancing together. Now I want to hear from them. No one speaks.

A bold voice breaks the silence. "Because I need another gym credit," she announces. This girl hasn't been feeling well for the past few days. She sat out the first class and warned she might have to leave this one to throw up. Her response is an easy one. Safe. Still, it cracks the ice. I know. It isn't an easy question to answer.

"I dance so that I can be better at sports. Stronger and more flexible," says one student.

"Me too, I want to be better at skiing," adds another. I nod and turn to my left, looking toward another girl who has not yet spoken.

"I dance because I love it," she says quietly. I breathe in. It takes a lot of courage to say what she did. Even here. I don't want to push too hard.

"Why do you love it?" I ask.

"Because it makes me feel connected with something greater than myself." I nod. I could go on and on in response, but I want to collect other voices first.

The girl to her left bashfully tucks her chin. "I know this is going to sound weird," she says. "I dance because it makes me feel beautiful." Others nod immediately. Their support is instant. It is obvious that they feel the same way, are reluctant to admit it, and are so glad that someone did. A couple of students speak in agreement.

I turn to the last girl on my right. I have noticed her in class. She moves well. She offers, "I dance because it makes me feel free. I have the freedom to move the way I want to. Even in ballet, there is no one right way to make the movement. You have to find out how to do it yourself."

I smile and ponder this range of responses. Some of these dancers have begun dancing this year. Yet already they *know* things that are unique to their experience of practicing dance. They are building knowledge in their bodily selves, of their bodily selves, that they cannot acquire any other way. That is why they are here. And they are also aware, at some level, of how radical it all is. I want to respond in a way that honors their honesty and affirms what I know they know. I open to the impulses arising in me.

"What I hear many of you saying is that when you are dancing, you feel *pleasure*—a pleasure that comes from dancing. You love dancing, yes, and you love it for how it makes you feel—strong, agile, free, beautiful, connected. I want to celebrate this fact. Regardless of why you begin dancing, you won't continue dancing unless there is some reward. Unless it feels good. There simply isn't enough cultural support for doing it.

"At the same time, our culture does not always value pleasure either. We are supposed to work hard and do well, not indulge ourselves. But, if you look at all the primary needs of our lives—the ones we need in order to survive and thrive—like food, warmth, touch, sleep, and belonging—you will find that they all yield intense pleasure. It is a pleasure that guides us to act in ways that are good for us—a pleasure that helps us know what to eat, how to be touched, and with whom to connect for our best well-being.[1]

"Sure, our sense of pleasure can be deceived, confused, and misled. In our capitalist consumer culture it often is. But even so, our sense of pleasure remains our strongest and best resource for knowing how to live, especially when we cultivate it.

"Dancing, we do. In dancing, we cultivate a sensory awareness of the movement we are making. We learn to pay attention to how those movements feel in our bodily selves—to the feelings of pleasure and pain—and we do so so that we can learn to make movements as easily and efficiently as possible. If the movement hurts, we pause, pull back, recalibrate, and try again, opening our bodily selves to flows of movement energy that will align with our bodily selves and build on what we can do.

"In this way, over time, we cultivate a unique form of knowledge: knowledge about how to become a bodily self, present in the moment to whatever the movement of the universe is creating in us. It is a knowledge at a sensory, visceral level of how to participate consciously in the rhythms of bodily becoming. It finds expression in spontaneous eruptions of kinetic intelligence in the moment, for the moment.

"Take your example of skiing. In order to get around the gates on a slalom run, you can't repeat movements learned from a coach, teammate, or book. You must be alert in yourself, attuned to the nuances of snow, light, and temperature, keyed to the pounding of your heart, the throbbing of your thighs, and the depth of your breathing. You have to create patterns of sensation and response in multiple split second decisions that align what you can do with what is required so you can make it down the mountain in the most expedient way. You have to *dance*. And when you do, whatever you are doing, you feel beautiful, able, connected. You find your freedom."

I gaze around the ring. Some heads are nodding. Some eyes are glazing. Enough words. It is time to experience this knowledge in the only form it exists: the movements of our bodily selves. It is time to practice dancing.

· · · · ·

The commonplace ideas that matter is real (chapter 1) and that matter evolves (chapter 2) find their match in a notion of objective knowledge that reinforces them both. In a materialist paradigm, "knowledge" describes a factual account of real objects, that is, of (something like) matter. Since matter is real, knowledge about "it" is possible. As seen in chapter 1, we assume that we can know "it" through our senses, or at least through their technological extensions. And what we "know" about "it" is that which resists change.

This knowledge, then, like the matter it aims to represent, remains what it is across differences in personal perspective and opinion. It is objective. This knowledge, like matter, can be lifted out of context and shared with other people at other times and in other places while losing none of its validity. It is abstract and stable. This knowledge can be tested using experiments that yield converging results. It is verifiable. To know is to know what is—not what might be or could be or should be; not what we would like it to be or prefer that it be. To know, in a materialist paradigm, is to have a true and certain purchase on what is real. What can be known as matter and about matter poses as the model to which other kinds of knowledge should aspire. Such knowledge is power.[2]

Moreover, within a materialist program, such objective, stable, verifiable knowledge is represented in forms that are considered equally objective, stable, and verifiable. It appears in the forms of principles and laws, classifications and definitions. It appears in graphs and charts and timelines. It appears as statistics and percentage points, ratios and probabilities. It appears in the shape of symbols that are abstract—words and numbers. Any exceptions that cannot be so represented—any points of data that do not fit the curve—are considered outliers, side effects, exceptions, or mutations and thus incidental to the reality that matters.

In Western culture, at least for the past five hundred years, the preeminent mode for circulating this objective, true, and verifiable knowledge has been the book. The book has arguably been the most important material object in the history of the West.[3] A book, like a body, is assumed to be a "thing." It has heft and weight. It can be held, opened, poured over, and handed down. And at least since the printing press put a Bible in many a home, the Book has stood as the Word of God, spoken to us and for us. The book has been perceived and framed as a material object with the inherent authority to convey essential knowledge about what is real and true and good—knowledge that matters.

These developments have led to a situation in which our Western ideals of knowledge are inextricably entwined with technologies of reading and writing. In the modern world we assume that everything that is important for us to know can be written down and, in fact, should be written down.[4] Whether we read, hear, intuit, or experience, we take notes and keep files, in cabinets or on a computer, surrounding ourselves with stored bits of verbal importance. Soon, some of us are so full of words that we begin writing our own. We become writers. And in every scientific or social scientific publication, every journal article, newspaper essay, or scholarly tome, writers authorize their cases by appealing to other examples of written knowledge. Authors cite, annotate, hyperlink, and compile extensive bibliographies. Authors base their authority on authors who have come before. We act as if many other writers are saying what we want to believe and claim as true.[5]

This matrix of values forms the scaffolding within which science and the materialist paradigm have ascended in range and importance to recruit nearly every aspect of human life into their service. It is the matrix whose rightness our subsequent emergence into a capitalist, industrialized, electrified, sanitized, computerized, globally connected world seems to prove correct. It is a matrix that finds expression in the latest scholarly trends—including those reaching for a path beyond materialism, dualism, and its political implications.[6] Objective, verifiable, written and read knowledge, we come to believe, makes a difference when it comes to achieving success in any profession. It is the key to inventing new energy systems and healing therapies. It is of utmost importance for making money, as well as navigating the challenges of relationships, desires, and daily life.

Of course, this definition of knowledge is not unopposed. Throughout the history of philosophy, writers and thinkers have been calling attention to kinds of knowledge that appear as "subjugated" relative to the objective written word.[7] Critics are and have been lifting up alternatives such as faith and intuition; emotional, social, and embodied knowledge; or practical, aesthetic, and spiritual knowledges and insisting upon their ability to represent dimensions of human experience that writing cannot.[8] Yet the dominant paradigm remains so strong that any substantive claim for an alternative to writable knowledge must itself be written. The case must be made in writing and preferably published by a reputable press, or else it does not rank as serious scholarship. As a result, critics of our Western push for writable knowledge, even in their most postmodern expressions, mirror the dominant trend along a line of argumentation they share.[9]

Regardless of bias, scholars describe particulars, formulate generalizations, generate hypotheses, roll out research, and report on their findings. They read and write and speak about "things" as if those things enjoyed an objective existence apart from their reading, writing, and speaking about them. They buy into a world where it is possible to say or write something that an other will be able to receive and recognize as having meaning, even when they write to deny the possibility of such others, such exchange, or such meaning at all.[10] Sure, a given author may protest that he has no control over the reader's experience and no message to send if he had. He may claim to play a minimal role in authoring the text he writes. However, to make the claim that words are not things or that words do not refer to reality is still to appeal to that "thing-ly reality" as a criterion against which the work and word can be measured.

If we hold that language is free of connection to what is, then we presume the flip claim that matter exists apart from any inherent meaning. Both sides of the debate cling to a materialism that, as we have seen in chapters 1 and 2, is no longer tenable. Neither side attends justly to the role of *movement* in the making of what is.

In sum, in a materialist program, where knowledge about matter that matters is knowledge that can be written down and where knowledge that can be written down is knowledge about matter that matters, then, in order to *know,* one must learn how to read and write. To read and write is to ensure that one will be able to know everything we can know, everything that it matters to know. So we practice reading and writing, exchanging books and documents, essays and texts as if they were useful things that entertain and nourish like balls or bread.

$$\cdot\ \cdot\ \cdot\ \cdot\ \cdot$$

In a culture where people focus most of their conscious energy pursuing or at least perusing writable knowledge, it is nearly impossible to conceive of—not to mention practice—dance as a vital art. In fact, dancing often appears as the opposite of what counts as knowledge. Dancing is nonverbal. Dancing is subjective. Dancing is emotional and physical. Dancing is ephemeral. Or so people believe. Thus dancing is assumed not to matter as much as words and books and other things. Even among those who contest the materialist paradigm, its foundationalism, and its dualism, dance, as noted in chapter 1, most often appears as a *metaphor* for movement that materialist methods cannot catch. "Dance" serves as the foil for what writing cannot encompass that allows writing to reflect its discontents back into itself.[11]

Those who dance or want to write about dance find themselves impaled on the horns of a dilemma. If they claim that it is possible to capture in words what happens in dance, then they undermine their own case: the action of dancing is not important. Conversely, if they defend dance as nonverbal and experiential, then what happens while dancing is not true knowledge. It represents a precursor to knowledge—knowledge in a less mature, more figurative form.[12] These options manifest in a range of familiar arguments about the value of dance. Dance is applauded as a kind of *technical* knowledge about how to make particular bodily movements—how to exercise muscular patterns so as to execute steps. Dance is heralded as an *embodied* knowledge that dwells in our bodies as the *experience* of making movement and of knowing how to make movement—an experience of subjective power and freedom.[13] So too, dance is lifted up as a kind of *symbolic* knowledge that functions like a text to communicate meaning, with gestures as words, sequences as sentences, and style as a form of syntax.[14] Finally, dance is embraced and celebrated as a *spiritual* knowledge, offering nonverbal experiences of communion with a divinity, presence, or reality that exceeds human being. Ego dissolves; ecstasy wells, and a person knows "the divine."[15]

However, in each of these cases, the attempt to affirm dance as vital art intentionally or inadvertently feeds the verbal economy in which writing remains the measure of authority. In each of these cases dancing involves material bodies making movements whose effects can be compared or contrasted to those conveyed through verbal expression. In other words, dance has value *relative* to the kind of knowledge that matters most. Dance counts as knowledge when it looks like a text, acts like a text, elaborates a text, exceeds a text, supports the sharing and dissemination of texts, or is nothing like a text. Dance is framed as some thing in need of—or forever immune to—textual interpretation and elaboration.

In order to embrace dance as vital art, then, we need to do more than defend dance as a knowledge that is like or unlike verbal expressions. We need to shift the discussion about knowledge itself so that verbal forms appear as a species and subset of the kind of knowledge invited and acquired in dance: reading and writing are themselves relational patterns of bodily movement. We need to redefine knowledge itself in terms of bodily becoming. When we do, as this chapter explores, we find new conceptual resources for advancing our vision of dancing. It will become possible to imagine how dancing itself, as a bodily practice, exercises the precise range of human abilities that enable us to know anything—including that which we claim as objective, abstract, and verifiable—in the first place. To know is to dance; to dance is to know. Could it be so?

Knowing Movement

I invite the dancers to lie down on the floor and begin, as I always do, legs bent and tucked into my chest, palms cupped under kneecaps, spine releasing into the cradle of mother earth. I invite them to exhale and let themselves drop into the ground, releasing all thoughts, all feelings, all effort. "Feel the points where your bodily self touches the earth. Allow your muscles to melt off your bones. Let your bones rest." I walk around the room.

"Let the earth support you. Feel its press upward. There is not a moment in your lives when the earth is not holding you, holding you up, enabling you to sit and stand and be. Let it. Acknowledge it. Appreciate it."

I want the students to use the weight of their bodily selves to clear away the patterns of thinking, feeling, and acting they have been rehearsing all day. I want them to open their bodily selves to new impulses to move.

Lying on my back in the front of the room, I demonstrate the first exercise. I stretch my feet up to the sky, bend my knees, and bounce my heels down for four counts before stretching, flexing, and pointing again. This sequence was one of the first dance exercises I ever learned, years ago.

I twist my torso and extend my legs to one side and then the other, guiding students to press their belly button to their spines, to feel the hollowing, emptying, and release of their lower abdomens. I invite them to send their breath deep into their bodily selves, there to awaken a sense of center—as a place where energy gathers and from which energy flows.

As the students begin to move, I add commentary, pausing between statements. "Center is not simply *there* like a thumb or a toe. We have to invite it—to call it into awareness. We have to make the movements that draw it into consciousness as the source of those movements.

"Center happens as a result of movements made. It is relative to movements made, and it serves as the cause of movements to come.

"Center is a capacity for perceiving and activating energy, so as to ride it into space. It is what every dancer develops in order to move as efficiently and effectively as she or he can.

"You cannot will center to appear. You cannot force it. You can only want it—and not just in your mind. You want it by breathing—by paying attention to your breath. Press all the air out, and, when there is no more to expel, release to welcome the inward rush. Center will begin to appear."

On the first day of the residency, when I talked about Martha Graham, I described how she designed a series of exercises based on the movements of breathing to help dancers cultivate a sense of center in the physical location—the pelvis—that would best align with the potential of the human form (or at least her human form) to make clear, powerful, bodily movement. The movements of exhaling, stylized and streamlined, became a specific move-ment called the "contraction"; inhaling a "release." In the Graham technique, the rhythmic repetition of these basic life-supporting movements is thus de-signed to track energy along the skeletal structure and its muscular rigging and so guide a dancer's sensory awareness deep within her bodily self. It is designed to help a dancer find and create within herself a sense of center. For Graham, a dancer's task is to engage her bodily self as potential and explore the limits of what she can do. It is all about discovery.[16]

As class continues, I invite the students to contract and release. Poised on our sit bones, soles of the feet together, we exhale and contract, pressing belly button to spine. Holding that contraction, we hinge our bodies forward at the hip, before inhaling, releasing, and extending out through the length of spine, one by one, lowest to highest vertebrae. Again we move through the gentle wave, exhale, over, release, and lift.

I make the movements myself, as I have thousands of times, animating the sensory awareness these movements have made in me. With every repetition, the sensation of moving changes. The pumping of the torso pulls energy up from the ground where it gathers, with the contraction, in a low-abdominal sense of center and then, with the release, flows forth through the spine, what Graham called the tree of life. Drawing vitality from the earth, my move-ments send it branching through my limbs.

I think about the knowledge these dancers are acquiring as they seek their centers. It is not just about steps or technique. In practicing these movements, these dancers are learning how to release themselves into their own breathing as a guide to future movement. They are hitching their sensory awareness to its currents and riding into new stretches of consciousness. They are learning to create and become patterns of sensation and response that will open their bodily selves to receive and transmit more energy in patterns that align with the health and well-being of their bodily selves.

This knowledge, though I can describe it for them, is not one that I can give to them. I can encourage students to look for it, but "it" does not and will not exist unless and until a person finds it for himself as a result of movements that he is making. Martha Graham called the capacity for coordinated action awakened by a rhythmically rehearsed sensory awareness "Spirit," or spirit-of-body, or "body spirit."[17]

· · · · ·

As with the ideas about matter and evolution discussed in chapters 1 and 2, so too with regard to a matter-based theory of knowledge. There is a contradiction lodged at its heart that attention to dancing helps us perceive: we cannot know what matters unless we learn how to read and write—that is, unless we *practice*.

But what is it that we practice? We practice making bodily movements—patterns of sensation and response—that enable us to use words and numbers and pens and books and keyboards. We train ourselves to make patterns of movement that are first and foremost physical. In order to read and write we learn to mobilize energy not only through tongue, lips, and larynx but through the eye that spies, the head that tilts, the arm that ranges, the hand and fingers that grasp and guide, and the entire bodily self that must sit calmly in order for rest to do their work. We must learn full-body patterns of coordinated sensing and responding before we can know what, according to a materialist paradigm, matters most. Before we can know what is real. The patterns of logic and argument that we aspire to master require an ability to make—or not—specific bodily movements in the world.

Is this fact important? Within a materialist paradigm, it is not. The bodily movements that we make do not matter to who we are or what we can know. When we make the movements of reading and writing, we assume that those movements do not change what we think or feel; they simply provide us with an ability to express ourselves. Our practice, we surmise, offers us a means for engaging verbally with others, for gathering information, and for accomplishing necessary tasks.

From the perspective of bodily becoming, however, the contradiction is clear. Reading and writing are not transparent to the knowledge they convey. Each and every movement that we make makes us who we are. Any knowledge that can be conveyed or received through verbal means has already been informed by patterns of sensation and response honed in the bodily acts of reading and writing, as well as by all of the social pressures and regulations to which those tasks conform. As a result, the "matter" that we "know" as "real" when we read and write is not what we claim it to be. It is a function of the movements we have created and become while reading and writing, as well as the movements made by us and for us in all other areas of our lives.[18]

What is it, then, that we know as a result of disciplining ourselves in practices of reading and writing? For one, we know what these movements educate our senses to notice. The movements of reading and writing train our attention to marks on a page and prime us to discern the minuscule difference among those marks. They train us to privilege our eyes over our other four external senses as conduits for knowing. They train us to ignore the inner sensations of our bodily selves, including any impulses to stand up and move around. They thus train our sphere of focus and awareness away from the lived and living moment so that we can more fully enter into a world opened and bound by the words we are reading or writing.

Patterns of movement we work hard to perfect become us. They become easy—so easy that they seem transparent. We read and write without having to sound out words, or think about how to shape each letter. The meaning of words jumps off the page and into our brains, seemingly without effort. And when we experience such meaning we feel a sense of achievement, purpose, and belonging—a pleasure of participating in a verbal world that exceeds us. We can communicate. We can understand. We belong. So affirmed, we come to believe there is a shared basis of common experience that can support general statements, rational consensus, or at least vibrant debates over the nature of the true, the good, and the beautiful. Reading and writing train us to act as if there is a knowable reality that exists independent of our bodily movements in speaking, reading, and writing. Reading and writing, we move in ways that make this matrix of thoughts and feelings real for us.

Likewise, as our skill in making the bodily movements required to read and write improve, we become people who interact with the world and everything in it as if they were *things* to *read*. We become people who look for meaning in marks and gestures, in visual patterns of what appears to be materially real.[19] We become people who revel in (or rebel against) linear, ordered abstractions—the very kind of ideas that our practice is leading us to believe are real.[20]

What is even more remarkable about the particular choreography that reading and writing exercise, however, is the extent to which the *movements* of reading and writing *erase themselves*. Reading and writing are forms of movement making that cultivate an ignorance of the fact that they involve any movement making at all. As readers and writers, we do not deny that we have bodies or are bodies, but we train ourselves to think and feel and act as if what we do with our bodily selves does not matter to our ability to think and read and write. What matters is not how we move but, more aptly, that we stop moving.

Even those writers who walk their ideas into view—and there are many—tend not to account fully for the impact of their walking on their writing.[21] They may appreciate their walking as a time when their minds are as free to roam as their feet or they may conceive of their writing as a kind of walking.[22] Yet rarely do walkers acknowledge that or how the bodily movements of walking—the patterns of coordination and balance—play a constitutive role in what one who walks can later write.[23] Until now, there have been few conceptual resources for doing so.

From the perspective of bodily becoming, our understanding of what reading and writing enable us to know shifts. We realize that there is no objective "reality" to know that exists apart from the bodily movements that our verbal engagement with it entails. The patterns of sensation and response we practice in order to read and write inform how we perceive, what we perceive, how we evaluate it, and what it can or will mean for us. What appears to us to as real are those aspects of experience that can (or cannot) be written. It is not that we intentionally select verbalizable aspects of what is for attention. Rather, the sensory patterns we have created and become in learning to read and write register aspects of life by which these honed senses are capable of being moved.[24] In this way the world that our words describe is a world that our words create—a world of which our word creating is an active part. Again, this word-world is not just a function of our words or of "the text,"[25] but a function of the bodily movements that those words and that text represent, rehearse, and require. This word-world exists as the feeling, thought, and capacities for action those movements create in us. It is the world that *matters* to us—the world that we can *know*—a world in which we care to dwell. And in order for it to exist we must keep making the movements in pursuit of it that bring it to life for us as real.

Within this movement-enabled perspective, the inherent limitations of reading and writing as media of knowledge appear. Not only do we not know what we think we know, we are creating realities we do not want to admit are ours. Reading and writing, as bodily activities, depend for their efficacy on dimensions of human life that their practice does not necessarily nurture. Just as capitalist corporations consume clean air, water, and soil without factoring the price of these "externalities" into their costs of production, so the bodily actions of reading and writing consume the resources of our physical health without replenishing them or counting the costs. As we sit for hours, blood pools, cell burners cool, metabolic rates fall, and we begin to feel sluggish and depressed. What we can understand, what we are able to think, what we are willing to know, all shrink accordingly to match the span of receptivity that our practices of reading and writing are creating in us, as us.

Once this state emerges, it is self-reinforcing. Once we train our senses to this split between our mental and physical activity, it remains within us as a movement possibility that we willingly, eagerly, and unconsciously mobilize in response to challenges or opportunities that greet us in any realm of activity.[26] Separated from our own bodily selves, enamored with our word-worlds, and feeling depressed, we start craving more—sharper edges, more ragged humor, life-threatening jags. We seek ever more potent verbal visions into which we can keep escaping from the pain that our own bodily movements are creating.

In short, when reading and writing, we move our bodily selves in such a way that we are encouraged to forget that the bodily movements we are making have anything to do with how and what we think and feel and act at all. Reading and writing, we train ourselves to do what we think we must do in order survive in a materialist, word-bound world—sit and think. We aspire to create value—sitting and thinking. We formulate ideals—sitting and thinking. And we orient our lives to enable us to do more—sitting and thinking.

• • • • •

Returning now to the connection between dancing and writing, it is not surprising that this idea of reading and writing as bodily practices carries implications for our understanding of the role that dancing can and does play in the pursuit of knowledge. Once we acknowledge that reading and writing require a precise calibration of physical and mental movements, we are ready to admit that acquiring knowledge of any kind requires skills that any kind of dancing exercises: the capacity to sense, respond to, and recreate patterns of bodily movement. In a world where movement matters, dancing exercises the cognitive capacities and physiological sensibilities that make reading and writing and the knowledge they yield possible.

From this perspective, it is not correct to frame dancing as a nonverbal, experiential act. Dancing is not nonverbal. Nor is it preverbal. Dancing may actually be an ongoing enabling condition required to keep acquiring verbal knowledge throughout our lives. Perhaps the (recently disproved) idea that our brains stop growing new neurons is simply an expression of the fact that few children in our culture learn to *dance*.

Furthermore, this idea of reading and writing as practices of bodily becoming helps pinpoint the sources of their efficacy. If we read and write without a sensory awareness of the movements that are making us, the words we think and read and write lose their connection to what our use of them is creating in our lives. Our visions of what we want, of what is good, of who we should be recoil into the virtual world our words are creating. We begin to align our thoughts and feelings and actions with what is necessary for the world of words to continue, rather with what is necessary for our moving, becoming, flesh-and-blood bodily selves to continue. The images in our mind of what matters and what is real grow increasingly detached from our lived sensory experience as creatures of earth.

What we create—how we move—*matters*; and the degree to which we are viscerally aware of our own movement making is the degree to which we notice. What are we—as bodily selves who participate in making their own word-worlds—creating?

Dancing, by contrast, exercises the very sensory awareness of ourselves as bodily movement that reading and writing both require and train us to ignore. It exercises our sensory awareness in nearly the opposite direction—in the service of mobilizing rather than stilling our bodily selves. Dancing wakes us up; it brings our senses to life. Dancing, we cultivate the sensory awareness we need to make sure that our words stay in touch, moment to moment, with the vast and varied enabling conditions of our health and well-being, our thinking, imagining, and knowing.

Thus, in a world where movement matters, dancing appears not only as a practice that exercises the skills that make read and written knowledge possible; it appears as a practice that provides us with the internal measure—the connection with our bodily selves—that we require in order to succeed in creating verbal worlds capable of guiding us in establishing life-enabling relationships with ourselves, each other, and the natural world. Dancing appears as an essential, enabling component of a knowledge that values life.

· · · · ·

We who live in contemporary world cannot refrain from reading and writing. Abstinence is not an option. Without the ability to read and write, not only can we not function as members of civil society, we cannot know *reality* as defined by those with whom we work and bond. We cannot sense the dangers or possibilities that exist in our word-worlds well enough to orient ourselves and navigate a path through.

However, even though we cannot *not* learn to read and write, we can cultivate the sensory awareness in ourselves that we know—from a movement perspective—is necessary for holding our ideas and values accountable to the bodily, earthen conditions of their ongoing production. We can engage in complementary practices that train our sensory selves to a center that is not located between our ears, but rather animates and enlivens our bodily core. We can *dance* to ensure that there is some nexus of reality in relation to which our words *matter*.

Writing, we train our sensory selves to receive impulses to move that come to us in the form of thoughts and ideas. Writing, we sensitize ourselves to a span of knowing that is both opened and bound by what we can think in words. We train ourselves to imagine forms of existence that can exist apart from our bodily selves and be handed from person to person. We train ourselves to locate our center in our heads.

Dancing, we train our sensory selves to the impact that the movements we are making have on our bodily selves in forming a (sense of) center. Dancing, we attend to sensations of pleasure and pain as guides to moving with strength, efficiency, and grace. We train ourselves to attend to the movement of life moving in us. We train ourselves to a sense of center that allows us to move our bodily selves through space with greater strength, agility, and ease.[27]

And when writers dance, the sensory education we practice while dancing begins to inform what we notice, think, feel, and write, even as our experiences of reading and writing inform what we rely upon dance to do. We begin to realize that reading and writing themselves may be best evaluated as dance. *What movement possibilities are we creating?*

· · · · ·

I admit it. The philosophy of bodily becoming that I am crafting, like the materialist model it seeks to overcome, is itself a word-world. Yet it is a word-world with a difference that the movement paradigm helps us acknowledge: it is word-world cracked open by my experience of dancing. It is a world that I hold accountable in every respect to my ongoing daily practice of dance and to all I have noticed and learned about dance from reading, watching, and studying the dances of peoples from farflung times and places.

I am spinning and weaving this word-world from ideas I have danced into consciousness—ideas that my dancing has drawn into reality. The words I write do not represent dance. They can never replace it. But they can mark the difference it makes to think through the lived, living experience of it.

Dancing Knowledge

We finish the warm-up, and I gather the dancers for today's assignment. I want them to improvise. I want to support them in finding their own movements. I know how difficult it can be. We all want someone to tell us which moves we should make to which counts in which direction. We want to make the moves we are supposed to make and we want to do them correctly. We want to be told what to do so that we can be right.

"If you are going to dance," I begin, "you are going to have to know how to improvise. You never know what is going to happen on stage. The music might stop, the lights go off, or your partner drop several steps. You have to be ready and able to respond."

Even as I speak, I sense what I really want to say. It emerges. "If you dance, whatever technique you study, there is always a dimension to that learning process where you must figure out for yourself how to move—you have to recreate the kinetic images that appear to you, and do so in a way that does not hurt. You need to find your own connection to any given pattern of movement, so that it comes alive in you as an expression of your being and your becoming in this moment in time. You need to become transparent to the movement that is moving you.

"How? You have to know how to play with your own sensory awareness, your center, finding and making movements that bring your senses to life. You have to know how to open yourselves to the movement impulses arising within you, using the push and pull of mental and kinetic activity to take you deeper and farther into your own expressive capacity."

The students glance at me with trepidation. I see the doubt in their faces. I read it as an expression of desire—they want to dance. They want to make sure that they are going to feel the pleasure they are accustomed to feeling—that they can find this pleasure by themselves. I know that they will.

I make it easy. "Lie on the floor. You have two minutes. Your assignment is to get from a fetal curl to an upright stance. Think of yourself as a seed. Which kind?"

I turn on the music and we begin. I have taught this exercise many times and never cease to be amazed. A room full of unfolding bodily selves is always extraordinarily beautiful. Two minutes to a simple stand, and, time and again, I am stunned.

Some of students finish unfolding before the time is up. Some peer about furtively, wondering if everyone else has arrived or not. I encourage them to stay in their own experience. The music softens into silence. The students wait. It is a poignant silence, and I am loathe to interrupt it.

What is happening? This exercise, as I see it, taps a knowledge the students don't know they know. It is not that humans all know how a plant grows, although most do. It is not that we all appreciate the unfolding of a seed as a metaphor for living, although we may. It is not that we are accessing some spiritual reality, although there might be one. We all know what it is like to emerge, experientially. We have seen it; we have lived it. We have a kinetic image of it, traced in our bodily selves by our own birth.

In this exercise, then, the suggestion of a seed, the two-minute frame, and the studio space occupy and orient our minds. The music creates a sonic, lyric support. And in this time and place we remember what we know. We *know* how to breathe ourselves open; how to reach, turn, and stretch into the light; how to be moved by sunrays and raindrops and the mycorrhizae around our roots. We know how to respond to the movement of life in us and around us by continuing its pulse. We know how to become the dancers that we are.

The exercise is short, easy, but even so. These dancers are enacting the paradigmatic movement of all human life: they are overcoming themselves. They are tapping into the potential for bodily becoming that is now, alive, and participating in it by recreating kinetic images of what appears to them. As they do, they know differently: they know themselves as becoming themselves through movements of their own making.

· · · · ·

When we acknowledge that movement matters and movement evolves, when we are able to appreciate reading and writing as bodily practices, and dancing as their enabling condition, then we are also ready to realize that the knowledge we humans need, our reasons for needing it, and our methods for gathering, recording, and disseminating it are all in need of revision. In a nutshell: we need to find dance in everything we do so that we can muster the will and desire and understanding to practice dancing in its own time and space apart from all that we do.

Given the creatures we have evolved to be, what we humans most need to know is how to work with movement. We need to know how to notice it, map it, recreate it, and align ourselves with it and we need to be able to do so in all realms of our living, whether physical, emotional, intellectual, or spiritual. We need to be able to do so on our own and with others, in our homes and in our communities. We need to learn how to open to impulses arising in us, unfolding along the limbs of our thinking, feeling, and acting.

Simultaneously, we also need to know how to discern whether the movements we are making are "good" ones for us to make. We need to cultivate a sensory awareness of what our movements are creating in us and through us—not a conceptual understanding of what is happening to us, but a visceral lived sense of what we are creating within ourselves as our center and source for action. We need a visceral sense of how and why our desires flow, our emotions erupt, and our will to act gathers. We need a sense of how to mobilize ourselves along vectors that strengthen our hope, our faith, our vulnerability to love. And we need to extend this sensory range as far as possible along the webs of life on whose vitality we ourselves depend.[28]

We need this knowledge, moreover, neither to secure power over other people or over our own bodily selves nor to protect ourselves from chaos, ignorance, or despair. We need this knowledge to succeed in creating mutually life-enabling relationships with sources of our sustenance, from oxygen to significant others to capitalist corporations to neighboring nations. We need the knowledge that dancing cultivates in us as a perspective from which to evaluate what our verbal, virtual worlds are creating around us, through us, and beyond us. Without this counterbalancing attentiveness, the decisions we make in our lives inevitably rebound to the messages of the virtual verbal worlds we also inhabit and their established patterns of power and privilege.

Correlatively, our methods of acquiring this knowledge can no longer be passive or "objective." To cultivate a sensory awareness of the movements making us, we cannot simply read, write, or listen. We need to practice actively grasping and recreating the movements we perceive in the fullness of their sensory expressions in order to discern their meaning. We need to move our bodily selves in patterns that exercise our kinetic imagination.

As we do, we will not be able to help engaging words and books differently than we had. From the perspective of bodily becoming, a book, like every "thing," is a pattern of movement. What its words represent are not the thoughts of the author but the patterns of physical, mental, spiritual movement that allowed the author to receive and tumble and polish and perform those thoughts (as well as the movements involved in its production and distribution). Conversely, the meaning that I, as a reader, get from a book is a function of the movements I make in sitting and staring, flipping and clicking, receiving and remembering; it is a function of all the movements I have made—mental, physical, emotional, imaginal—that have made me who I am. It is not just my experience or expertise that informs my reading, but the degree to which I have cultivated a sensory awareness of the movements I am making and how they are making me.

Words succeed when they move. They succeed when they invite a reader to recreate the physical and mental moves—the patterns of attention and inattention—that the writing process expresses. Words communicate, if and when they do, kinetically and viscerally. They cannot communicate any other way, regardless of whether they deliver the most sensuous poetry or a rigorous logical proof. Words can guide a person in making moves that sensitize her to the dawning of particular sensations—of ideas—but those ideas will not and cannot be hers unless she can make the moves that make them hers—unless she can recreate them in herself as expressions of her own capacity to move.

As we pursue the project of gathering knowledge through the acts of reading and writing, then, it behooves us to keep dancing—to take the sensibilities aroused and play with them so as to deepen our understanding of what we are reading and writing. We need to dance so that our writing does not simply rearrange the furniture of our word-worlds. We need to dance so that what we read retains the power to fund movement that matters.

· · · · ·

Our minds are limited by what we sense, what we remember, and what we can predict. Our minds are what the movements we make create as the sense of who it is that created them. Our bodily selves, on the other hand, are infinite.[29] Our bodily selves are movements of connecting, relating, and interacting with incalculable dimensions of existence extending far beyond our sensory range. We sense what we need to sense and know what we need to know so as to make responsible successful movements with our bodily selves. But our presence in the world is infinitely open, infinitely more.

Dancing, we can cultivate a receptivity to what lies within and beyond the granularity of our sensory range by growing increasingly attuned to the microscopic differences between those bits of matter we would otherwise identify as the same. We can do so by making movements that draw our attention to our enmeshment in an endless rhythmic tapestry.

At this point in history, we need this dance-enabled knowledge more than ever. We humans have succeeded in driving our lives inward along the trajectories of movement opened by our use of words and books, images and texts. We have succeeded in making ourselves at home in these virtual worlds. The words we read and write reinforce our perception that these worlds are the ones that matter most. In so doing, we have nearly succeeded in splitting our sense of what we can and do and should know from the bodily selves who beat and breathe. We are killing ourselves and our planet in pursuit of a perfect, perfectable virtual world.[30]

When it comes to knowledge, dancing is not an evolutionary holdout. It is a means to a kind of knowledge, without which we can no longer live: the knowledge of how to participate consciously in the rhythms of bodily becoming. As chapters 4 through 7 elaborate in detail, this knowledge that dancing affords is, for human beings, a biological, ethical, spiritual, and ecological necessity. These chapters do so as they revalue those tenets of the materialist paradigm that concern the nature of a human person and retell the story of human development from the perspective of bodily becoming.

• • • • •

Class is over. Our time is up. I look around the room. Something has happened here. Cheeks glow. Faces bloom. Bodily selves move with released ease. We are all sorry to go. I can see it: these young people feel beautiful, free, connected, and alive. And they are. These dancers have moved and been moved by the movements they have made and by the movement that makes us all.

The energy in the room crackles. I encourage the dancers to lift up their hands and feel it. Feel what they have created. Take it in. Many of them smile. They know love. The love of dance. Love for what it can do. Love for all those who made it possible. Love for themselves. Life is flowing through them, creating new connections, new relationships, and new possibilities for further movement. And that knowledge, that receptivity, that sense of center is something these dancers will take with them when they leave this room and venture into all areas of their lives.

Martha Graham's words peel through my mind: "Wherever a dancer stands ready, that spot is holy ground."[31] In this moment I know these words as true.

4

To Dance Is to Be Born

In order to work, in order to be excited, in order to simply be, you have to be reborn to the instant. You have to permit yourself to feel, you have to permit yourself to be vulnerable. You may not like what you see, that is not important. You don't always have to judge. But you must be attacked by it, excited by it, and your body must be alive. And you must know how to animate the body; for each it is individual.

—MARTHA GRAHAM, *BLOOD MEMORY*

I am lying in a long, white tub. Somewhere beneath me are its clawed feet. On each side of me its porcelain sheen slopes up, scrolls over, and spills out. When tapped, the tub rings. I am not tapping. I am waiting. I am waiting for the breathtaking squeeze of a contraction. It is coming. My pregnant belly juts up and out of the watery depths, an island of hope that this arc of experience will soon end.

The contraction is near. It is inevitable. I try not to be afraid. Breathing in and down through my bodily self, I invite all my thoughts and feelings, edges and ends, to soften and dissolve into the warming water like so many cubes of sugar. *My bodily self knows what to do. Trust it. Trust yourself. Trust me.*

The rim of a contraction enters my sensory awareness. It comes slowly, then rapidly, storming through my soaking cells. Sensation is everywhere; I am swimming in it. I begin to flail. I cling to what my bodily self knows—the cycle of breaths that I discovered years ago and that I have been practicing.[1] I want to help myself align my attention with the unimaginable transformation that my bodily self is driving and undergoing, all at once. *Become who you are.*

I focus hard. With the earth breath I intentionally let go of muscular tension. I don't need it any more. *Sink. Dissolve.* With an air breath I fill myself with white light until every cell glows brightly. *Beam. Whiten.* With a fire breath I feel the flames beneath my belly button ignite, bringing focus and vitality to the core of my bodily being. *Intensify. Quicken.* With a water breath I allow streams of awareness to flow from my center, carrying this wide-open, light-infused, burning warmth out into space, out into the world. Out of me.

As the water breath completes the cycle, a new sensation pops into view, small but clear. Something in my pelvis is shifting. Stretching. Revealing. The contraction releases.

I smile inwardly. This tiny sensation is a huge reward. I am so encouraged. Something is happening. I feel it. The contractions are working. My hands float on the water. Affirmations bubble through me. It is happening. I am happening. My bodily becoming is happening—is being born.

I am dancing this birth.

From early on in this pregnancy it is what I have most wanted: to dance this birth. I have wanted to call upon the dance-enabled sensory awareness that I have spent years cultivating as the primary resource in navigating safe passage for my little one and for me. I knew that I wouldn't be able to do so in a hospital setting, wrapped in monitors and measured by machines, held high above a cold linoleum floor by a narrow bed.[2] I knew I had to be at home, on the farm, in a warm bath, surrounded by the family who would support me in being as present as possible to the rhythms of bodily becoming.[3]

Through these rhythms life is becoming what it is. How I participate determines who I am. *I choose to dance.*

· · · · ·

When it come to materialist conceptions of the human person, we find one of the most pernicious conceptual obstacles to acknowledging dance as a vital art—one whose validity the three tenets of a materialist paradigm discussed in chapters 1, 2, and 3 all presuppose and reinforce. It is the notion that "we" humans are first and foremost thinking minds living in, over, and against material bodies that "we" minds own and for which we are responsible. It is this mind, this "I," that evolves to study, understand, and master matter. Without such a mind, there would be no way to know that matter is real or that matter evolves or that knowledge about "it" is possible and important. *I think, therefore I am.* Subjectivity is cognitive.[4]

We humans, or so this story goes, are rationally minded beings, the wise ones, Homo sapiens sapiens. We *think* that our capacity to *think* is our distinguished, distinguishing quality. It is a capacity we imagine resides in the byways of our large brains. Perched atop our slender necks, these organs are presumed to act as headquarters for our bodily selves—a command center located primarily in our extensive frontal lobes that processes impressions gathered by our inner and outer senses and generates responses. These minds send messages to the farthest reaches of our bodily selves, demanding obedience and assigning function and meaning to what would otherwise be merely material, even mechanical functions. And they accomplish these tasks, or so we have believed, by wiring trillions of connections among billions of neurons, thereby generating a sense of "self" as the one who can do and is doing the firing and wiring, the thinking, feeling, and knowing.

It follows, according to a materialist paradigm, that our telos, as humans, is to realize the potential of our brains and become minds who can know, own, and control matter. We become human, it is assumed, when we learn to think rationally and logically in response to problems; when we learn to manage our bodily desires; when we learn to rise up above our bodily conditions and converse with others in pursuit of a common ground, good, or goal. We become human when we learn to follow an ideal, take an oath, obey a law, or love God. Whether scholar or artist, scientist or carpenter, caregiver or housekeeper, we evolved to think, and the rest of what we do serves as a means to that end.

This idea that humans are minds over bodies compounds the devaluation of dance that we have already seen occurring within a materialist paradigm. In a world where humans evolved to think, dance not only appears as one way in which a material body can move (chapter 1); or as a form of social cohesion (chapter 2), or as nonverbal knowledge (chapter 3). Dancing also appears as a means by which a thinking mind proceeds to attain a rational end. I choose to dance in order to build strength, burn calories, express emotions, access spiritual states, or seduce a mate. I choose to dance because "I" want to, whether or not it hurts. From a mind over body perspective, the dancing humans do is proof that we are minds capable of instructing our bodily selves what to do and how to do it. *See?*

Moreover, as a means to a thinkable end, dance appears as one of many, and not the most effective or prudent. For exercise, I can choose to run, ski, skate, play football—or dance. For creative satisfaction, I can write a poem, paint a picture, compose a piece of music—or dance. For fun, I can go to a movie, stroll in the mall, take a hike—or dance. But I don't have to dance. I can be human without it. Or can I?

When we shift to a movement paradigm, the answer changes. Once we acknowledge that movement is real, movement evolves, and movement is the medium in and through which we know what we know, then the idea that "we" can control "our bodies," not to mention "matter," is riddled with contradiction. "We" cannot exist as conscious or cognitive selves without the ongoing, unconscious bodily dynamics "we" aspire to control. From a movement perspective, humans are not minds; we are bodily selves whose movements are making us. We are rhythms of bodily becoming, ever creating and becoming patterns of sensation and response that relate us to others in life-enabling ways.[5]

Thus, if we aspire to acknowledge and practice dance as a vital art, we must dislodge the riddled concept of ourselves as minds living in bodies that has been engrained in us by our own movements in modern culture. We must reinterpret the arc of conception and birth by way of our convictions that movement matters, movement evolves, and movement gives rise to knowledge worth knowing. We must retell the story of what it means to be conceived and born as a story of bodily becoming.

Once we do, the implications for our understanding of dance are profound; and it is the task of this chapter to begin to ferret them out. For, once we are able to conceive of a human as a rhythm of bodily becoming, dancing appears as a biological *fact* of human living. Dancing appears as the distinctive kind of movement that pulls a uniquely human bodily self into form. It even makes sense to claim that dancing is what "we" are doing before birth, spontaneously, without example or instruction, in order to build the brains and bodily selves we have the potential to be.

At the same time, from the perspective of bodily becoming, dancing not only appears as a biological fact, it also appears as a biological *necessity*. For if we are born creating and becoming relational patterns of sensation and response, it is all too easy for us to learn to do so in ways that do not support our ongoing becoming. We can discipline ourselves to patterns of movement—thinking, feeling, and acting—that do not express careful attention to our bodily selves. We can learn to ignore our sensations of pleasure and pain. We can learn to ignore the impulses to move arising in ourselves that would guide us to move in life-enabling ways. Thus, the claim that humans are born dancing carries with it a call for ongoing practice: we must learn how to *continue* the dance that we are in ever changing circumstances as ever changing bodily selves. We must dance our own births, again and again. At stake is our humanity.

Beginning Again

I am resting in the wake of another contraction. Ripples of relief cascade through my sensory self. Once again the cycle of breaths brought me through. I marvel at how helpful it is proving. I feel deeply, interminably grateful. But to whom? For what?

It is hard to say. I am grateful to whatever movement of mine pulled this cycle of breaths into my sensory awareness. I am grateful for the lake in which I was swimming, the pain I had been feeling, the sun that was beaming, the strong strokes I was making. I am grateful for my ability to remember the movement pattern, reflect on it, and recreate it. What first seemed like a small sensation of a passing moment, over time and with attention, grew into something quite remarkable with its own persistent pulse that multiplied itself through me, my dancing, my books, and now this birth.

How did it happen? Waiting for the next contraction, my thoughts drift through time. The idea for the cycle of breaths seemed to pop into my mind. I had the thought while making the movement of what would become the first in its series. The earth breath. I was exhaling, breathing down, and releasing myself into the weight of the water as if it were solid ground. My swimming suddenly got easier. I was curious. I repeated this pattern of sensory awareness, extended it, elaborated it. I decided to expand and apply the idea. My thought branched out to other elements—air, fire, water. I experimented and discovered new sensations and possibilities for movement that intrigued me. I opened through them.

My experience of my own self changed then and there. It felt good and right, so I continued. It was exciting. Earth breath to water breath I knew: *every move I make is making me who I am.* With every move I conceive something new. I am born again, regardless of whether I want to, care to, or know that I am. As I practice, because I practice, everything changes. I participate in the elemental currents of creation.

The furrow of a contraction approaches again, dispersing my thoughts. I inhale and plow down into its squeeze. Following the streams of my breath—earth, air, fire, water—I find my way through the tight tunnel into a clearing where I am once again released, floating, eyes closed, quiet and still; me and my belly, in a white porcelain tub, dancing this birth, giving birth to myself.

· · · · ·

Birth is not the beginning. It is a model and metaphor for beginnings, but it never is or was the beginning. What is born must be conceived. In a materialist paradigm that conception occurs as a collision between two microscopic bits of material that unite to form a new entity: an embryo that floats into the uterus and strands on its supple shore. Once attached, in this telling, the embryo proceeds to divide and multiply itself according to explicit instructions written in its cells like letters pressed in wax.[6] Heeding these written commands, the bundle of cells builds itself into a neural tube, sprouts limb buds, and wires the parts together via a neural net that will eventually bring the organism online as a self-conscious mind, capable of exerting coordinated control over its many parts. Being conceived, in this view, is the first step in an inexorable march to becoming someone who can think—or conceive—(for) herself.

In a materialist paradigm, the birth that follows is inevitable. It realizes what is already true: the embryo is its own material entity.[7] As such, birth serves as a model for the breaks that will happen as a human develops into an independent individual, distinguishing himself from caregivers, objects, animals, and the natural world so as to secure an emotional, intellectual, and spiritual autonomy. To become human, in this light, is to be born again as mind or as spirit.[8] Our first birth is a break from the material ground of reality—the mother/matter—that frees us to be born again as the thinking selves we are. We live for this rebirth, ready and willing to spring forth from our own bodies as deftly as Athena leaps from Zeus's skull.

When we approach conception and birth from the perspective of movement, however, the story changes. We realize that we humans are not individual minds born to think ourselves free of our mother/matter bodily beginnings. Rather, in a world where movement matters, we humans are conceived as impulses who are always already *moving*, creating and becoming relational patterns of sensation and response that sustain human life. Our big brains, active minds, and sense of self represent patterns of movement pulled into reality as an expression of the ongoing process they exist to serve: the rhythm of bodily becoming.

Re/Conceiving

Sweeping across the ovary's bumpy surface, fallopian follicles test for a ripening egg—an enfolded movement-potential flooding with hormones. On the inner walls of the fallopian tubes cilia brush back and forth, creating a suction that pulls the swelling egg-ripple into the tube whose peristaltic contractions wave it down toward the uterine hold.

Meanwhile, whipping tails propel sperm squiggles from vas deferens into testicles. Dropped in a sea of semen, they await the squeeze that will carry them forth. Surging against gravity, en million masse, through caustic tides, these squiggles blindly go, not knowing where or why or how. They move because they must: movement is what they are.

Two humans ride toward one another, surfing the currents of mutual desire. Lifted high, they meet and meld, but not all the way. Skin rubs and resists, inside and out. Male and female come close enough to enable smaller movements within each one of them to continue moving toward one another.

While woman and man pull apart, ripples carried by waves, riding tides pulled by gravitational arms, hurling through space in a seemingly infinite round, meet. Within each ripple molecules surge and retreat, their electrons whirling in empty space. A few swimming sperm bump into the egg; the egg lets one wiggler in before sealing her surface shut.

Within the egg's outward press, ripples collide. Each carries memories of movements made in the past that succeeded in expressing life within the womb of a woman and the cradle of a human community. Each ripple carries movement-memories ushering forth from earlier eras, before mammalian mentors and amphibian ancestors, to a time when there were no bodies, no mates, no sex. They come forth from a time when the repertoire of movements made was, to our recently evolved eyes, invisible.

Nothing has changed. Everything is different. The movement that life is still gathers into streams by which it flows, creating and becoming patterns of sensation and response. Now, however, these gathered patterns have the potential to form complex bodily selves who can sense and respond to one another as real, as resources, as relatives. As human.

Two ripples cross and cancel each other's movement potential. They interfere with one another. They do not unite. In their meeting, a new ripple issues forth, a whorl of the current in the river of life. An embryo pulse bobs downstream in time with the wave of the fallopian wall.

Like woman and man or egg and sperm, embryo and womb do not become one. They move close enough to alter each other's movement patterns, allowing for other movements between. They come close enough to weave parallel webs of blood vessels whose contents, seeking parity, flow from one to the other through porous walls. Pulled by absence, pushed by plenty, quotients of oxygen, nutrients, and hormones equalize. Moving in response to their sense of one another, womb and embryo cocreate a placenta that connects and separates them in mutually life-enabling ways. They exchange cells, becoming parts of one another, while each keeps time for its own life flow. An embryo continues to move in relation to itself—doubling and dividing. It swells and splits and pulls into shape a hollow ball of cells along trajectories made possible by the patterns of movements it is making and remembering.

With each twist and turn, cells register the presence or absence of resources circulating around them, within them, and respond accordingly, mobilizing possibilities that promise further movement. With each round of replication the multiplying mound absorbs nutrients and generates waste, in reciprocity with its surrounding space. With every internal rupture it creates and becomes new patterns of sensing and responding—new potentials for moving again, differently, along the paths opened by the previous pose.

In this movement medley there are no determining directions. There is no map to follow. There is only resistance to guide the way—the resistance of movement moving in relation to itself. Each movement is rhythmic—a sensing and responding, reaching and retracting, releasing and contracting. Each phase of the wave is reflexive, doubling back on itself in time, moving against the direction of its own flow, creating a friction that energizes, a swell that fortifies. The resistance arising in movement's relation to itself creates pull and pressure, suction and slide. The most basic units of this emerging organism are not binary bits, but variable wavelengths.

The first asymmetrical patterns of movement potential expressed by this multiplying mass are those with the capacity to register and respond to sensation—the sensations of moving, and from moving. A neural pipe forms along a fold, bending over and into itself, taking shape as a tube within a tube, as a possibility for connection. A neural network threads through projections that press outward as limbs. With every movement of this form, the movement that it is goes one span farther than it did, running the course tracked by a previous arc of sensation.[9]

As the fetal bodily self moves, a brain blooms as record, recorder, and repertoire of movements made. This brain does not direct or determine the process; it undergoes it. It forms to serve the movement that is making the brain what it is. The movements of the bodily self pull the brain inward as a complementary and mutually enabling expression of the movement patterns it is making. Movement makes the brain matter.[10]

A fetus is a kinetic exploring of its womb-world; it is a capacity to remember what ensues. A fetus moves in order to sense. It senses the movements that it makes. It senses the effects of doing so. It moves again, differently. Electrical impulses course through meshing muscles. A heart beats. Pliable bone folds along flexible joints. A thumb wiggles; a mouth opens; legs sweep. Energy patterns leave traces in the brain. The brain expands. Awareness of movement possibilities grows. The fetus's increasingly sophisticated movements continue to fold its brain into shape as an inward expression of the sensations these movements are creating. A thumb finds a mouth. A hand spreads and closes. Soon a mother can sense the quickening. Tiny taps of fists and feet impress her uterine wall.[11]

So too, with each turn and twist of its bodily self, a fetus is not moving alone. Its every move returns to it as a sensation that its mother's movement has crossed and bent. Its every sensation responds to the movements of mother, her womb, their placenta. When mother is active, the small traveler rides quietly. When the womb stills, the fetus echoes her exertion. Every move a fetus makes, every move it remembers, is thus a function of its relationship to whatever movements are impressing it as it moves and so too is the capacity for sensory awareness of itself and others that grows along the way.[12] A fetus, from conception on, builds its bodily self and nascent brain in dynamic relation to the resisting, rubbing walls of mother's womb. A fetus is made by the movements that make it what it is in relation to what is on hand to support the ongoing movement of life, and it does so until, finally, it is hugged so hard that it finds itself finding a way out.

· · · · ·

In this rendering of conception, the brain that a fetus's movement makes exists to serve a bodily self who can and does and must become what it is through movements of its own making. This point is worth pondering. From the perspective of bodily becoming, all that a brain can know and do and process and direct is a function of the movements made by the bodily self of which it is but one expression.[13] Everything that a brain thinks and feels and wants is a *result* of bodily movements made sensory impressions of its bodily self and the world in which and through which it moves.. The brain is a "reality emulator."[14] It exists to create a sense of earth within.

Correlatively, in doing so, a brain does not simply reproduce a picture of the world out there. The images that it makes and remembers are images of what its own bodily movements allow it to perceive—images of its own movement patterns as moved by whatever other movements there are. This emulation, in other words, is not visual or aural or even verbal. It is kinetic. It is relational and multidimensional. The kinetic images of which it is comprised represent possibilities for moving in ways that produce visually, verbally, or audibly perceptible results in relation to others. These kinetic images exist as potential patterns of coordinated action—patterns that reside in our bodily selves and not just between our ears. What "we" remember is how to move and be moved by movements other than our own: how to move with and against, toward and away, for and because.[15]

What a brain does, in this account, by creating and becoming kinetic images of ourselves in relation to our environments, is to serve as a clearinghouse for discerning how, when, and where to express and realize the movement potential that our budding bodily selves already are. A brain does not and cannot act over and against a "body." It does not direct or control bodily action. Rather, it exists in a bodily self, for a bodily self, as an awareness of its own movement possibilities. It exists to aid and enhance the efficacy of the movements that a bodily self is making and to imagine movements it could make—including and especially movements that will grow the ability of its brain to keep it moving effectively. Said otherwise, a brain *expresses* and *exercises* and *enables* the bodily movements that make the brain what it is. A brain exists to become aware of its "self"—that is, of the dynamic rhythm of bodily becoming of which it is one moment—in such a way as to make its ongoing movement likely.[16]

Is this fetus *dancing*? Does it make sense to think of this prenatal movement as dance? Yes, no, and neither. On the one hand, this movement does not rise to the level of sensory awareness identified by the definition given earlier. The self-consciousness required to choreograph a quartet is far from realized. On the other hand, the movements of a newly conceived bodily self do enact the rhythm of bodily becoming—participating, with whatever degree of sensory awareness is extant, in creating and becoming relational patterns of sensation and response. Further, this rhythm of bodily becoming is what will gather and grow the shapes of sensory awareness into a "self" who could choreograph a quartet. In this sense, the movements of a fetus represent *dance in the process of becoming itself.*

Shifting to conceive this fetal movement as a nascent dance allows us to build further on the analyses in chapters 1 and 2. First, we realize that an embryo is, like every apparent material "thing," a potential for movement making. Every movement that it is and does exploits an existing potential of latent movement possibilities. Yet every embryo floats its own path, traces its own route, and sprouts its own placenta. No particular movement is guaranteed. If a spine forms or a limb unfolds, that forming represents a synchronicity—or sync-ability—of movements that life has made in past generations with the challenges and resources of the ever-moving-womb-sustained moment. It represents a life that is ancient, human, and new, pushed and pulled into existence by the multiple conflicting impulses through which life is expressing itself all at once.

Said otherwise, fetuses are living pumps whose every movement draws shapes of life forth from infinite flux and hurls them into the future. Insofar as the shape of a human emerges, then that movement is a unique coming-into-presence of a distinctively human bodily self and its movement-enabled awareness.

Second, by perceiving this fetal movement as emergent dance, we also realize that "we" who have been born have always already been creating and becoming patterns of sensation and response that mark us and make us human. We are always already growing *as* a sensory awareness capable of guiding ourselves from one moment to the next and we do so with as much consciousness as we have folded inward. In this sense dance appears as the *means* by which any bodily self becomes what it is. Dance is the *medium* whose pulses generate the kinds of sensory awareness that distinguish a human being as capable, in time, of participating more and more consciously in the rhythm of bodily becoming.

No human exists whose unique inner-uterine bodily movements do not pull and push its unique brain into form. No human exists whose bodily movements do not channel streams of movement potential reaching back through generations of humans, animals, and elements to the beginning of what we can know. No human exists whose movements do not express the vast matrix of relationships in relation to which it is presently moving. Without this dance, there would be no human life at all. Every human bodily self is a microcosm of the whole, and a macrocosm of the smallest movements made.[17]

Dance, once again, as I am using it here, is not a metaphor for a kind of relating, becoming bodily movement that constitutes human life. Dance is the concrete activity by which humans emerge able to act as distinctively human bodily selves capable of being born—and giving birth. Dance, in this sense, is a biological fact of human life.

Re/Birthing

My thoughts yield to an incoming wave. As another contraction erupts through my entire sensory space, my bodily self grips uncontrollably in response. The breaths are not helpful now. The wave is too big. I am tumbled.

I desperately try to imagine myself as an empty, hollow tube. Empty. Hollow. Done.

I need help. Now. Where is Geoff? Where is my midwife?

Suddenly Geoff enters the room and sits by the side of the tub. He holds my hand. I hold his. We clasp tightly. The stress of being alone eases. I feel him present with me. The kids are downstairs eating dinner. He has served them their favorite meal. The midwife is on her way. There is nothing else to do but wait. Be here. Move together.

Another contraction nears, casting a long shadow before it as it comes. I focus all my attention on the palm of my hand, where it meets Geoff's. The site of our current connection. Skin to skin. Touch to touch. Shingles of fear and effort drop away. I can do this. We can do this. He nods. *Let it happen.*

The wave hits. I squeeze his hand as hard as I can; he squeezes back. I dive into the heat of sensation. Outwardly calm, I am inwardly frantic, searching for a way out. A way through. To be born. Just like my child.

My conscious mind scours my bodily self, desperate for signs, for action, for movement of my own. I look through every cell for proof that this birth is happening. I yearn to dissolve into the rip tide of transformation. I am making these moves. I want to be the one who has made these moves.

The contraction eases, finally, releasing me into a huge space of sensory awareness. Eyes closed, body calm, I feel myself moving across a wide open plain. I am running, flying, dancing.

· · · · ·

Human birth is difficult. In most cases, in most cultures, it is not easy for the mother, for the child, or for anyone in the listening vicinity. Compared to that of every other mammal or primate, human birth is longer, harder, and more dangerous.[18] A human infant's head is so large; a woman's pelvis so narrow. Safe passage is far from guaranteed. While every birthing species courts mortality, the risk is greater among humans. To aid this ostensibly natural process, human birth is wrapped in practices and rituals that are specific to communities and cultures. Around the world and throughout time, human birth has been sustained by shared patterns of movement that members of a community believe are most likely to succeed in bringing forth healthy humans.

When we unpack this observation, we find evidence for why dance is not only a biological fact but an ongoing biological necessity in the process of becoming the human bodily selves we have the potential to be.

Why are human births so difficult? Scholars tend to wrap the reason around an evolutionary "bottleneck" that they predict occurred around the time that Homo erectus disappeared and Homo sapiens appeared, approximately 250,000 years ago. Very few humans survived. Most died away. Many scientists argue that all human genetics can be traced back to one African Eve alive at the time.

When this bottleneck occurred, scholars surmise, hominids had already moved out of the forests and onto the plains. They had been walking upright, on two legs, for at least a few million years; and their skeletons reflected this change. The spinal column attached underneath the skull and not from behind; the face looked forward; the arm rotated around but could no longer swing its body's full weight from trees; the pelvis had narrowed and its front rim tipped up; a big toe and arch structure had formed in their feet, which allowed humans to gather forward energy with every downward press of their springlike step.[19]

For food, it is thought, these early forest-departing hominids first scavenged prey left by larger animals and then, by watching these predators, learned to hunt for themselves. They probably ran after game in packs. They controlled fire, cooked and shared their food, and so maximized their calorie load. They cared for their young collectively. They bonded together in groups of up to 150 people for protection at all hours. And to keep track of all of these activities and social relationships, the story goes, they added a large prefrontal cortex to the typical primate brain, which would come to serve as the basis for later humans' symbolic action, language, law, and culture.[20]

According to evolutionary scientists, it was these pinching pressures—an upright stance and a larger calorie-engorged, socially challenged brain—that created a nearly unworkable situation for females of the pre–Homo sapiens lines: how to move an increasingly large skull through a long and narrowing pelvic ring.[21] The answer was a compromise that did not solve the problem but at least tipped the balance, making birth more likely than death. Evolution selected for infants born earlier than normal and for mothers able to move them out.[22] Homo sapiens survived. By 195,000 years ago, the fossil record suggests that the human head had stopped growing.

Aside from difficult births, this "solution" to the bottleneck carried other implications as well. Human babies, then and now, even when carried a full forty weeks, are born effectively premature relative to other primate babies. They need extensive care, for they are completely and utterly dependent on other humans for their survival. Human infants cannot feed or transport themselves. They cannot hold up their heads or raise a hand. What they know is how to latch mouth around nipple and suck. If allowed to develop in the womb to the level of brain and body maturity common among other mammals and primates, a human infant would emerge a year later, after twenty-one months of womb care.[23] A newborn chimp can haul himself up his mother's belly by gripping on to her chest hair. A newborn human does not have the neural control, kinetic coordination, or muscular strength needed to make such movements and will not for at least twelve months. Given this degree of dependence, the practice of cooperative breeding, already in use, would have proven even more advantageous for human survival.

While the communal caring costs of earlier births are high, scientists surmise that those costs were borne willingly by all who benefited from living upright in large groups.[24] Further, once humans progressed through the evolutionary bottleneck, it is thought that their large brains proved useful for purposes other than managing social relations. Homo sapiens had the bandwidth to develop tools beyond the Homo erectus stage of hammer stones and flint chips and to invent symbols and language beyond the stages of gesture and grunt.

In a matter-based reading of the human story, then, the hull of a fetal head plows into a woman's pelvis and something must give. What gives does so by chance. Genes mutate. Matter evolves by natural selection. Some infants are born earlier. Some mothers (and significant others) are able to care for them. The genes these pairs carry live on. The resulting big brains hold advantages for which they were not initially selected, namely, creating culture.

· · · · ·

When these data points are viewed from the perspective of movement as a case of bodily becoming, a different story appears—one without material collision, compromise, or a coincidental connection between walking and words. Rather, the development of upright walking, early births, and big brains happens together in a mutually enabling, mutually resisting branching of movement possibilities that distinguishes humans from other creatures as dancers.

To begin, the trend toward an earlier birth would have emerged before humans congregated in larger groups and before they felt peer pressure to build social brains. It would have begun as hominids stood upright for longer periods of time. Upright walking induces labor. When a female animal walks upright, the weight of the fetus is held in and up by the same muscles of the pelvis that must open for it to be born. When women are interested in starting or sparking their birth process, they walk. They walk to take advantage of gravity's downward pull, to coax their muscles to release, to relax the tension of anticipation building in their tissues. For any upright animal, the ability to walk, the desire to walk, and the rewards of walking create a matrix of movements within which earlier births are more likely.

At the same time, as noted, when hominids spent more time walking, they freed their primate arms for doing more of what those arms were already doing—holding objects. Walking, humans could use their arms to catch and carry the children whose birth their walking induced.[25]

In this reading, then, the movement patterns of walking and early birthing emerged together, in cooperative and mutually enabling relationship with one another. They emerged as a continuation of movement trajectories already established. They emerged as a possible combination that enabled hominids to move in new directions and take advantage of resources—like sources of food and shelter—farther afield that would further support their ability to keep moving. The entwined movement patterns would have enabled as well the discovery and creation of new patterns of physical, emotional, and mental intimacy between those who carry and those who are carried.[26]

What then of bigger brains and harder births?

While meat eating and cooking were both changes in human movement patterns that delivered greater caloric resources into bodily selves, those calories need not necessarily have flowed to brains. While complex social relations may have called upon our neural capabilities to notice, remember, recreate, and repeat movement patterns, our brains could have responded to this challenge, for example, by perfecting patterns of synchronized movement common to the Canada geese who rest on the beaver pond in front of my farm or by practicing the hierarchical herd consciousness of Jersey cows. (Having horns helps.)

From the perspective of bodily becoming, while sufficient calories and stressful social relations may have precipitated the growth of big brains, that growth would have had to appear along a trajectory of brain activity already in play. The pressure that upright walking exerted on birth created a challenge for infants that was unique among other primates or mammals: *they needed to engage in brain-building bodily movements while outside the womb*. In this telling, the pressure to build a big brain and the ensuing difficulty of birth came from an infant's need to create and become the patterns of sensation and response that would secure for her the relationships with the multiple caregivers she needed in order to survive as the utterly dependent creature she was.

While a primate brain is formed at birth, the brain of a human grows another third during the first year of life.[27] During this time, the newborn human continues to do what it has done since conception: create and become relational patterns of sensation and response that pull and push his potential for movement making into existence. He creates and becomes patterns of sensation and response, cultivating a sensory awareness of the rhythms of bodily becoming. He participates as the level of his consciousness allows. In a word, he *dances*. However, he does so in an environment that is variable and insecure to a degree that life in the womb can never be. Born so early, a human infant cannot rely on instinct to the extent that any other primate can. He must have the ability to wire his own patterns of preferred movement. And insofar as he is raised by a collective of caregivers—as a dependent infant requires—the stakes of such movement pattern creation are high.[28]

The movement patterns of walking and early birthing, then, required human infants to exercise and thus fund and develop to a unique extent a set of movement-making abilities they were already practicing in the womb. A human infant must be able to notice, remember, and recreate patterns of movement occurring in her and around her. She must have a sense of pain and pleasure to guide her in coordinating these movements. And, most important, she must be able to experience her own sensations of pleasure and pain as catalysts for receiving new movement possibilities along the trajectories of movements she is and has already made. In other words, in order to continue becoming the *biological* self she has the potential to be, a newborn infant has to continue *playing with movement*. Only then will she be able learn how to connect with caregivers and communicate her needs in ways that will entice these others to respond.[29]

The ability to move with and in relation to others is not equivalent to empathy, though it enables it (see chapter 5). It is not mere imitation, though it sometimes looks like it. It does not require self-consciousness. It is not something that can appear in the fossil record. It is not even exclusively human: all animals respond to aural or visual or kinetic stimuli in site-specific ways. Nevertheless, in humans, this ability to create and become relational patterns of sensation and response is of necessity more highly developed than in any other species. Movement making is as important for our species-being as thumb and big toe. Once infants emerge from the womb, they cannot continue becoming the biological beings they have the potential to be unless they are continually learning and relearning how to *dance*.

Thus, from the perspective of bodily becoming, the Homo sapiens shift toward earlier birth appears as a movement possibility prompted by walking that created a situation in which a movement-making capacity already at work in the animal world was exercised and developed to be more responsive, relational, and creative than ever before. The task of learning to play with movements so as to find ways of moving well with others pulled into existence the brain that had done it. In short, it was the action of learning how to make increasingly complex and differentiated bodily movements when walked and squeezed early from our mothers that grew the hominid brain.[30] We grew big brains in order to dance, and keep dancing, well.

In turn, these brains, as they grew, redoubled the press toward early birth and prolonged, attentive cooperative caregiving that was already occurring among hominids. In fact as brains grew, their enhanced capacity to create and become movement patterns served this progression toward bigger brains and earlier births. Because humans were already exercising their ability to record, remember, and recreate the myriad movements of their social and natural environments, mothers and infants were able to imagine the creative responses needed to navigate harder births. Caregivers were able to handle the challenges of relating with less able infants. The brains that required earlier births also enabled human women to dance those births.

Once we acknowledge its constitutive role in a human's bodily becoming, the ability to dance appears as a capacity that may even mark the "phase transition" that catalyzed the emergence of Homo sapiens.[31] As brains grew larger, humans were those hominids who could survive their challenging births by pulling together and dancing their way through. Infants, mothers, and others could mobilize their movement-making ability to create and become relational patterns of movement capable of supporting them all.

Organisms do not need brains in order to sense, respond, or remember. Maple trees and seaweed do just fine without.[32] But organisms do need brains in order to *move* themselves intentionally from place to place. They need brains in order to create and become patterns of movement that are responsive to the resources and requirements of a given moment. And it is the evolutionary exploitation of this particular capacity that the human species represents.

In this telling, then, the push to early birth is not a solution to a problem of colliding materialities. It emerges as one movement possibility within a web of existing movement patterns that opened up along established trajectories of movement. Humans stood and walked; births occurred earlier, and brains grew bigger to accommodate the challenges of being born so immature: they had to learn how to move. These brains could grow bigger because the potential for them to do so was already in place: that growth was simply a continuation of the rhythms of bodily becoming that had been happening in the womb. So too, as brains grew bigger, births could grow harder because humans were already able and willing to use their sensations of pain to help them discover patterns of moving with one another, in support of one another. They could dance their births. Homo sapiens emerged from this "bottleneck" as creatures who can and must learn to make patterns of movement in order to become *biologically* human.

Subsequently, these movement-enabled brains did not just work to improve the birth experience or the relationships between infants and caregivers. They opened up new possibilities for infants in relating to their own bodily selves—for playing with the movement potentials of inherited patterns given in a hand, tongue, lips, and larynx. Playing with these movement patterns would have accelerated the discovery of what can be done with bones and hides, with food and fire, and so forge new movement-enabling alliances with resources (other than caregivers) in their worlds. In this account, Homo sapiens could fashion new tools, create dance rituals, and begin to circulate symbols *because* they had been exercising their ability to create and become life-enabling patterns of sensation and response in relation to birth. Their movement-enabled brains created the conditions within which evolution could select physical and metabolic features for their *movement-making potential*—that is, for their adaptability within an uncertain ever changing world.

When conceived in terms of bodily becoming, the culture and language that Homo sapiens went on to create were not offshoots of a material solution to an evolutionary bottleneck. They represented expressions of the potential for movement-creation released by a walking-induced change in the movement patterns relating mother, newborn child, and the community. Such hominids evolved into humans: creatures for whom dancing is a *biological* necessity.

• • • • •

Everywhere I turn, I find new evidence that our bodied brains and the "mindness states" they support have evolved for the express purpose of helping us move our bodily selves in the most efficient, expedient, and expressive ways. That evidence is appearing in fields ranging from neuroscience and developmental psychology to nutrition and exercise physiology. Although few follow through with the implications for the ongoing practice of dance as a vital art, these scientists are blazing the trail by rooting our self-conscious thinking in the movements of our bodily selves.

For example, as scientists have determined, in the brain, the largest band of grey matter spanning ear to ear, separating the older and newer parts of the brain, is the sensory-motor cortex. In this arc of flesh, scientists have located maps of our bodily selves that correspond point by point to anatomical locations. While the techniques of neuroscience and the metaphor of a map encourage us to think about this cortex as a set of *visual* representations—pictures of body parts—scientists admit that these maps form and reform constantly as a function of the movements we make in sensing and responding. These maps express and guide the movements we have made and are capable of making with tools, instruments, and objects. They express a play with the movement capacities remembered in the patterns of our muscles and bones.[33] From the perspective of bodily becoming, then, it would be more accurate to think about these "maps" as kinetic images. Each "place" represents a set of movement patterns made and remembered. Any body part "appears" on the map if and when "it" can be mobilized in spontaneous, formal, relational open-ended movement. The map is less topographical than it is choreological.[34]

Further, once thought to operate as discrete systems, the sensory and motor systems are now generally understood as braided together.[35] How we move influences how and what we sense. How and what we sense impacts how we move. Sensation itself is a form of being impressed. Movement itself is a form of sensing in action. There can be no pattern of sensation that is not also a pattern of responding, and vice versa. And in some cases we respond as we are sensing, before the signal of sensation even travels to the brain. Every pattern of movement—from cardiac to conscious, from cellular to systemic—is what I have been calling a pattern of sensation and response, and every pattern of sensation and response is a pattern of movement. What we can think and feel and do and know is both limited and enabled by the movements, willed and otherwise, that are making us.[36]

Scientists are also discovering that the prefrontal cortex, so-called seat of our executive thinking functions, or "mind," does not operate in isolation from the older parts of the brain as their commander, as once thought. The relationship is nearly the reverse. At every turn, the processing that the prefrontal cortex performs is wired through sections of the brain responsible for emotions, memories, sensations, actions, and other physiological processes.[37]

It is increasingly evident that the prefrontal cortex is equipped to serve these older parts of the brain by helping clarify and execute the most life-enabling movements—like those of giving birth—where the criteria for life-enabling remains accountable to our basic physiological functions.

Further, that primary service provided by the prefrontal cortex is not, as once imagined, one of inhibition and self-control. It is not one of predicting, planning, and suppressing emotional and instinctual drives in pursuit of a rational goal. The prefrontal cortex does act to stop reflex actions and habitual patterns. However, this action is not about inhibiting primal desires; rather, this stopping serves to clear a space of sensory awareness—to hold open a space for the activity of bodily creativity—so that a person can receive impulses to move that respond to the moment in ways that will best honor, express, and satisfy those desires. The prefrontal cortex serves to encourage and allow receptivity as much as it does action. It enriches perception and experience as much as it generates ideas.[38]

This interdependent relationship between the prefrontal cortex and other areas of the brain extends to the human use of language as well. The area of the prefrontal cortex that is responsible for sending signals for making sounds, Broca's area, is also the portion of the brain whose mirror neurons (discussed further in chapter 5) fire when a person watches another person use a tool. This coincidence suggests that the capacity to manipulate movement and the capacity to manipulate sound coevolved, perhaps in Homo erectus. It not only suggests that the first symbols human used were patterns of bodily movement but also that our ability to manipulate symbols at all is thickly dependent upon the bodily movements we make.[39]

Correlatively, as neuropsychologists are establishing, our brains, in all these bodily entanglements, are also and thus inherently relational. Because our brains grow by a full two-thirds while outside the womb, their very biology is informed by our experiences in the world—or, rather, by the movements we make in and in relation to the world. Our neonate brains need our bodily selves to move and be moved in order to keep developing, and the experiences we have influence the creation of neural pathways that serve as the default patterns of thinking, feeling, and acting.[40] In describing this phenomenon, scientists use the term *experience-dependent development.*[41]

What we are only beginning to acknowledge, however, is that (in a situation similar to the case with epigenetics, chapter 2) *experience-dependent* might be more accurately rendered as *movement-dependent* or *movement-interdependent*. As noted earlier, it is not just what we experience that shapes us—as if "it" existed out there as a material thing or person whose qualities we passively perceive. Rather, the movements we make in sensing and responding pull our brains into shape as biological powerhouses capable of supporting and guiding us in finding and exploiting future movement possibilities. "Experience" itself is a function of how we are moving and how the movements we are making, in concert with all of the movements in whose flows we swim, are making us.[42]

In short, current research is coalescing around the radical idea that how we move as bodily selves matters to the biological development of our brains. The movements that humans make in being born early have precipitated a need to create and lay down relational movement patterns in the physical structures of our brains that then exist in us with the same compelling force as a womb-readied instinct. In creating and becoming relational patterns of sensation and response, infants develop both a sense of their bodily selves as moving and a sense of the world out there capable of supporting that ongoing action, with one as a function of the other.[43]

This shift in our understanding of sensation and experience again recalibrates our understanding of what consciousness or mindness is and does. Consciousness itself is nothing more or less than patterns of relational bodily movement. It exists as a rhythmic oscillation between inner and outer sensation pulled into awareness as we move and are moved by others. At no time is our sense of one wholly independent of the sense of the other. We feel the smooth surface of an egg and the feeling of being touched by it.[44] Everything that appears to us in consciousness and as consciousness expresses movements we have made and been moved by. Consciousness arises in us as patterns of sensory attention that our bodily movements have made possible. As conscious beings we are not only able to discern which movements will be best for us to make in a given moment, we find ourselves making them spontaneously, as a function of an attuned sensory awareness. We hold the glass gently. We adjust our sitting positions to release the crick in our neck. So too, we can also learn to make these movements "consciously," as a function of our thinking, where all that "thinking" has to go on are past experiences we have already had moving and being moved.[45] We can learn to do what we are always already born doing—we can learn to dance—and we must.

This movement-enabled reading of consciousness sheds further light as well on what seems unique in humans: *self*-consciousness. Humans have a sense of "self" that, as we can now appreciate, develops as a function of the movements those humans learn to make. As noted, a fetus in the womb senses and responds. She is aware. As electrical pulses contract her muscles, she picks up sensations. Gravity and mass, bars of light and thumps of sound, impress patterns of movement that move inward. The fetus's movement changes, spontaneously, creatively, in line with its movement potential; as her movements shift, a fetus not only experiences her own movement, she feels the experience of being transformed by (that) movement.

Once born, the infant's experience of how his movements make him only intensifies. A fetus not only feels the experience of being moved, he finds himself spontaneously recreating movement patterns in response that travel along pathways of electrical flow opened in the womb. Soon the infant is remembering both the pattern of movement as well as the sensations it yielded— the easing of discomfort and appeasing of desire. Over time, as we shall explore further in chapter 5, this sense of learning to move—of being able to make a new move—forms an organizing node for an accumulating collection of kinetic images. A sense of "self" takes shape as what has moved, can move, and will move again in particular patterns of sensation and response.[46]

Here again, humans differ from other animals, but only in degree. All animals are conscious of being a "self." All animals learn to move in response to sensations of pleasure and pain, and often do so in response to changes in their environments that our senses can barely perceive. Yet we humans, with our duller senses and uncoordinated movements, because we are born early, are present to our learning process in a way that no other womb-readied animal is. We have an experience of our "self" as creating, as learning, as becoming; we have a sense of ourselves as feeling the pleasure of doing so. We love the sensation of receiving and making a new move. We seek out this experience of playing with movement possibilities and we do so as much for the pleasure the experience gives us—for the sense of "self" it yields—as much as for any particular result. We humans are born yearning to conceive and give birth to ourselves.

As adults, we cannot call to mind the events that happened to us when we were infants and young children. But we do remember patterns of sensation and response that we created and have become. We remember how to roll, crawl, walk, stand, beat a spoon on the table, and tip a cup. And every time we mobilize a pattern of sensation and response in response to a new moment—every time we fire and wire that neural-muscular connection—we build upon those memories in shaping a sense of "self" as the one who did. This self-who-did is thoroughly relational and thoroughly embedded in the bodily matrix that her movements are creating. It represents an ability to be open in the moment to sensing other movements that honor and extend her bodily potential.[47]

In this account, then, human self-consciousness is not identical to thinking power; nor is it simply a matter of reflection. It is not due to a spiritual or transcendent entity that resides within us, nor a soul or spirit that promises to fly from us. It is neither constant nor continuous. Rather, the bodily movements we cannot not make pull into awareness a sense of our "self" as *moving* that floats in us as a kind of radar for recognizing and receiving impulses to make new moves. "Self" is what the movements we make pull into consciousness as an expression of movements we have made, can make, want to make, can conceive of making, and can plan to make—that is, as a condition of our ongoing movement. It is a "self" that the movements we make constantly recreates along the trajectories of its ongoing movement. It is a self that functions as a center—a sensory range where we are vulnerable to moving and being moved.

Moving and being moved, we seem real to ourselves. We make ourselves matter. While this experience of our own multiplicity may even lead us to imagine that "we" are thinking minds existing over and against material bodies whose movements we own and control, that idea is simply an expression of a capacity to move in a given direction that we are exercising in ourselves.[48]

Finally, also relevant to this discussion is a recent finding among neuroscientists that this rhythm of bodily becoming as I am describing it is coextensive with human life. Our mature brains maintain a *plasticity* characteristic of young in other species.[49] We can continue not only to make new neural connections among existing cells; we can generate new brain cells. Within a movement paradigm, the implications are immense. Humans never lose the capacity to keep creating and becoming new patterns of movement and recreating their sense of self. There is no end to the shoreline of sensory awareness. More to the point, humans never lose the *need* to keep learning new movements as the enabling condition of their health and well-being. The act of moving our bodily selves—of playing with movement patterns and discovering and learning new ones—is precisely the kind of exercise that keeps our biological brains alive. It keeps our sense of self alive. Without such exercise, we lose neural, muscular, and (as further chapters elaborate) emotional, intellectual, and spiritual tone.[50]

In these discoveries lies further support for the claim that dancing is a biological necessity. The lifelong ability to create and become new patterns of sensing and responding carries with it an ability to unlearn at least some of the patterns we have made earlier in our lives. Once an infant is born, it is not assured that she will continue to create and become movement patterns that align with her best bodily becoming unless she is consciously cultivating a sensory awareness of herself as movement.[51]

Most children, raised free from trauma or abuse, readily retain their sensory awareness for several years at least. Children will still move spontaneously, freely, open-endedly, in response to movement that appears to them. They move to music; they recreate the movement patterns of animals; they run and skip and dance in nature.[52] However, as a child progresses within the realm of culture, learning to read and write, he also becomes fully capable of creating and becoming movement patterns that arrest this capacity to sense and respond to movement patterns.[53] He becomes capable of creating and becoming movement patterns that sustain the forward pulse of life forms other than himself—patterns that express a lack of attention to the enabling conditions of his ongoing movement.

Humans can learn to want food that makes us sick, drugs that fry our brains, and behaviors that overwhelm and dull our senses. We can internalize patterns of violent behavior, repeat the abuse, and recreate situations of depression and despair. We can mature into creatures who aspire to forms of self-destruction from which healthy animals would turn away in disgust.[54] We can grow to love our virtual worlds more than our own bodily selves. Because our brains are so movement dependent, we are fully capable of learning to move in ways that deaden us to the sensation of what our own movements are creating, and of where our center is taking hold. We are capable of unlearning patterns of pleasure and pain that guide us in knowing what is *good* for us to think and feel and do.

To become healthy humans, then, we need to keep cultivating the sensory awareness that will give us a purchase on how we are moving and being moved—on the movements we are making and what they are creating in us, as us.[55] We need to invest the ample mental powers our movements have engendered in the project of becoming a bodily self, of moving in ways that help us discover what a human bodily self can do. We need, in other words, to practice dancing, and we need to do so for life.

Dance is not only a biological fact; it is a biological necessity. We need to practice creating and becoming relational patterns of sensation and response, consciously and deliberately, throughout our lives, in order to build brains and bodily selves capable of making movements that will serve and enable our ongoing vitality. We need to cultivate a sensory awareness of ourselves as rhythms of bodily becoming, alert to the movements we are making. And we need consciously to internalize a sense of self—a self-conscious awareness—that is capable of not only guiding us but *enlivening* us to the possibilities of action in the moment.[56]

Dancing, in this sense, is not a question of learning steps or mastering technique or performing on stage; it is a question of discovering and disciplining ourselves to our own capacity to move. It is a question of learning how to participate as consciously as possible in the rhythms of bodily becoming so that we can align our actions with creating a world in which we want to live—and being born into it.

Because we humans are born early, we are biologically primed to dance as the enabling condition of our best brained, bodily becoming. The question is not whether but how.

· · · · ·

I reach up inside myself and feel a soft squishy film covering a hard head. It feels so far away, so deep within me. Panic flashes again. How will this baby ever get out? Suddenly pressure releases from somewhere inside. A gush surrounds me. The water has broken. We are closer—the baby and me. I feel a hard head now. A circle of bone.

A contraction seizes me as we drain the tub. It drains me. Bent in a deep plié, with all weight on my toes, I wrap my arms around Geoff, whose arms are wrapped around me. I am desperately trying to let go, let be, let live.

A wave of love and desire and yearning surges forth in me, rises up, and crashes as my lips meet Geoff's. A passionate kiss seals the circle we are completing. The contraction releases.

I sink back into the tub. My gaze is pulled to the door. There are my four children, looking over at me. Watching. Waiting. As their mother cleaves in two. Seeing them releases in me a burst of hope and confidence. *I have done this. I can do this. It is so worth it.*

A mighty roar of a push turns me inside out. A head appears. The baby is out, on the towels, in the cradling curve of this now dear tub. Trembling am I with effort, relief, cold, happiness. It is a him. I lift him up onto my belly, and press his compact self against my emptied balloon. He was in. Now he is out. He was far. Now he is near. We made it apart, so we can spend the rest of our lives getting to know one another, growing closer than we ever were.

He is all curled up—fists clenched, legs curled, arms pinned to his sides. Slowly he will stretch out and up, sensing and responding along the trajectories of his bodily self. He will open to the energy of the universe flowing in him, as him, through him into the world. He knows how. It is all he knows. He is a dancer too, after all.

Re/Birthing

It is a lingering fantasy of Western minds: to undo our birth and reunite with the mother. Nostalgia for the oceanic feeling of floating in the womb pervades art and literature, philosophy and psychology, ritual and religion.[57] Raised with these images, we learn to make these moves. We learn to want to be plugged in, tuned out, returned to a place where all our needs are met. A place where there is no desire. No longing. No want. No pain. No reason to move. Constant coitus. A land of milk and honey. A heavenly garden. Nirvana. Bliss.

From the perspective of bodily becoming, we see anew. This desire for union with the mother in both its secular and religious expressions is a materialist fantasy.[58] To our matter-trained sensibilities, she appears as the original Mater for whom we cry out as we walk and wander in search of food and shelter. We were born too early, too young, too helpless, and too immature. Convinced that the way back is forever barred, we struggle forward, seeking a second home in the peace and power of our womblike minds. We immure ourselves in word-worlds of our own making, denying our bodily selves, striving to be born again into a place where we are (with the) divine. The pure, disembodied *I am*.

Yet, from the perspective of bodily becoming, we realize that this yearning for senselessness is itself a pattern of movement we have made and mastered that keeps us moving in sync with word-worlds where matter is real, matter evolves, and matter is worth knowing by minds who can. When we retell the story of human conception and birth in terms of bodily becoming, we realize that what we most desire may not be communion with the mother after all. There are other moves to make.

As we cultivate a sensory awareness of ourselves as movement, we begin to sense, woven through our physiospiritual selves, a deep desire for the primal squeeze of being born—for that swell of contraction that wrings us dry, snaps open our senses, and releases us into a feeling of being alive. We realize that we want this rhythm, this contraction and release, this movement across the surfaces of our sensory potential. We want the difference, the generative tension that nourishes us and keeps us moving.

Birth is the squeeze shared by mother and child that brings sense to life. That brings desire to life. Literally. Birth marks a surge of intensity where the movement of life ruptures into a new relationship, divides internally, and expresses itself in the release of new movement. Birth is an opening, a connecting, a flow. It is ecstatic. It is always singular, always one, never guaranteed. It marks a pattern of coordinated movements that neither mother nor infant nor anyone present can make before they do. It cannot be rehearsed. Every time, every birth, is a completely unprecedented occasion that sets the entire dance of our lives on a new course. And, once it happens, it is a pattern of movements made that remains within us as an invitation and guide to recreating that sensation of being brought to life.

Perhaps what will give us the greatest satisfaction is not merging with Mom but having her hug us into health. Perhaps we are happiest not when dissolved into her ocean, but when feeling the resistance from her shores that enables us to find our own swirling center within. Perhaps our deeper biological longing is not to become minds who can direct our bodily selves to sit—but to become bodily selves with minds primed to help us dance our ongoing birth.

5

To Dance Is to Connect

We must consider the relation with others *not only as one of the contents of our experience but as an actual structure in its own right.*

—MAURICE MERLEAU-PONTY, *THE PRIMACY OF PERCEPTION*

The midwife hands Geoff a pair of scissors. He cuts the cord, which is more like a rope—thick, slick, and knobby. At first the cord resists, as I did, and then yields to the sharp press of the shears. It is over. We are two. Little Leif is one, an individual, his own person, breathing. I am alone in my bodily self.

I am flooded. Waves of relief, joy, and discomfort splash through me. It is over. I did it. My legs shake beyond recognition. The tub that was once a comfortable, holding arc is now hard and cold. My fifth birth—I thought it would be easy. I couldn't have done it without the practice, the concentration, the support. I am so grateful.

I did it. We did it. I look down at him, snugly tucked against my spongy belly, wrapped in my arm. I scan his face, his wrinkled limbs, his barrel torso, and the cut end of the cord that connected us. I feel utterly happy yet deeply sad. I miss him inside of me. I can barely sense his weight. I can smell him, squeeze him—he is with me—and, still, he remains apart. On his own. On me. I try to fathom the thought. The reality. The moment.

His eyes are open. His gaze wanders. I move mine in an effort to catch his, thinking I might be able to see inside, into his future, and know something about who he is. But "he" is not yet there in a way with which my "I" can connect in words or thoughts or feelings. Conceived in me, emerging from me, dependent upon me, he confronts me as a stranger. A moving bundle of sensory potential. Precious. Fragile. Foreign.

He cries. The movements his diaphragm made in the womb, contracting and releasing, now pull warm air across his vocal chords, sounding him out. His call to life reverberates through every exhausted, ecstatic cell of my bodily self. We are still one.

I close my eyes and lie back against the tub, holding him tightly against me. I know that I am supposed to care for this child. I am supposed to feel love for this child—whatever that is. But how? How do I love this scrawny, squalling, slippery armful of movements made and remembered? This little with-me without-me? Little Leif? How can I learn?

I place a nipple in his mouth.

· · · · ·

Once the dance-limiting idea of a human being as mind-in-body falls away (chapter 4), a twin idea appears close behind, ready to topple as well. It is the idea that we human beings are individuals first and foremost—autonomous units who evolved to protect, preserve, and reproduce our genetic fingerprints. This companion idea, equally rooted in a matter-model of reality, is as detrimental to affirming dance as is the notion that we are thinking minds living in matter-bound bodies.

Yet, as this chapter tells, a shift to a perspective of bodily becoming reveals a dance-friendly story at the heart of our attachment to individuality. Building on the discussions of evolution in chapter 2 and chapter 4, this chapter explores a corollary that is also a paradox: we humans are as *individual* as we are by virtue of the *relationships* our bodily movements create with those who support us in becoming who we are. In other words, every movement "we" as individuals make expresses an *impulse to connect* with whatever other movements have enabled and will enable our ongoing participation in the rhythms of bodily becoming.[1]

With this shift in our notion of human individuality come ample resources for affirming dance as a vital art. For not only does dancing appear to be necessary for building *biological* selves (as discussed in chapter 4), but dancing appears to be necessary for building *ethical* selves as well. As this chapter elaborates, dancing may be fruitfully envisioned as an activity that provides humans with the knowledge we need in order to *connect* with other humans in *mutually* life-enabling ways.

The knowledge that dancing affords is the same sensory awareness of ourselves as moving that we discussed in chapters 3 and 4. Yet here we tease forth an added dimension of its importance. This sensory awareness can not only guide us in finding movements that build our brains and bodily selves, it can guide us in cultivating, over time, ways of moving in relation to others that respond and contribute to the ongoing health and well-being of those others as well as of ourselves. The act of dancing is the experiential source and the guiding solution of a distinctively human paradox we enjoy in being irreducibly singular yet ultrasocial creatures.

Because we humans can and must dance, we have evolved into creatures who need to live in loving relations with others as the enabling condition of our individual bodily becoming. We have evolved into creatures for whom the act of dancing is an ethical necessity.

Almost Individual

The idea that a human being is an individual first and foremost currently enjoys a sphere of influence so large that its territory is difficult to map. In a conceptual world where matter is real and evolves, "individuals" are autonomous, body-bound agents who are inherently self-serving. Individuals use their mental and physical skills to compete with one another for access to resources they each need to thrive. Those who secure more for themselves pass their genes onto the next generation, enacting a "natural" selective pressure for traits that clinched their victory. Such individuals, the story goes, can and may choose to enter into relationships with other individuals if and when it furthers their own chances of surviving and reproducing. "I" come(s) first.

Within modern culture, this idea of a human being as an individual serves as the basic conceptual unit for nearly all forms of social organization and knowledge. An "individual" is the unit we use not only to chart evolutionary trends. It is also the *one* to whom we accord legal rights, grant political representation, and apply laws. Individuals are the ones whose behavior we monitor and measure, reward and reprimand. Individuals are subjects who can act freely, and bear the responsibility of doing so. Individuals drive, vote, pay taxes, join organizations, and befriend whomever they want. Given the right person, they may choose to marry. Becoming such an independent, responsible subject is considered the goal of psychological development, and encouraging that development is the goal of effective parenting, education, and personal counseling.

In short, the idea that humans are individuals first looms in our culture as an ideal, a value, and a guide to action. We grow up believing that we are individuals, and in nearly everything we do we work hard to prove ourselves true.

· · · · ·

Despite its ubiquity, the idea that humans are individuals first is one whose reign has always been contested and is again under fire for the simple fact that it is haunted by a contradiction: humans cannot exist as the individuals they are *without* other humans. It is not only helplessly dependent infants who need other humans, but children and adults too. From our earliest days on earth, as we have seen, humans have needed other humans in order to hunt and gather and cook food, to raise young, compete with predators, and defend ourselves from attack. So too today, humans need friends, partners, colleagues, and acquaintances in all professions in order to eat, dress, own property, act properly, set up house, travel, or earn a livelihood.

In fact, as noted in chapter 4, the demands of human social life are frequently pegged as a driving force behind the evolution of a human-sized neocortex. Seeking evidence for this theory, a team of researchers correlated the size of the mammalian neocortex relative to body weight, on the one hand, with group size, on the other, across a range of species. They found that the bigger the front brain, the bigger the social group; and humans ranked at the top of the mammalian graph. Based on the size of the human neocortex, scientists predict that humans are creatures who evolved to live in proximate groups of 150 or so. The examples of the few existing hunter-gatherer societies, as well as the average membership of church congregations and military units, are data points that support this view.[2]

It is fair to say that humans have evolved into creatures who cannot become *human* without regular, close engagement with other like-minded, like-bodied beings. Humans need such interpersonal challenge, stimulation, and support in order for their brained, bodily selves to manifest their processing power.

Moreover, as scientists are realizing, humans are not just social animals, we are *ultra*social animals. Although our immediate circles of association may range to 150, we live comfortably, sometimes preferably, in colonies of thousands and even millions of other humans. Even those of us who opt for rural life are generally connected with urban multitudes through channels of production and consumption, not to mention communication.

So too, we humans are the only known ultrasocial creatures who organize their extensive societies on some version of male-female bonding, mostly involving one of each. Other ultrasocial species (e.g., bee, wasp, ant, or naked mole rat) live in communities comprised of children born to one "queen," the egg maker and mother of all. Humans, perhaps uniquely, have evolved an ability—and a need—to establish extensive networks of intimate, cooperative relations with fellow creatures who do not share their genetic movement-potentials.[3] We not only need to be in relationship with other people, we need to learn how to *love* them.

Hence the ethical paradox with which modern, postmodern, and new materialist studies of human relationships from ethics to psychology, philosophy, theology, and political theory frequently wrestle: if we humans are individuals first and foremost, why do we want and need so intensely to bond with other humans? Conversely, if what we most want is to bond with one another in relationship, why are our relationships so fraught with conflict? Why is it so difficult for humans to stay married, govern cooperatively, or avoid war? If we want (to) love so much, why is it so hard for us to learn how? Then again, is it so easy to be an individual in the first place?[4] In short, how do we, as individual humans, create cooperative, caring, just communities? Or how do we, as members of communities, foster the development of healthy individuals?

Individuals Who Attach

I am resting now, or trying. Leif is nursing, and, as he does, his pulling triggers wrenching uterine contractions. The labor is supposedly over. I want a break. I feel myself relaxing, baby in arms, and now the knife! I know I need it. My bodily self is making the movements that will help me close up that plate-sized placental wound inside of me. But I am not prepared. It may be the hardest challenge yet. I hold my breath and try to breathe both at once.

The seizing pain finally releases, leaving ripples of ease in its wake. I breathe deeply. The pleasure of nursing returns. I look down at Leif's small head and feel pulses of warm affection. I smile. I am feeling what I recognize as love. Is it? I am sure some test could track the oxytocin, prolactin, and pain-released endorphins charging through my blood vessels. But what would those plotted points mean? Is love a chemical reaction to physical stimulation—one that I share with my mammalian kin?

Certainly, my bodily self and Leif's bodily self are making movements made by generations of species before us—patterns of movement remembered in the form and function of our interlocking organs, muscles, and nerves. I am also making movements I have learned to make from other humans who have gone through this process—humans I know personally or whose stories I have heard. Leif and I are biosocial patterns of movement that have proved life-saving for many mother-infant pairs.

Making these life-saving movements feels good. Nursing, as medical experts encourage me to do, I feel a pleasure that orients me to my child, reminding me to seek him out, hold him close, and give him what I have to give. Nursing, as my movements in relation to Leif enable him to do, he feels the pleasure of warm nourishment flowing from my bodily self into his, reminding him to turn toward me when he feels discomfort. I know his pleasure by the way he moves: he gives himself completely to the act of receiving. Bearing witness to his pleasure amplifies mine: I want more and to do more for him, in a spiral of escalating intensity and often joy.

My baby and I are chemically, aesthetically, emotionally vulnerable to one another's movement. We each exist as an ability and desire to connect with the other as the best possible circumstance for enabling our own ongoing movement. Our bodily selves move toward one another, with one another, to nurture and be nurtured by the other. I am not an individual; neither is he.

Yet the connection between us, latent in the movement patterns of our bodily selves, is never guaranteed to manifest or endure. At this moment I could lose Leif and live. He could lose me and never remember who I am. For our connection to persist, we must keep giving ourselves to the movements that the movement of the other evokes in us. What matters most to the endurance of our life-enabling, pleasure-yielding connection is whether and how we *dance*.[5]

• • • • •

In the psychological sciences the dominant models for describing how individual humans learn to establish loving relationships with other humans fall under the umbrella of "attachment theory."[6] In this line of thinking, the key to a person's ability to form lasting relationships with others lies in whether or not she forms positive "attachments" with her caregivers as an infant.

Attachment, in this view, describes an emotional bond characterized by trust. A well-attached infant trusts that his caregiver will meet his needs. He "feels felt." Such an infant wires this emotional reality into the biological structure of his immature brain. He develops a sense of being safe and secure in the world that grounds and pervades his emerging sense of bodily self. As he matures, he is able to find comfort and comfort himself because he knows at a cellular, neuronal level that his needs will be met.

Later in life this sense of comfort enables a person to trust that others will care for her, respond positively to her, and move with her. She is thus able to open to others, and to share herself with them, because she has already had positive, life-enabling experiences of doing so. She feels secure in doing so. She knows love as something that matters. Something real.[7]

Of course, infants do not always form healthy attachments with their caregivers, and much of the literature on attachment describes what can go wrong and the implications of what happens when it does. For example, if an infant has caregivers who do not respond to his needs consistently, then he may not learn to trust others. If he does not have an experience of feeling felt, he may lay down patterns of self-protection that interfere with his ability to build interpersonal bonds across differences, whether in friendship, marriage, or community. He may be bound by anger, grief, or fear and reluctant to open and share with others. As a result, these others may turn away, perceiving him as cold, unsympathetic, and not interested in the love he most wants.

What determines whether or not secure attachments form between infant and caregiver? In evaluating the most important variables, psychological researchers generally assert that the lion's share of the responsibility falls with the caregiver. A caregiver must be able to respond to an infant's needs and desires

114

regularly and consistently with empathy. If a caregiver does not, the helpless infant has no place to go for help and comfort except farther inside herself. Yet, as noted in chapter 4, researchers also acknowledge that infants must be able and willing to act in ways that draw their caregivers near in order to secure a proper attachment; both individuals must act in relation to the other.

Hence the ethical paradox characteristic of the human species assumes a familiar contemporary formulation: how do infants and caregivers *attach* to one another in mutually life-enabling ways? What cultural moves can we make to support that process of attachment? It is a question that lurks at the core of current debates over daycare, working mothers, and stay-at-home dads; gender roles, family values, and parenting styles, as well as questions concerning the origins of autism and the morality of abortion. It is a question that motivates ethicists and social scientists to examine and assess the efficacy of social institutions. It is a question whose implications are political, economic, religious, and, of course, deeply personal.

· · · · ·

Not surprisingly, this notion of humans as individuals who attach pervades modern Western theories of dancing as well, especially those that have appeared in the last century. From a mind over matter, individual-first perspective, dancing can and does appear as having value for the project of establishing cooperative and intimate attachments between material bodies. In fact, as introduced in chapter 2, scholars not only assert that dancing is one of the earliest forms of culture, they often argue that it evolved precisely to ensure the coherence and stability of social relations. Dance is social cement. That "cement," as noted, is thought to function as a result of physiological changes induced by the experience of communal bodily movement, resulting in an "expanded emotional solidarity."[8]

Here the assumption of humans as individual comes into view. The theory of dance as social cement not only presumes notions of materiality, evolution, and mindedness. It also presumes that individuals are individuals first *before* entering into social relations. Once they dance, individuals *become* bound to one another by their own personal experiences of pleasure. They feel loyalty to the group, even love for the group, for granting them this experience of themselves. In pursuit of their own pleasure and power, they thus align their actions with those of the rest so as to help the group endure.[9]

Alternately, in a related line of argument, scholars argue that dancing is effective in attaching individuals for the way in which it teaches social virtues. According to this view, when individuals spend time learning to make patterns of movement handed down to them from ancestors and elders, they learn to pay attention to others, to cooperate with others, and to discipline themselves alongside others. They practice patience and perseverance; they experience the benefits of rigor and repetition. Dancing, individuals make movements that make them into community members who are capable of acting in accordance with ethical codes—individuals who are willing and able to submit.[10]

In a third, related line of argument, dance connects individuals by providing an effective forum for potential mates to find, assess, and entice one another. Dancing, individuals watch each other and display themselves to one another. They stir in themselves and one another a desire that funds their willingness to commit to one another and assume the requisite degree of responsibility that the privilege of joining the other's family and community carries. Dancing with one another, couples foreshadow their coming together in sex. In this reading, then, dancing is a form of foreplay, preparing people for more intimate and demanding modes of attachment.[11]

Nevertheless, as generous as these matter-linked theories of dance are, they are limited by an assumption they share with attachment theories: the idea that an individual is an evolutionary unit whose survival depends upon its ability to bond with other individuals. In each of these theories, *individuals* dance and choose to continue dancing because dancing mediates an exchange between the individual and a group (sometimes rendered as the individual and social aspects within a person). Dancing, an individual submits to the rhythms of the group; she surrenders degrees of freedom and autonomy in order to receive benefits of membership, whether she is old or young and whether that group is a couple or a colony. In this view, dancing forges the "naturally" selfish interests of individuals into socially efficacious links. As a result, these theories fall short of appreciating what I am calling the *ethical necessity* of dancing—that is, the role dancing plays in teaching wholly dependent infants *how* to keep connecting with others in *mutually* life-enabling ways.

When rendered as a means of social cement, dance does not register as necessary for the development of a human *into* an individual. What is necessary is something akin to a secure infant-caregiver bond. In fact, attachment theories often cite as ideal the child-rearing practices of hunter-gatherer peoples whose nomadic mothers carry young children, skin to skin, for up to four years.[12] These same traditional cultures are the ones whose dances comprise the evidence for theories of dancing as a prelinguistic, nonverbal social technology.[13] As noted in chapter 2, even scholars who aver that dancing may have once been necessary to secure attachments among adults profess that we now have more expedient means. Ethics and religion, social values and ritual practices guide individuals to act with respect, fairness, and love for one another. Police forces and courts; sacred laws and social customs; bible-sworn oaths, public schools, and legally binding promises now corral individual will into life-enabling relationships. Because dancing worked so well to attach individuals, the story goes, humans no longer need to dance as we once did.[14]

When we shift to a perspective of bodily becoming, however, new questions arise that call our attention back to the definition of human being at work in these theories, and open up new avenues for considering humans as primarily relational and for considering dance as an ethical necessity.

What if a human being is *not* an individual first? What if there is no *one* who wants to attach and no *one* to whom to attach, but simply an ongoing rhythm of bodily becoming from which two movement makers emerge and in whose ongoing life they participate? What if a human person, whether infant or adult, is nothing more or less than an impulse to connect?[15]

In this case the challenge of social relationships, including those between infant and caregiver, is not a question of individuals learning to attach to one another through feelings of empathy and trust. It is a question of whether utterly dependent impulses to connect can learn to *become* bodily selves— that is, whether we can learn to create and become patterns of sensation and response that draw other impulses to connect into such a proximity that we move and are moved by one other in ways that release us along trajectories of our respective bodily becoming. It is a question of whether we, as enfolded, emergent capacities to move, can learn to move *with* one another so as to discover and release our own movement-making potential.

· · · · ·

Asking these questions begins to reveal a more robust defense of dance hidden in the narrative of an individual who attaches. Implicit in the idea of dance as bonding agent lies an acknowledgment that an individual capable of cultivating relationships of trust and respect with other humans *becomes* so *because* he dances, *insofar* as he dances, *by virtue of how* he dances *with* others—whether those others are caregivers or community members at large. An individual is *one* by virtue of the movements he makes in relating to others in the social, ecological communities of which he is a part.[16] In this account individuality and an ability to attach emerge in generative tension with one another, forming a distinctively human paradox that is rooted in the lived experience of dancing.[17]

In sum, from the perspective of bodily becoming, an individual is not one when the cord is cut. A human becomes individual by virtue of relationships that grow her sense of self long before she can think or feel or say "I."[18] These relationships take shape as a result of the patterns of bodily movements she is and has been making from conception, through birth, and into infancy—movements that express a fundamental impulse to connect. As a result, the ability of a person to cultivate fair, respectful, and compassionate relationships as she matures into adulthood is a function of how well she keeps this *dance* alive as the enabling condition of her singular, ultrasocial bodily becoming.

If we are to embrace dance as an ethical necessity, then, the path is clear. Continuing the story of a fetus as a rhythm of bodily becoming (chapter 4), we need to retell the story of infant-caregiver relationships in terms of coupled impulses to connect. In so doing, we need to consider seriously that humans, while *individual,* are not *individuals,* and that whatever individuality we enjoy derives from our ability to *give ourselves to the movements that others inspire in us.*

Once this task is accomplished, toward the end of this chapter, we will be poised to recognize dancing as the *experiential source* of the ethical paradox humans express as creatures who are both ultrasocial and individual. In the dancing that begins before we are born, humans exercise this generative tension of becoming ever more connected and ever more individual as a function of one another.

We will also be ready to recognize dance traditions as *culturally specific practices* of movement patterns that evolve as a resource for sharing movements that prove effective in negotiating the generative tension of this ethical paradox. In learning a particular dance technique, people practice recreating movements made by others *as* the path to discovering, deepening, and realizing their own potential to move, become, and give. They practice giving themselves to the movements that proximate, relevant others quicken in them. In so doing they create themselves as ethical persons: individual members of the community made real through their dance.

An Impulse to Connect

An infant is born moving—moving out, moving through.[19] Electrical impulses twitch through her muscles propelling her bodily self in patterns she has been making for months. This movement is constant and spontaneous, relational, and open-ended. While guided by limb shape, structure, and size, it is inherently creative. A newborn infant moves because *movement is who and what she is.* Movement is what she does and what is making her. And her moving creates her as a connection to herself that must feel good, for she keeps going. She moves constantly until she crashes into sleep. Even then, the work of movement-creation and bodily becoming proceeds apace.[20]

So too, every movement an infant makes is not simply a movement. It expresses an impulse to connect with whatever movements appear to him through his own movement as real. An infant knows nothing of object or person or place. What he knows are the sensations of moving and being moved.[21] Every movement he makes is an invitation issued by his bodily self to sensations that will support him in extending and amplifying the pleasure of moving itself.

Yet, once born, every movement an infant makes in this wide-open realm ushers in results that are stunningly different than they were in the womb. As she wiggles and squirms, blinks and breathes, these differences arrest her attention—squares of light, shadows cast by window blinds, degrees of taste and temperature. Blanket and mattress, skin and sun, the milk that nourishes and the air that dries and crinkles, all meet and move her otherwise, catalyzing responses whose potential is already present in the patterns of movement remembered as the shape and structure of her rhythmically becoming bodily self.

A pillow or thigh presses against an infant's flailing feet, and his legs push back. An adult finger opens his cupped palm, and his fist squeezes around. Rhythmic rocking releases him into sleep. As an explosion from below fills his diaper, he startles into stillness and then cries.

As these post-womb patterns of connecting form in an infant, each one releases a sensory hue: pleasure or pain. When she latches onto an approaching nipple with womb-rehearsed sucking strong enough to alter its flow of milk, she feels the pleasure of doing so—a pleasure of moving and being moved that she did not know in the womb.[22] This new pleasure becomes part of what this movement is and means to her. This pleasure shades the full-bodied pattern of movement she is making, marking the memory of it and making it more likely that she will mobilize it again. Alternately, when a pattern of movement registers as pain, she shrinks away, marking the memory with a resistance to repeating it. In this way desires form. Every movement made lays down a neural-muscular track along which energy and attention run, branch out, and find new routes leading to further experiences of pleasure or pain.[23]

With every movement, then, an infant not only creates patterns of sensation and response, he becomes them. It is not just that an infant's movements teach him about the world or even about how to move in the world. Rather, his movements make him into a bodily self who can sense and respond to the world in a variety of ways. His movements are creating in him, as him, a nascent capacity for evaluating the movement he is making (pleasure or pain?) in any given situation. His movements are not only providing him with a sensory motor map of who or what lies "out there," they are creating him as a capacity to respond and relate to enabling or aversive others in ways that further his well-being. With every movement of his bodily self, external reach and internal depth open in reflexive tension with one another.

Further, the connections that her movements create in her and as her are not external links with "things" or even "people." Every movement she makes connects her with something or someone who is *moving* in relation to her in patterns of its own. In response to her squirming, a caregiver rocks and pats, cradles and clutches, trying to find the movements to make in relation to her that will move her toward ease. The infant's cry shifts an arm to snuggle her tighter. Her writhing impels a caregiver to place her gently on his shoulder and firmly tap her back. Her movements connect her with pleasure when her caregiver moves with her and for her as an expression of moves she cannot yet make for herself—a promise of what is yet to come.[24]

As a caregiver's movements move an infant, the infant begins to learn patterns of moving in relation to other humans that are culturally specific. Not all cultures hold, pat, and rock in the same way. The way an infant is touched, held, addressed; the places he goes and the people he meets all impress him and draw him forth. Because his every movement invites and responds to movements made in relation to him, he necessarily engages cultural and social values at a biological, neurological level. Moving and being moved, an infant builds into his most basic sense of the world cultural patterns of interacting with those who are in proximate, enabling relationship to him. Who he is is not only irreducibly relational, he is inherently ethical. The most basic movements that he is creating and becoming are imbued with cultural value.[25]

As an infant creates and becomes the patterns of movement that connect her with sources of nurture and nourishment, the pleasure she feels calls her to give herself again and again *to the movements* that she has been making. She is not (yet) interested in "attaching" to some thing or some one out there. She has no sense of self or other. She is movement, patterns of movement, criss-crossing ripples of sensation and response that are ever seeking opportunities to move some more. She is participating, to the degree of her budding sensory awareness, in creating and becoming the movement that is making her . . . happy. Her movements express the relational values most likely to bring her pleasure.

· · · · ·

At first an infant, as an impulse to connect, is open to whatever will move him—open to whatever is appearing within him and around him as a result of the movements his bodily self is spontaneously making. When his own fingers find their way to his mouth, he does not wonder what they are or what they can do; he gives himself to the sensation, waits for an impulse to move that that will connect him with them. He sucks. It is different from a milk source, but not bad. Another sensory surface pops into view, associated with the fingers themselves. He continues sucking until the fingers disappear again.

Within a couple of weeks, however, an infant's play evolves. It is as if the electrical impulses contracting and releasing the infant's muscles along their potentially infinite range settle into grooves. The infant not only plays with *sensations* notched along the trajectories of her bodily movement (as she has been doing), she begins to play with the *patterns of movement*, the kinetic images, that she has been making as well. She rehearses those patterns, using them as resources for exploring what is and gathering more experiences of pleasure. Sucking becomes a strategy. So too does the up-down movement of her arm. She lifts her arm up and bats it down, smiling with the sensation of downward thrust. She lifts her arm again, thrusts it down, and smiles again. Put a ball in her hand and she makes the same movement, launching the ball forth. Put a rattle in her hand and she makes the same movement, shining at the noise. Put mom's hair in her hand and she makes the same movement. Mom squeals.

In movement, with movement, an infant starts to ask questions. What will happen if this pattern repeats, lifting my head from the blanket again, high and higher? A new view! What will happen if this pattern repeats, locking my eyes with the eyes of another? A smile! What will happen if this pattern repeats, holding my legs up high? A roll!

Meanwhile, the movement patterns an infant is making not only build in him new strength and coordination, they quicken his movement-making potential. The infant's legs, for example, assume a regular pumping action like pistons moving back and forth, running in space, marking time. Making these movements, over and again, an infant animates the muscles in his core, front and back, pulling the length and lever of his torso into sensory awareness. Each movement hurtles along the path opened by the previous pump to stretch a little bit farther and faster. The infant thus makes movements that exercise and unfold the movement potential of his own trunk and limbs. His movements fund muscle growth, enhance kinetic facility, and expand the range of both external and internal sensory awareness, all as a function of one another.[26]

So too, as an infant rehearses this growing repertoire of movements made, she does so in every domain of sensation, hearing to touch. She does so spontaneously, playfully, in an overflowing exuberance of life energy until she drops into sleep. Every move is made for itself, unconstrained by prescription or goal. Every move aligns with what is best for straightening bones and mounding muscles. Every move is responsible to what the movements she is making allow her to perceive. Every move opens her to new sources of sensation along its length, like the plunging tongue of an anteater gathering ants.

• • • • •

Within a month or two, an infant's play expands again along trajectories that his play with both *sensations* and *movement patterns* is opening up. As he repeats movements he has made, he begins to accumulate a varying range of patterns of sensation and response that his movements have accrued. He experiences situations in which patterns that worked to one effect in one instance are now blocked, altered, or amplified. The patterns of movement he is and remembers coalesce into patterns of possibility and vulnerability. Common sources of resistance and stimulation begin to impress his consciousness and take shape as faces, places, and objects. He starts to play with these constellations of kinetic images—with what we call things.

Soon the infant is not just hurling the ball every time it appears in her hand. Nor is she simply sucking on it. When it crosses her visual field, she reaches for it, fingers it, explores it. Replace the ball with the rattle or the spoon and she will barely blink. But handed one or the other, she does not simply repeat the same down-thrusting arm movement patterns either. The infant gives her attention to "it," greeting it as a source of resistance and opportunity that guides her in moving differently. She plays with the resistance it offers to familiar patterns of movement—with its shape, texture, and weight—as a stimulus to receiving new impulses to move. She allows the fork to mobilize her movement patterns along pathways only it allows. She pokes and thrusts and waves, open to "it" as an enabling condition of her own bodily becoming.

Yet what this newborn wants is still not "it." He wants the pleasure of moving in patterns that exercise and extend his sensory kinetic range. He wants to move in ways that allow "it" to become real as something that gives him pleasure.[27]

. . . . .

Soon again, within several months, an infant's movement experiments stream along the riverbeds of movements-made-and-remembered into new territory. Not only does an infant rehearse particular movement patterns she has made; not only does she recognize patterns made in relation to her, she begins to recognize these patterns of movement, her own and others', as answers to questions that her sensations pose. She begins to perceive her own sensations as a desire for "it"—as an impulse to move toward, to grasp, to mouth, to have. She wants the pleasure she feels when she moves with it, because of it, in relation to it.[28] What the object "is" for her is a relief from the pain she feels when she is not in active relation with "it."[29] In psychological parlance, she is beginning to "attach."

But is attaching what the infant is doing? From the perspective of bodily becoming a complementary interpretation arises. This infant is learning how to *dance* within the circumstances he inhabits. He is learning how to make patterns of sensation and response that connect him with others in life-enabling ways. He is doing so as consciously as he is able, and growing that consciousness in the process, as a function of his movement making. At this stage in his development, then, the patterns of movement he is making are gathering within him as a felt sensation of desire—an impulse to move toward an other, with an other, and for an other, *as* an enabling condition of his own bodily becoming. He is exercising an ethical self, moving toward and with his caregivers, because doing so brings him pleasure.[30]

In this reading, the infant does not "trust" the caregiver. If an infant can be said to "trust," then what she "trusts" is the impulse to connect that her caregiver's movements quicken in her. She trusts her own movement responses; she gives herself to them. She moves as them. And insofar as she has not been unduly blocked from doing so, she will keep receiving and recreating these impulses to connect. She will be the place where relational patterns of sensing and responding arise and go forth. As a result, when caregivers give themselves to their own infant-quickened impulses to connect, the infant will not just "feel felt." The infant will feel moved to keep discovering, creating, and becoming relational, life-enabling patterns of sensation and response.[31]

In this view, infant and caregiver are not attached in the manner of two material objects coming together at a common point. Rather, they are two sources of movement making, each funded by the ongoing rhythm of their mutually entwined bodily becoming. They are not two entities who merge with one another; they are two movement potentials that emerge by way of one another. They are not individuals who choose to move with one another; they become individual as they allow themselves to be moved by one another. Infant and caregiver each give themselves to movements that draw them close enough to one another to be moved again some more. They literally express themselves in movement. *They dance.* They play with movement patterns, discovering and creating sequences of movements that they repeat and perform for one another. And when both infant and caregiver are willing and able to welcome their respective impulses to connect with the other as causes of their being, then the ever evolving movement of life continues in the shape of them both.

Infants in particular emerge from this dance having created and become patterns of sensation and response that comprise the ethical paradox at the heart of human existence: they have learned (or not) to give themselves to the movements others inspire in them as the enabling condition of their best and most individual bodily becoming.

· · · · ·

Leif is curled up next to me, lying on his side, sleeping. One foot rests softly on the other. His arms cross. I study his fingers and toes, his hairless head, smooth brow, and soft lids. I try to burn the images into my brain. I will forget what he looks like now. As he grows, I will see who he is, not who he was. I want to remember.

Remembering him is my job. I am his ecosystem, his unconscious, his past, present, and future. I am a possibility for shapes of pleasure and pain that he may learn to make or not as he moves in relation to me. I am his dancing partner—or one of them.

At this point, whether and how he and I connect is largely up to me. Am I aware enough of my own movement making that I can receive and trust the impulses to connect that being near him stirs in me? Am I open enough to able to discern how to move toward him, with him, for him in ways that bring me pleasure? Can I learn from him how to *dance* with him?

· · · · ·

Infants call caregivers to participate consciously in the rhythms of bodily becoming by which all humans are pulled into existence. Infants teach us to dance again; they keep the dance alive in us. They do so by moving spontaneously, freely, and fiercely in ways that stir in us a desire and a willingness to find ways to move with them.

It sometimes happens, however, that a caregiver does not or cannot engage the infant in a play of movement patterns. When this happens, its effects are more profound than suggested by a "failed" or "faulty" attachment. The idea of a faulty attachment leaves the individual who cannot do it relatively intact. However, if a caregiver cannot or will not dance, then an infant is in danger of losing the desire to participate in the rhythms of his own bodily becoming. A caregiver's responses to an infant can break the connection that otherwise would exist in the infant between the action of making new movements and the pleasure of doing so.

If a caregiver, for example, responds to an infant's attempts to make new moves by shutting her down with critical words or acts, then the infant will not only feel frustrated in making those particular movements. Over time she will learn that participating in this bodily becoming is not pleasurable. She will learn to respond to the crackling of her own sensory creativity as a source of stress and anxiety. She will be afraid of making a new move, afraid of acknowledging her emergent desires, afraid of what movements in others her actions might provoke.

So too, if a caregiver responds to an infant's moves with anger, disgust, or dismay, the infant will pick up those emotional patterns as the meaning of his creative attempts. He will learn to be angry or disgusted at himself for "wanting attention"; he will learn to distrust his own upsurges of energy and rail against others who are making similar emotional moves.

If an infant's impulses to connect are blocked or ignored in these ways, she will learn *not* to give herself to the movements that being with others stirs in her. As noted, an infant *is* an impulse to connect. More often than not, the swells of energy she fields and transmits are impulses to give herself to caregivers in ways that will bring pleasure to them—or at least in ways that will allow them the pleasure of taking care of her. As a result, if a caregiver is not responsive, not only does the infant learn not to enjoy the pleasure of making life-enabling moves, she learns to deny her own natural *generosity*.

A child who learns that what he has to give is not wanted or needed or appreciated is one who will learn to take whatever he can from others. He will learn to deny the sensory awareness in himself that remains his surest guide to connecting with others. He will lose the oscillating balance between inner and outer sensory awareness that grounds his sense of self as ultrasocial and individual. He will be increasingly vulnerable to influences from outside himself, which he has neither the conceptual tools nor the inner resources to evaluate.

Here, reasons surface for why dance is not only an experiential source of a distinctively human ethical paradox but also a practice that we can and must engage throughout our lives. In order to raise persons capable of empathy, it is not enough to have the time, attention, and (mind over body) will power to respond consistently to a child's needs. Such perfection is impossible. Instead, caregivers must be willing and able to *move with* a child in ways that fund that child's own ongoing movement making. Caregivers must not forget that they too are first and foremost movement makers, ongoing sources of movement potential, able to create and become patterns of sensation and response that relate them to others in mutually life-enabling ways. Caregivers must be able and willing to *live* the ethical paradox of being inseparably entwined and irreducibly singular by allowing the challenge of caring for young to serve as a catalyst in the unfolding of their own movement-making potential. Caregivers must be willing and able to discover and play with movement patterns that nurture both their wards and themselves—that is, to *dance* in relation to their children as they want their children to dance in relation to them.

Mirror Neurons

In the work of scientists attempting to identify a neurobiological basis for human attachment, the human capacity to perceive and recreate patterns of movement is enjoying a star turn. Critical to this project is a class of brain cells identified in 1996 as mirror neurons. When one person observes another person making a physical movement, these mirror neurons fire in various parts of the brain, creating in the observer the pattern of neural connections that the observer would need to activate in order to make the same movement. It is a discovery with the potential to support the claim that dance is an ethical necessity.

For many scientists, this seemingly innate human ability to make an internal image of observed movement provides the biological template for empathy.[32] It is what enables humans to discern what it must feel like to be another person. I can watch what another person does and know how it feels to act likewise. I see a person grimace and punch the air. I know what it feels like to make those movements. As a result I can relate to what that person must be feeling as "anger" and respond accordingly. In this way, it is thought, human beings can establish bonds of empathy with one another strong enough to compete with those that rely on shared genetic material. Thus the abundance and sophistication of these mirror neurons in the human brain relative to other primates supports the idea that humans evolved as creatures who can and must form relationships with other humans in order to survive. As scientists conclude, human individuals evolved to *attach*.

Yet this description and interpretation of mirror neurons is, as with attachment theory, bound by matter-models of reality and evolution and corresponding assumptions regarding minded individuals. The metaphor of the "mirror" implies that some *thing* is out there. *It* is moving. It is seen by an *individual* who passively registers a visual image that is transmitted to her brain. Her ability to do so was once a genetic mutation that has since proven advantageous to her in the effort to reproduce her genetic material.

Mobilizing the perspective of bodily becoming, however, shifts both the description and interpretation of these neurons in ways that shed light on the ethical import of dancing. For one, even as defined, a mirror neuron exists as a potential pattern of sensation and response. It exists as a capacity to *notice* movement and to *respond* to this noticed movement. Mirror neurons exist as patterns of movement that can be activated by the appearance to us of movements other than our own.

So too, what appears to activate these neurons is not a thing that is simply there. As noted in chapter 1, every sensation we receive appears to us by way of bodily movements we are already making. How we move impacts our ability to notice and grasp; it influences whether and how our senses work, and what resources we have at our disposal for perceiving. Any kinetic image that mirror neurons register, then, is not simply a *reflection*, as the metaphor of the mirror implies. Any image expresses movements we as sensory selves have made in relation to the movement patterns by which we have been moved. The activity of mirror neurons is *movement dependent*. Any image that mirror neurons allow to form in us is an *interpretive re-creation* of what our own movement has allowed to appear. It is a recreation comprised not of visual cues but of patches of sensory awareness that our own movement has awakened in us.[33]

For these reasons, the term *mirror* is not only misleading; it erases the constitutive role played by bodily movement in the reception and recreation of kinetic images. Concomitantly, it masks the implications this kinetic-image-recreation carries for the role played by bodily movement practices in our capacity to mirror and bond with others. Research into mirror neurons suggests that bonds of attachment form between humans who are able to move with one another.[34] Such persons must be able to perceive the movements that another person makes, to recreate kinetic images of those movements within themselves, and be able to receive corresponding impulses to connect with those others that arise within them as a result. For all these actions, however, we must first have a sensory awareness of our bodily selves as movement and an ability to participate consciously in the rhythms of our bodily becoming. As scientists confirm—without yet discerning the implications for acknowledging dance as a vital art—there is a measurable correlation between people's degrees of visceral awareness and their capacity for empathizing with the feeling states of others.[35]

Taking one step farther, inasmuch as our bodily selves *are* movement, the only way to gather this kind of empathy-enabling sensory awareness *is* to *move*, and not just randomly. From the time we are born we need to practice moving in ways that draw attention into and through our bodily selves. We need to study and practice recreating patterns of movement that comprise the cultural and even environmental contexts of which we are a part. When, and only when we do, will we become persons with the skill and sensibility we need to move with relevant others as they are moving in relation to us and so become individual members of the community our movement patterns engender.[36]

Further, given what we know about bodily becoming and brain plasticity (described in chapter 4), it follows that this ethical need for practice never ends. Learning to move with others is not a one-shot deal. Because every movement we make makes us, our bodily selves are always changing. The same is true for any other with whom we are involved. As a result, in order to sustain relations of empathy with others, we must constantly renew a sensory awareness of ourselves as movement, bringing it in line with the current scale and size and capability of our ever becoming bodily selves. And we must constantly stay open to being moved by new patterns of others as they appear to us.

The discovery of mirror neurons, then, has profound implications for understanding dance as an ethical necessity. Without an ongoing practice of cultivating sensory awareness, without a studied engagement with cultural patterns of relational movement, we will not grow our mirror-neuron-enabled potential to be moved by other people. We will lose our ability to discern the impulses to move with others in ways that would nourish our own bodily becoming and we will not have the attention or patience to notice.[37]

From a movement perspective, mirror neurons represent part of the neurological network—the patterns of sensation and response remembered in the form of our bodily selves—that makes it both possible and necessary for humans to *dance*.

Dancing Humans

The dancing that humans do and have done is a manifestation of life energy coursing along trajectories laid by patterns of movement made and remembered in forms, spaces, and times that extend far beyond any individual human lives. Every human is born of a dance, born into a dance, as a participant in the ongoing matrix of movements that is making him or her *human*. And once we begin to fathom the *degree* to which humans *are* the bodily movements that they are creating and becoming, we come to the point of considering a new perspective on the role of dance in human relationships.

If a largely unconscious practice of dancing created in human infants the experiential matrix of an ethical paradox, then perhaps a largely conscious practice of dancing emerged as a way for humans to help themselves negotiate the challenges of this paradox—the challenges of being both singular and ultrasocial. Perhaps a conscious practice of dancing arose in humans as a way to help learn from others how to move in relationship to them and thus learn what they most needed to know in order to thrive as the individual humans they had the potential to become.

Here the human capacity, need, and desire to move and be moved by others, on the one hand, and the conscious practice of dancing, on the other, would have evolved in tandem as the length of our gestation shrunk, the size of our neocortex and especially prefrontal cortex grew, the range and quantity of mirror neurons increased, the span of our childhoods stretched to more than a decade, and the territory of our nomadic explorations expanded around the earth. Dancing, early humans would have created themselves into highly adaptive, inherently creative creatures, equally capable of going with a group or leading it in new directions.

Is it so? Did the dancing of our ancestors help pull into existence a recognizably human sociality and self? If so, when? When did hominids begin to invent, repeat, and teach patterns of movement in a time and space dedicated to such work? When did we begin consciously to practice dance as a skill, art, and ideal?

· · · · ·

Leif is now three weeks old. I am watching him closely. Not only does the mere sight of him hug my heart and leave me drenched in milk, I want to know: why is he smiling?

I know that at this young age his smile is most likely the result of random muscle twitches. He smiles in his sleep with his eyes closed. Awake, he smiles at patterns on the wall, at bubbles in his belly, at the gyrations of a mobile, for no apparent reason, and, sometimes, when looking at me. Asleep and awake, he runs through facial expressions like a lock picker running through combinations, as if looking for the key. At this point a smile is simply one pattern of potential facial movement without much meaning. Yet he *seems* to be smiling at me. My heart is heaving. Why am I so moved? I'm sure I could graph a mountain range of my postpartum hormones. My mirror neurons are undoubtedly firing. But why?

Rationally speaking, his smiling doesn't make much sense. There are so many other tasks he must master before he can fend for himself. He cannot yet roll over, sit up, crawl forward, or wield a spoon. Why spend any energy at all learning to smile? Doing so involves activating at least forty-four muscles in the face.[38] Shouldn't he be devoting that brain space to something critical to his survival? Or could it be that smiling is? Could it be that smiling is, for him, a life-enabling pattern of movement?

When Leif cracks a smile, I fall in. Maybe that is its purpose—to catch me, a caregiver. Maybe I am so moved because I know what it *means* for me to smile. I have learned over time how it *feels* when I smile. I know how *good* it feels to smile and how good *I* feel when I smile. I know because at some point in my life someone smiled (back) at me.

When Leif smiles, I imagine that he feels good. I imagine that he feels good to have been born, good to be alive, and perhaps happy with me. I smile back. I smile because I share his joy—I feel it in me as mine—and I know: if he is happy, then I must be taking good care of him. I like that. I want that.

When he smiles at me and I smile back, Leif and I connect: we are each moved to move toward one another for our respective, mutual pleasure. We are encouraged to give ourselves to the movements the other inspires in us. It is not that I will myself to give to him. Rather, when I see him giving himself to the movements that draw him close to me, his patterns of movement, as learned and culturally enabled as they may be, bear witness to a visceral, transcendent immediacy that moves me to respond in return. I want to participate too. Eyes locked, faces beaming, we exchange ripples of delight.[39]

• • • • •

Most likely, a humanizing dance sprouted where it was already happening: in relationships between infants and caregivers.[40] An infant moved; a caregiver responded; the response moved the infant to move again. Or not. And vice versa. Over time, the matrix of movements that emerged to connect and coordinate the movement patterns of infant and caregiver conducted cultural expectations and values through a placental-like osmosis, enabling both infant and caregiver to survive the event of birth and get, give, and grow as a member of a community. In this dance, as we have seen, both partners are actively engaged in creating and becoming patterns of relational movement and cultivating the sensory awareness that will guide them to do so effectively.

This reciprocal movement making between infant and caregiver, while present in other primates and mammals, is not as necessary, as intense, as biologically effective, or as prolonged. Because humans can and must create brain-forming, relational patterns of movement while outside the womb (chapter 4), we have developed a capacity to feel deep pleasure in moving with others and being moved by others—a deep pleasure in giving ourselves to movements that others inspire in us. We smile back. It is not a need or ability that humans outgrow. Unlike other primates who stop imitating others after several months of life, we never do.[41]

This dance between infant and caregiver, where successful, because of its success, would have created expectations in both infants and their caregivers for experiencing the same kind of movement—the same depth and pleasure of moving and being moved—in their relationships with other living things. The experience of moving with and being moved by an other would have created in infants a bodily, sensory pattern—a felt desire—for similar kinds of responsive engagement with others, beyond the team of caregivers on whom their early lives depended, such as friends, allies, partners, or clan. This desire for connection would have been expansive, unconscious, always searching for new enabling relationships, new occasions to smile.

So too, the experience of moving with and being moved by an infant would have created in caregivers a felt desire for the intimacy of beginnings, even after a child had grown. Bearing witness to the benefits of moving with an infant, caregivers would have felt the pleasure of being able to care for another, connect with another, receive from the other, and nurture life. Among caregivers who cared for more than one child, the desire for intimacy, as a pattern of sensation and response, would have kept reaching beyond particular wards in patterns of openness, ready and able to find and respond to opportunities as they arose, even in relation to potential mates.

Thus a dance between infant and caregiver that was largely, initially unconscious may have created barely conscious expectations for intimacy and connection—for relational patterns of sensation and response—that infant and caregiver carried beyond their relationship into other areas of their lives. A yearning among members of a breeding cooperative to recreate the feeling of moving and being moved they had experienced as children may have given rise to an impulse to repeat movement patterns that evoked it. Such an impulse would not have emerged as a mind-over-body intention to move. It would have erupted in bodily selves as a spontaneous response to feelings of lack or disease or desire reminiscent to ones they had felt as infants. It would have erupted in their bodily movement as a pattern that evoked a comforting, enlivening sense of moving-with—a pattern that already existed within them as memory and potential for movement.

What might these recreated, repeated movements have been? It is impossible to know for certain. However, given this analysis and the examples we have of hunter-gatherer peoples and of children themselves, it may be that the movements of the first dances were ones that enacted movements of caring and being cared for—movements of cradling, rocking, holding. Movements that encompass, encircle, and protect. Movements that sound out a (mother's) heartbeat or a comforting rhythm while stepping, hopping, and walking. Movements that manifest the power of protection.

Then again, the movements may have been more "abstract," that is, inspired by the feeling of moving with and being moved by. The movements may have expressed comfort—not in the sense of pressing out an inner feeling, but in the sense of recreating a movement pattern that allowed the feeling to coalesce within. The movements might have expressed the thrill of loving and being loved, as with the leaping or jumping that create feelings of excitement.

Such movements would have appeared in those people who were particularly adept at sensing and responding, perceiving and recreating the movement patterns of others—those, perhaps, who had had or were especially attuned caregivers. The movements they made would have helped them feel the yearning they were feeling and respond in life-promoting ways. And those who made the movements would have experienced the pleasure and power—not only of making the movements but also of continuing to exercise the movement-making, symbol-forming capacity of their early-born, brained, and bodily selves.

In turn, these movements, once made in the company of others, would have sparked the movement-responsiveness of those others. These others would have recreated and repeated the patterns, setting in motion a chain of influence. Various points of infant/caregiver connection could thus have collectively constellated a movement matrix that could have spread via the rhythms of bodily becoming to draw those who could already, to some extent, dance into a connected community of those who wanted the experience that dancing together could provide.

Humans who dance know a power and pleasure that comes with the action of moving their bodily selves in rhythmic patterns. Humans who dance know a power and pleasure that comes with moving as part of a group. And these two sources of power and pleasure are linked in a spiral of increasing intensity—an intensity that manifests in the creation of bonds that enable and support individuals in becoming bodily selves who realize their potential to give what they have to give to those who enable them to be. Humans who practice cultural forms of dancing beyond the infant-toddler stage cultivate their individuality and relationality, and do so as a function of one another. They learn about themselves, who they are and what they can do, as they learn how best to create life-enabling connections within the specific social and natural environments they inhabit. And, in reverse, they learn how to create and advance those relationships by way of the experience of themselves that moving like others, with others, affords.[42]

In this way the dance forms that have congealed into cultural practices may be best conceived as neither social cement nor individual empowerment but rather as a means by which people ensure that the movements they are creating and becoming as they learn to relate to others will express the same careful attention to their bodily selves that the dancing requires. *They learn to*

134

love. While that attention may not always be loving, there can be no love without such attention.

Here the case for dancing as an ethical necessity touches down. Dancing is an ethical necessity because humans, without it, do not develop the visceral sensibility they need to divine ways to move that are not too individual (and self-absorbed), too social (and self-sacrificing), or insufficiently either. To be human, we are, and must be, always becoming both. Our capacity to nurture others as they need and want to be nurtured is thoroughly entwined with our own need to participate in the ongoing rhythm of our bodily becoming. Dancing cultivates the sensory awareness of ourselves as movement we need to guide us in making movements that preserve the ethical paradox constituting a human bodily becoming as both social and individual.

· · · · ·

From the perspective of bodily becoming, the fact that humans have danced for hundreds of thousands of years appears vital to understanding who we are. The fact that we have danced has changed our bodies, our minds, our hearts; our metabolisms, our chemical composition, and our capacities for pleasure. Dancing, we have become large-brained, big-hearted creatures who can bond with nearly every life force. Dancing has created us into caregivers more able to move with the needs of their charges, hunters more able to understand and stalk their prey, cooks more able to respond to the flesh of plants and animals and so reveal their potential to nourish and heal, and young with a far longer list of movements to master than any other species. Our dancing has pulled and pushed us into existence as individual persons with an unimpeachable need for intimacy and as ultrasocial creatures with an undeniable requirement to realize a singularly specific potential to move. Dancing, humans become creatures who can and must love others for their own good.

From the perspective of bodily becoming, ethical questions of how to bend an individual heart, mind, and will to the good of these enabling relationships, or how to attach individuals to one another, appear misguided. There has never been a human individual whose heart and mind existed independent of shared activity in the first place. Rather, the primary ethical questions concern whether and how humans *dance.* The task in becoming an ethical human involves learning how to draw close *enough* to others so that we are moved *by* one another to unfold our capacity to give *to* one another in mutually life-enabling ways. It involves learning how to cultivate sensory awareness of how and why movement matters and to participate *consciously* in the *dance* that is always already happening. In this work lies the secret to healthy humans and healthy communities, to fierce loyalties, enduring friendships, and astonishing sex.

When this learning occurs, cooperation among humans happens and just, equitable social relations are far more likely. For what we then desire from one another is not love or attention or union per se. What we desire is for the other to draw close enough to us that we may be moved by him or her to move in relation to him or her in ways that give both of us the pleasure of participating in the rhythms of bodily becoming. What we desire is the pleasure of this dance. While there is no one way to dance humanly, there is no way to become human without it.

• • • • •

Leif smiles. I smile back. He smiles more. I do too and add a squeeze. He giggles in response, and I am flooded with love. Leif's smile is an invitation to dance.

I accept.

6

To Dance Is to Heal

Understanding ritual practice is not a question of decoding the internal logic of a symbolism but of restoring its practical necessity by relating it to the real conditions of its genesis, that is, to the conditions in which its functions, and the means it uses to attain them.

—PIERRE BOURDIEU, *OUTLINE OF A THEORY OF PRACTICE*

My eyes crack open to a promising glow. Morning. Spring light hums through the room, rounding out hard walls and square corners. I feel no pain. I am encouraged. I lie very still, savoring these moments that I know, too soon, will end. I breathe in, exhale slowly, and begin to think about getting up. A stab of fear punctures my heart. Will it hurt?

To be safe, I begin by moving my toes, ankles, and feet, rolling this way and that. I point and flex, point and flex, and then straighten my legs hard enough to stretch my bones. I release and wiggle my pelvis from side to side. No pain.

Feeling bold, I draw my knees to my chest, roll to my right side, and press my left arm into the bed with hopes of sitting up swiftly. Suddenly a blade of pain slices down the length of my upper spine and flares wide. I fall onto my back, back on the bed. Floored. It is still there. The pain. This pain is not a good pain. It is not a healthy pain. It is a sick pain—a getting sicker pain. It hurts. Despair wraps its fingers around my throat.

I take a deep breath, drawing in courage mixed with oxygen, and push against the despair. *I have to sit up!* I will. I will.

I spend the next twenty minutes trying to find a way to get vertical that does not trigger the same slicing spasm. I rock and twist my hips, experimenting with one unsuccessful pattern of movement and then another. Eventually I straighten my right leg far beneath me, cross a bent left knee over, and sink my attention deep into my pelvis. My lower leg comes alive as a lever that presses my upper body up. I inch along the edge of the pain. I move and pause, release and rest, and move and pause again. Nearly there, I give a small grunt and push past a yawning cavern of potential discomfort, arriving suddenly upright, with only a slight tremor, awash in relief.

I breathe deliberately to slow my beating heart, as my attention turns to the next goal. *I have to get outside. I have to go for a run.* I cannot put on my socks or tie my own shoes; I cannot pull my shirt over my head. But I know that if I can make my way to the road and move my legs, my own movement will wake me up, open me out, and take me to a place beneath the pain—a place of hope and joy from which I will be able to move without pain.

I will feel so much better. I just need to run. I know because it has happened every morning since that day several weeks ago. I hadn't been running in years. I had been dancing. Running had hurt. But now dancing was hurting. So, desperate to move, I decided to try to run. Miraculously, the running had not hurt! It helped! Every morning since I have repeated the same movements, seeking the same relief—the same experience shift that transforms my pain into something with which I can live. My morning run has become a ritual.

Geoff helps me tie my shoes. I close the door behind me. Bright air kisses my skin, teasing forth an unexpected pulse of pleasure. I smile and start to jog, holding my upper body erect against the pull of its natural sway. It happens again: as my feet take turns touching down, a waterfall of sensations streams gently down my back, bathing frayed nerves, releasing muscle tension, and finding ease.

The threat of pain recedes; I move without spasm. My sense of the world shifts. I feel a happiness stronger than the pain. I release into a sensory awareness of my own movement making, and I begin to dance. Down the road I go, skipping, weaving, and turning; old movements yield to new movements that do not recreate the pain.

· · · · ·

We humans are wounded. We can and we do feel pain, every day, along every dimension of our bodily selves, until we die.[1] This "pain," whether we name it as physical, emotional, mental, or spiritual, appears within us as an invasive, aversive sensation. Every surface of our selves is exquisitely calibrated to register such hostile imprints—our thin skin, pliant tissues, soft hearts, meld-able minds, and desiring spirits. When pain flares across our bodily selves, unless trained to do otherwise, we feel it as a desire to make the feeling stop.

Within a materialist paradigm, as this chapter elaborates, pain is generally perceived, not only as a defining fact of human life, but as a problem. Pain is what an individual feels when his machine-body breaks down. Given this understanding, the best response to pain involves mobilizing the power of a mind to correct the malfunction. "We" aim to stop the pain and repair what went wrong.

Not surprisingly, this perception of pain, like the notions of matter and mind it expresses, leaves little room for affirming dancing as a vital art. In a world where matter is real, people dance when they are free from pain. They may dance in spite of their pain or they may acknowledge that dancing can cause us pain. Rarely do they consider dancing itself as a resource for transforming or healing pain.[2]

Yet, as with the concepts addressed in earlier chapters, this notion of pain as a problem, as commonsense as it may seem, is plagued by contradictions that the perspective of bodily becoming reveals and overcomes. The idea that pain is something to *stop* implies that pain is itself a pattern of *movement*. As we shall see, pain simmers or glows, slices or cramps in a particular shape at a specific location relative to movement that we, consciously or not, want to make but cannot. Feeling stuck or arrested, unable to stop or unable to begin, *hurts*. Pain, in this view, expresses a desire to *move differently* than we are doing. Perhaps, instead of working so hard to kill our pain, we should learn to honor it as an expression of the movement that is making us.

Once we appreciate pain as a desire to move differently, we are ready to add another twist to our understanding of the role dance plays in human nature and culture. Dancing, as earlier chapters indicate, is an activity in which humans cultivate a sensory awareness capable of guiding us to create and become relational patterns of sensation and response that promote bodily health (chapter 4) and ethical relating (chapter 5). This chapter fleshes out what that guidance entails and how it works. Specifically, it considers dancing to be an activity in which humans learn to perceive pain as an invaluable catalyst to sensory creativity. And once we affirm that dancing is and has always been a medium and agent of healing, we will be ready to consider the process of healing as one of learning to dance.

While this further step affords a new view on all forms of dancing, it is especially revealing of rituals—the earliest known forms of communal dance.[3] Continuing the argument of chapter 5, this chapter proposes that movement patterns crystallized into dance rituals within human families and communities as people began consciously rehearsing patterns of bodily movement that they found effective in transforming the kind of pain they were facing in themselves, their relationships, and in their communities. In this account, rituals evolved out of the site-specific movement patterns that people were already, spontaneously making as a way to enhance and expand, remember and repeat the pain-transforming efficacy of those movements. By this logic, rituals, even to this day, work insofar as they guide people to access and amplify the powers of healing latent in the movement-making potential of their bodily becoming. That is, they work insofar as they engage and activate a human ability to dance.

In order to affirm dance as a vital art, then, we need to retell the story of human pain—the story of our physical-emotional-spiritual distress—from the perspective of bodily becoming. We need to reconceive of any and all pain as patterns of sensation and response—the result of movements, conscious and not, that we are making and being made by. We need to reconceive of healing as a process of cultivating sensory awareness and inviting impulses to move differently. When we do, ritual will appear as an expression of dancing through whose practice humans evolved into persons able to conceive of "spirit" as a power they could possess, pursue, and purpose for their own healing. In this figuring, human "spirituality" or spiritual life appears as a process of becoming rather than escaping our bodily selves, and dance appears as an ongoing spiritual necessity.

The Problem with Pain

In a world where matter is real, where minds manage bodies, and where individuals come first, most people learn to perceive pain as a symptom of some material process gone awry. Individuals get sick. Injuries and accidents happen. Genes mutate. Organs collapse. Relationships break up. Projects fail. In every case, it is assumed that there is some material event, encounter, or invasion responsible; and it is assumed, by those in the medical profession and beyond, that the best response is to stop the pain and fix the problem.

What this intervention entails depends on whether the locus of the pain appears as "physical," "emotional," "mental," or "spiritual."[4] For most people in the medical profession, the proximal cause of any pain is *physical*. Some virus, cancer, rupture, foreign object, chemical imbalance, electrical malfunction, or muscular weakness impinges upon an otherwise healthy body, impeding its ability to function. A person feels pain. In response, medical professionals work to identify the offending agent and its impact pathway. They then isolate, cut, radiate, medicate, or otherwise divest "it" of power to harm. They sew, splint, suspend, or cast the injured part, fixing it in place. In the process, practitioners generally arrest a bodily self's responses to what is occurring by administering drugs for reducing fever, shrinking swelling, and anesthetizing feeling. They kill the pain.

Even when the locus of the pain is perceived as *mental*—as in the case of neuroses, obsessions, addictions, paranoia, or depression—fixing generally entails a similarly matter-modeled intervention. For a large number of professionals, the cause of mental illness is still a chemical or electrical aberration that can and should be adjusted with matter-manipulating drugs. Yet even professionals who locate the causes of mental illness in emotional pain and psychic wounds also rely on a model of fixing and arresting derived from materialist assumptions.[5] Patients, with the help of their therapists, revisit and release memories of actual physical or emotional injury; replace traumatic, traumatizing thoughts with healthier, life-giving ones, and thus return to normal function as quickly as possible.[6]

So too, even where people subscribe to a notion of illness and injury as *spiritual* in source and locus, they often rely upon the logic of a materialist paradigm to explain the problem and justify the cure. Here the task is most often to identify a karmic or demonic cause, a sin or disobedience that is affecting a person, and then intervene through practices of prayer, meditation, exorcism, and/or confession that may be personal or communal. Even in this realm the affecting agent is still often conceived in terms of an object or substance, and treatment still involves calling upon expert powers to remove the offensive entity and patch up what "it" left behind.

In sum, the prevailing responses to pain in contemporary culture espouse treatments that explain their efficacy in materialist terms. Insofar as such matter-modeled treatments succeed in promoting health, their success is taken as proof that pain is a problem, matter is real, and minds rule.[7] Beyond the obvious role of helping practitioners locate its material cause, sensations of pain are considered incidental to the process of healing. It is as if pain is an alarm. Once it sounds, alerting us to danger, it is no longer necessary. We can ignore it, while experts tackle the issue at hand.

· · · · ·

Within this matrix of responses to pain, there is some room for affirming the healing potential of dancing, provided that its efficacy can be explained in materialist terms. For example, for a person recovering from stroke or hip replacement, sprained ankle, tennis elbow, or too much typing, good physical therapy is deemed vital for helping her restore healthy patterns of physical movement. For such patients, movement practices play important roles in recovering lost movement potential, learning new movement patterns, and developing additional strength. Children are referred to ballet classes to straighten sclerotic spines. Elderly patients take tango classes to preserve brain health and balance.

In the realm of mental illness as well, there are practitioners who welcome dance as a therapeutic tool for helping people give outward form to troublesome thoughts and feelings they would otherwise be unable to express. Dance therapists guide autistic children, angry teens, addicted adults, and depressed seniors to move in ways that release them to feel what they are feeling, relate it to others, and so share the sensory load of their emotion.[8]

Moreover, in the realm of spiritual healing, dance-friendly modalities have taken hold alongside more traditional ones. Techniques of energy work and bodywork from acupuncture to Reiki to hands-on prayer to massage are gaining acceptance as catalysts for healing every sort of pain. Body/mind/spirit approaches to healing that were indefensible decades ago are now for sale in spas, storefronts, and hotels. Practitioners of such methods are generally favorable to the practice and experience of dancing as having therapeutic value. Traditional cultures, such as Navajo or Aboriginal or shamanic, are cited as models of healing dances. Dance, in this view, is greeted as an ecstatic ritual that offers individuals experiences of communal catharsis, of solidarity with greater powers, and thus of support in relieving spiritual, emotional, and physical anguish. Dance is thought to heal by drawing mind and body together in a harmonious unity.[9]

Even so, in each of these cases, the reasons given for the efficacy of dancing inevitably conform to a materialist logic. Dancing manipulates matter; it releases repressed emotions; it generates feelings of empowerment that overwhelm the scars of social interaction. Dancing "works" because it helps to dislodge some "thing" and defuse its pain-producing potential. It works because it brings "the body" back within the fold of what "I" expect and want from "it."[10] The net effect of this union is to *dissolve* the body, its boundaries, its finitude, into conscious awareness.

As a result, even apparently dance-friendly moments in modern culture tend to confirm rather than refute the point: modern Western cultures lack a theoretical matrix that would enable us to understand the healing efficacy of dancing in terms that do not reinforce the materialist beliefs that otherwise deny dance access to "higher" realms of human achievement.[11] Without a clear voice in our word-ridden culture, the healing potency of dancing is perceived as experimental at best and as marginal by most. Concomitantly, even though practices of healing dance are many and varied throughout history—even frequenting the fringes of Western culture—practices of dancing have been, until recently, largely absent from mainstream Western medical, educational, and religious institutions. We do not usually find dancing in hospital wards, school classrooms, academic conferences, government ceremonies, or worship services. We are missing out.

Moving with Pain

All I can do is run, and not very far. I stop lifting buckets and children and five-gallon pots filled with milk pulled by my kids from our three cows. I stop doing yoga or swimming. The pain prods me to take a hard look at myself. *What am I doing?* What movements am I making that are making this back of mine hurt?

I take a closer look. What am I doing? Slumping, really. I slump forward at my computer, head down while cutting vegetables, or shoulders rolled when kneading bread. Every time my chin tucks under, my collarbones curve in, my chest sinks, and my back hurts. I am amazed. I practice moving creatively every day, and yet I still, without thinking, repeat and reinforce this slumping pattern in nearly everything else I do. So much for sensory awareness. I seem to ignore it regularly. This pain is proof. I am getting the message. I need to move differently. But how?

I begin to expand my movement explorations. I stand up straight, pushing my crown to the sky. I lie down flat, pressing my upper spine into the earth. I stretch and rest and reposition. I move through the patterns of different dance techniques I have studied. I practice the cycle of breaths. I learn a lot, but nothing seems to reverse the trajectory of injury. The pain keeps poking deeper into my sensory self. Only running saves me from despair.

Unwillingly, I admit it. I need help.

On the first visit, the physical therapist puts his finger directly on the spasm-ridden spot and names it. It is a rhomboid: a small triangular muscle, awkwardly attached, that holds a scapula to the upper spine. He gives me a brief massage and slaps a piece of wide tape across my back. He hands me a stretchy band, demonstrates some exercises, and sends me on my way in about twenty minutes. I have waited two months.

I drive home, sifting through the physical therapist's assessment, searching for insights. If the rhomboid holds me together and mine hurts, then I am being pulled apart. Somewhere inside says: *yes.* Emotions swirl. I am frustrated that I cannot move. I am afraid that I will not be able to move. I am doubtful that the tape will do anything. I am reluctant to do exercises that seem boring to me. I punch and pout: *Why this? Why now? Why me? This is not what I want! Will I ever get what I want?*

My physical pain bubbles into emotional pain that erupts as intellectual and spiritual distress. My sense of the world is at stake. *Why isn't it working to dance?* Am I silly to have faith in dancing as an agent of healing? Am I wrong to believe in the creative movement of my bodily self? How is it remotely possible that this obstacle is a path? With every pulse of pain, my confidence flickers.

Nearing home, gazing upon green fields, I push hard against the dead weight of doubt. I breathe deeply, drawing on what I know from my long experience of practicing dance. I know. This pain is not robbing me of my pleasure or my belief in dance. It is simply letting me know that I need to learn some new moves. There is more of me to discover, more to enjoy, more to give. Perhaps.

Oh good. (Sigh.) At least I can run.

· · · · ·

In the womb there is no pain. Or at least we do not remember feeling any. When we are born, a primal squeeze imprints every cell: our senses come to life. Pleasure and pain arrive together. As noted in chapter 4, movements we have been making in the womb register new sensations of one and the other. We begin to play with these sensations, with the patterns of movement that render them, and then with the objects that those patterns of movement make present and real to us.

Along the way, making the movements that we do, we compose ourselves as a repertoire of pain-pleasure patterns. We feel the pain of getting hurt, being left, and not having; we feel the pleasure of moving freely, being held, and receiving. We remember these movements by way of the sensations they yield. The sensation of making the movement and the sensation of what happened as a result meld together in a memory of that moment, creating a movement pattern that is as much emotion as it is kinetic image.

When making movements toward what has given us pleasure, we feel joy; when watching something we want move away, we feel sadness. We feel anger when our best efforts to catch it fail and pride when we finally succeed in reaching, holding, and having. In each case the emotion forms as the internal sensory perception of movements made—as the feeling of what we feel.[12] In each case the emotion arises spontaneously in anticipation of what will happen based on what has happened. Moving toward and away; curling in, extending out; pulling and pushing, we feel happiness, sadness, anger, and fear, which propel us to make movements that connect us with others in ways that generate feelings we associate as "good."

So formed, emotions serve as support for the movements we most want to make. They serve as tags to our patterns of sensation and response, helping us to coordinate them into ever more complex and refined combinations. Memory and expectation wrap around and through every physical cue. Soon, these internalized movement patterns prime us to look out for circumstances in which the pleasure or pain of these emotions will be forthcoming. Emotions branch out along movements made, reaching for new regions of awareness and mobility in an effort to find a way through. Patterns of movements-made erupt in the form of intentions or directional action. We develop reasons for why we can and should feel what we are feeling and get what we want or not.[13] Consciousness of our movement, of ourselves as movement, takes shape along the trajectories of physical and emotional movement that we make, as what those movements are making. And at every step along the way, from sensation to emotion to thinking, pain acts as a catalyst. It sets consciousness in motion, pushing it further and further, as our primary resource for finding and fielding impulses to move that will not recreate the pain we feel or fear.

Given this dynamic, any pain we feel, whether the cause is injury, illness, or lack, is never simply a material matter. Any pain we recognize as such is immediately enmeshed in a matrix of movement patterns—sensations, emotions, intentions, and ideas—that we have learned to make and remember in similar situations. Sensations of pain cannot *not* pull into consciousness—as consciousness—the emotional and intellectual choreography we have developed for navigating such moments. We not only ache, we curse, cry, and call for help. Or we bite our lip, suck our thumb, and wait. We have faith that help will come or we despair at the indifference of the world to us.[14] Even insofar as we believe that our pain can be physical, that too is a learned pattern of sensing and responding to our own bodily selves.

Finally, as much as we might like it to be, this process of sensing and responding to pain is not optional for humans. As dependent infants and ultrasocial adults, the only way we can survive is by feeling the pain of our discomfort strongly enough, acutely enough, to be moved by it to move differently—to ask and amend, to question and create. The infant who responds to pain by shutting down her emotional register; a child who responds to pain by withdrawing into a virtual world; the teen who responds to pain by not eating, cutting, or sleeping around; or the grownup who responds to pain by turning to drugs or alcohol or affairs to dull and distract his senses are indeed creating and becoming patterns of sensation and response. They may even be creating and becoming movement patterns that help numb their pain. But they are not cultivating the ability to discern in pain ways to move that will not recreate it. Healing has yet to happen.

In sum, pain, from the perspective of bodily becoming, is never simply a problem. The fact that we feel pain at all is an indication that we know, consciously or not, that there are ways to move that will better align with the potentials for movement-making present in our bodily selves. Pain is proof that we are able and willing to advocate for our own well-being. Pain is a sign of health. It marks both a potential for movement-making that we have yet to tap, and our desire to do so.[15] It is a sign that healing is underway and it is an invitation to participate. The pain that grabs our attention is calling us to align our thoughts and emotions with the healing that is already at work in us, preceding our emergence into consciousness and persisting even when that consciousness wanes.[16]

· · · · ·

Once we are able to conceive of pain as a catalyst to health, our perception of healing shifts as well. Where pain is a pattern of movement, healing is a matter of finding a different pattern of movement—one that does not recreate the same sensations. Or it is a matter of learning to make a given movement pattern differently in ways that do not hurt. In either case, healing appears as a function of an ongoing rhythm of bodily becoming—one in which we can participate consciously or not. How, then, do we participate in the healing that is happening in us and to us in every moment—even and especially when we are feeling pain?

First, we need to realize that just as pain is never simply physical, the same is true for healing. In most cases there is not one quick physical fix that will cure the pain. Healing is holistic. Any healing that happens does so in the context of a person's singular emotional/intellectual matrix. It happens as an expression of bodily becoming, as a bodily self creates and becomes the movement patterns that make her who she is.

Then again, since pain patterns are inherently riddled with emotions and ideas, they, like all our movement patterns, are not properly "ours." They are imbued with cultural practices and values we have imbibed in relation to those who care for us. As a result, healing is never simply personal. Healing is interpersonal, social, and even cultural. The felt vibrations of our pain—as personal as they appear—only make sense within the context of the patterns of relational movement they express.[17]

Nevertheless, despite its communal genesis, healing never occurs through a process of imposing cultural solutions on a bodily self in the name of arresting or repairing "it." As noted, healing is always already happening, and so cultural forms have a specific and limited role to play. Such forms can be helpful—lifesaving in fact—but that efficacy is a function of how well they engage and animate the ability of a singular bodily self to create and become its own patterns of sensation and response. Patterns of movement that have worked for others can be valuable as catalysts for our sensory creativity. Conversely, it is also possible for cultural patterns to guide a person in making movements that impede his ability to learn from his pain how to move differently and thus make the pain worse. When cultural prescriptions do not fund our sensory awareness, then healing involves rejecting those patterns in search of others.[18]

Finally, given this process, the healing toward which pain points is far more than a restored normal function. Healing evolves us. To the extent that we use pain to help cultivate our sensory awareness and discover movements that will better support our healing, these movements change us. Insofar as the movements we make relieve the pain, they create in us a sense of "self" as an open, generative space where such healing movements emerge— a sense of self as a site for resisting movement patterns imposed upon us that would deny us the right or the ability to participate consciously in our bodily becoming. Every move we make in responding to our own pain thus pulls a sense of self into existence as capable of responding to whatever occurs, regardless of whether or not it hurts. Healing, we create our bodily selves anew.

Because we move, we humans *will* have experiences of not being able to move in ways we know we have or can or want. We will have experiences of not being able to relate to others as we have or can or want. We will have experiences of not being able to secure for our selves the certainty or comfort we desire. We will feel the pain of being arrested, lost, or left, regardless of how progressive our politics or how hale our constitutions. As such, the primary task for a human being—the best way to participate in the ongoing healing at work in our bodily selves—is to cultivate a sensory awareness that allows us to welcome our pain as a catalyst for making better movements that will connect us with others in more life-enabling ways. Our primary task is to learn to discern the wisdom in sensations we wish would disappear.

How do we unpack aversive sensations and find the impulses to move locked within? How do we teach ourselves to embrace pain as our ally along the path of healing?

The logic of bodily becoming points tantalizingly toward dance. As we have seen in earlier chapters, the act of dancing can serve to open wide sensory fields within ourselves, and, given what we now know about pain, we can appreciate the usefulness of these spaces. A dance-enabled sensory awareness is a "place" where we can embrace our pain as a catalyst to our fundamental sensory creativity. It is a place where we can begin to learn from pain how to invest our conscious selves in the ongoing healing work of the universe as it is happening in us.[19]

• • • • •

All creatures feel pain. It is a primary element of sentience. Plants remember and move away from sources of past trauma.[20] Animals avoid situations in which they might get injured. If hurt or sick, they take action by retreating to a quiet place, curling up in a ball, and sleeping. Humans, however, tend to respond by creating and becoming new patterns of sensation and response. We too retreat, curl, and sleep, but we also imagine, invent, build, and sew; we adjust, wrap, and experiment. We find new ways to move that will prevent the pain from occurring, and then we repeat them. We respond to pain, in other words, as a catalyst to creating *culture*—to extending our bodily selves in the creation of technologies designed to support our ongoing bodily becoming.

Perhaps, then, our human ability to feel pain so precisely and acutely, on the one hand, and our ability to dance it out, on the other, emerged together, pushing and pulling each other into existence, as the oscillating rhythm that has enabled humans to make ourselves at home wherever we are. Perhaps dancing arose in tandem with this physiological sensitivity as the cultural act that enabled humans to learn from pain how to relate, adapt, evolve, and thrive in vastly divergent contexts. Perhaps dancing, as medium and agent of healing, is coextensive with the development of human self-consciousness.[21]

• • • • •

At some point in time, probably before Homo erectus disappeared and Homo sapiens emerged, a conscious practice of dancing came to life in early humans as what their own movements were making.[22] This dancing was their consciousness. It was the form in which "consciousness" appeared.[23] These

149

movements may have initially erupted as a spontaneous response to sensations of pain—an unplanned eruption of a movement memory. That pain may have been taken shape as increasingly strong feelings of wanting to connect with other humans arising in increasingly intimate relationships, as suggested in chapter 5, or as a response to the travails of birth, as suggested in chapter 4. This pain got their attention and may have triggered movement memories that they associated with comfort and pleasure.

Following this logic, when humans felt sick or sore or sad; when they felt conflicted, confounded, or rejected, ways of moving erupted in them that were familiar, soothing, rhythmic, and repetitive—that felt good. These movements expressed their capacity to feel frustration at being unable to move and connect as they wanted to; they expressed an ability to create and become patterns of sensation and response that relate to others in life-enabling ways, and they expressed a desire to do so. This movement may have erupted as a bodily self's attempt to heal the rupture in its sense of itself.

Once impelled to move their bodily selves in response to pain, early humans would have felt the transforming relief of doing so. The movements would have opened spaces in those making them for welcoming new impulses to move along the trajectories of pleasure those movements represented—movements that were responsive to whatever emerging challenges they were facing. This dynamic would have occurred whether those sensations of pain were due to physical injury, illness, interpersonal conflict, or mourning. The movement patterns that erupted spontaneously in response to pain—in accord with the logic of bodily becoming—would thus have made these early humans into persons who were primed to make those movement actions again in response to other instances of pain. In a dynamic akin to the discoveries of an infant, early humans would have remembered these movement patterns with pleasure, tagged them with positive emotional resonance, and, at some point, begun to repeat them strategically.[24]

Given human vulnerability to movement patterns—and as that vulnerability increased—such eruptions within families or among friends would have been contagious, provoking responses in nearby others. In turn, that contagion would have become contagious—with people seeking out opportunities to move with one another, for one another, in the manner of one another, to surprise and please one another, and all for the pain-transforming pleasure of it.[25]

At first these gatherings would have happened in an impromptu fashion. Movements that people had learned from one another, alongside one another, would have emerged in response to some familiar cue and then rolled through persons gathered like a wave, animating every reed. The experience of this wave would have impressed those through whom it passed. It would have flexed through emotional patterns of stress and fear, anger and longing. It would have charged their sensory awareness and set their sensory creativity free. Opened to the possibility of making new movements, those gathered would have received impulses to move arising in the moment and for the moment in response to whatever patterns of pain or desire the dancing was helping them to feel, individually or as a group.[26]

Moving repeatedly, rhythmically, in response to pain, to one another, and to their experience of dancing, early humans would have cultivated an extraordinary sensory awareness of themselves as makers of movement. They would have created in themselves a sensory ability to notice more pain, feel it more acutely, and engage its nuances as assets and guides to greater pleasure and fuller connections with what is.

In this telling, early humans danced themselves into creatures who were able and willing to find in the act of dancing (alone and with others) the resources they needed to make pain not meaningful but *generative*. They made themselves into creatures who could dance and wanted to dance as an ongoing, enabling condition of their best birthing, bonding, and bodily becoming. Such education of sensory awareness, fostered by the repetition of movement forms, would have strengthened the cognitive matrix and neural networks humans needed in order to develop symbols and verbal language into instruments of abstract thinking.

• • • • •

To the extent that early humans' movement experiments proved pleasurable, memorable, and emotionally resonant, they may have begun to repeat certain known and trusted patterns of movement in response to situations that were not immediately painful but rather were remembered as having the potential to produce pain—situations that were risky or that might go awry or that required special attention and effort, such as mating, birthing, hunting, or gathering. Persons may have come together before such events to remember and repeat movements they had found comforting and enlivening in the past—walking, clapping, circling, and skipping. Perhaps they broke into such movements to highlight and deepen the experience of joy and pleasure when they were full or well.

Again, by the logic of bodily becoming, as humans made these movements, they would have made themselves into creatures who related to the "things" of the matter-seeming world as patterns of movement potential—powers, forces, or spirits—that could be engaged and moved by means of their dancing. They related to these spirits in the same ways as they related to one another; they learned to move with those spirits by recreating the movement patterns that appeared to them. The key to good outcomes and right relationship with the movement-potentials of their environments was to make the right movements—that is, to make the movements in the moment and for the moment that would align with those powers. The key to such interaction was to dance well.

In the process the visceral experience that dancing granted humans of their own rocking, rollicking movement—the lived experience of their own power to transform sensation—would have had the effect of strengthening in those dancing humans a sense of themselves as the people who, as they dance, connect with forces larger than themselves, a sense of themselves as people who are constantly healing and being healed through this connection, and thus as potent sources of movement-potentials, or spirits, themselves.[27]

When conceived via the rhythm of bodily becoming, an idea of spirit or force, so crucial to theories of religion and ritual, was not originally projected outward from a human experience of toolmaking, cooking, hunting, or even baby birthing. Nor did it originate in experiences of dreaming or death. Rather, it emerged as a function of the dancing humans were doing. It emerged as a function of the transformation or shift in their experience that occurred as they learned to make and repeat movement patterns that relieved their pain. The idea of spirit may have initially referred to the experience of being moved—that is, of receiving impulses to move that had not been previously imagined. It may have referred to the experience of expanding in space and time—of transcending the present moment. By this account, the experience of dancing pulled and pushed a lived sense of spirit into human consciousness as an animating principle of their movement and the enabling condition for the ongoing occurrence of the dancing itself. People may have started dancing in more formal and repeatable patterns in order to experience this spirit—and its pain-transforming, creativity-catalyzing, healing power.[28]

The more humans danced, the stronger this sense of spirit would have grown as the medium in which a self dwells and the more adept these spirited selves would have became at accessing and becoming effective, adaptive patterns of sensation and response. Humans who danced well felt empowered to move further, faster, atilt and off balance, taking greater risks in the pursuit of their desires. Moving as they did made them into more expertly agential and highly relational persons as a function of one another. Ritual leader. Shaman. Mystic. Subject. Self. Their movement-making empowered them to seek out new movements and again call upon these movements—physical, emotional, intellectual—in response to new sources of pain.

As the human ability to respond to pain improved, it is also possible that their capacity to feel it would have continued to increase along the lines of the very movement patterns that proved previously effective in promoting healing. Each pattern of pain-relieving movement became a pattern of pain-discerning movement. *Is this pain like that one was?* Humans could risk feeling the pain not only of a difficult birth but also of a broken heart, a prey's escape, or god's indifference because they had resources for converting related pain into a catalyst for bodily becoming. Patterns of bodily movement, made and remembered, provided the ground for increasingly nuanced thoughts and emotions that formed as the very pathways by which those sensations entered into and opened within a person.

Finally, as humans danced to heal, they would have not only danced themselves into conscious, relational, spiritual subjects; they would have danced themselves into creatures who *needed* to move with others repeatedly over time in order to plumb these depths of their own sensing, healing capacity. Humans developed a sensitivity to pain in relation to spirits of their worlds, human and otherwise, that only movement with those others could relieve. Humans danced themselves into creatures who could not only feel wounded within a relational matrix of emotions and ideas but who also needed healing at that relational and abstract level—creatures who needed *ritual* action, ritual dancing, as an ongoing condition of their bodily becoming and their species being.[29]

This feeling of dancing—of moving, being moved, and moving with one another—took shape in humans as the emotion—the pattern of sensation and response—we call love. Love. The form and content of god. And dancing acquired its role as a spiritual necessity.

· · · · ·

In this account of the "origins" of ritual dance, there is no founding instant of human intention. There is no moment when a person or persons sat down and decided to invent a dance for a particular reason. Nor is there any over-arching or underlying intelligence driving the process. There is only the movement of life, expressed in the rhythms of bodily becoming, seeking to continue moving along the trajectories opened up by the shape and form of early-born, ever interdependent, inherently ethical human beings.

Moving together in time, humans experience a pleasure they can not achieve any other way—not the pleasure of communal bonding per se, but the pleasure of exercising the creative, transformative healing potential of their movement-making bodily selves. The pleasure of becoming spirit. The pleasure of *dancing*. Events thus emerge constantly, to this day, to mark, cele-brate, extend, and elaborate this lived experience.

· · · · ·

The pain is gone. I can't believe it. I feel so happy—so in love with life! A day with the tape and I feel no pain. I can sit up and lie back down, go to sleep and wake up again, without the long, torturous clawing my way to upright living. All because of this tiny piece of tape?

This tape is holding me together. It didn't take much, but it had to be right. I couldn't put it on myself. I can't even reach it to take it off. Someone else had to put it on—someone who wanted to help me. The tape works like any other cultural form—to guide my movements. This tape is teaching me how to hold myself together. I am grateful. I revel in the feeling. *No pain!* I love everything and everyone. I keep up my running ritual.

Twenty-four hours before my next appointment, I take off the tape, as the physical therapist had instructed me to do. Fear quickly curdles. The pain might come back! Sure enough, hours later, the pain returns. I feel raw, weepy, and weak. Discouraged, I hobble to my next appointment, wanting nothing except more tape. I'm willing to pay.

A different physical therapist greets me this time. She is chatty and kind. She does not use tape. I explain why I need it. *I have to be held together.* I share a suspicion that has been sneaking into my mind. *The pain may stem from my center—it is too weak.*

"Let's take a look," she replies. She invites me to lie down on my back and lift my head, while she presses her fingers into my abdominal wall. "Hmm," she says. "I can fit my two fingers in here like this, between the muscles that run vertically down your abdomen. Your muscles have not come back together again as they need to do after giving birth." I am split apart, mother and child, and this split is reproducing itself in my belly and in my back, in patterns of pain. I remember when the pain began—during those two long high school music concerts, when I held a sleeping Leif on my lap without adequate support for my left arm.

The therapist tells me directly: "You need to coax the muscles back together again so they touch, side to side." She gives me more exercises, another orange stretchy band, and, thankfully, has her coworker give me some tape. I feel instantly relieved.

Leaving the office, I ponder her words. Tape is not the answer. It will not heal me. I need to learn to sustain the movements of my coming together myself. I vow to fuse my abdominal groove into an abdominal wall.

My vow slams into slabs of anticipatory trepidation. I hate stomach work. It is the one aspect of dancing that haunts me. I cannot do it, and when I feel that sense of not being able to do it, I hate myself. I am sure the world hates me. I am sure I will never get or be or become what I want. I will never dance. Life implodes, and I am sucked into a spiraling vortex of depression and despair.

As emotions careen wildly within me, I try talking to myself. *I don't have to go there.* I tell myself again. I don't have to take this emotional freefall. What if, instead, I embrace this pain as an occasion gently to awaken more deeply the centered sensory awareness I need to dance faster and farther than I ever have? What if I could find a health beneath the hate?

Behind my fear is nothing other than desire. A desire to move. To love and be loved. It is a desire that consumes me, inflates me, and elates me. It is big. It is crying out. I vow to let myself be moved by the movements that will release my capacity to heal. *I vow to dance.*

Ritual/Dance

In the scholarly literature, rituals are identified by the bodily movements they require. A ritual is something people do—a set of actions they perform, often over and again for years.[30] Rituals may be communal or private, local or universal, formal or improvised, as vibrant as a charismatic revival or as silent as a Quaker meeting. They may be simple or complex, occur in a few minutes or across weeks and even years. They may burnish long histories or erupt spontaneously in a given time and place. They may or may not be associated with a religious tradition.

Yet all rituals involve patterns of bodily movement that a person or persons choose to repeat. While these bodily movements may accomplish some identifiable task for those who execute them, such as preparing a meal or raising a barn, the actions nevertheless acquire a significance apart from the task itself. The fact that they are performed, how they are performed, when they are performed, and by whom matters, and it matters, for those involved, to an individual, a community, a nation, and the planet. In the performance of such bodily movements, transformation happens. Healing happens. Prayers are answered. Fears calmed. Spirits appeased. Insights revealed. Conflicts resolved. In short, rituals appear to those who perform them as necessary for life itself to continue. And scholars trained in materialist methods wonder why.[31]

How does the mere repetition of bodily acts acquire such importance to human beings? How does transformation happen? By what means is it effective? Is ritual a disciplinary practice or a symbolic act?[32] Does the action of making bodily movements make a difference, or is it simply people's belief that action is meaningful that makes it so? Is that efficacy a matter of habit? Or a function of people moving together?[33] And what, in the end, does ritual actually accomplish? Does it preserve order or foment dissent? Empower individuals or subsume them within a collective?[34] Does ritual make meaning possible, or does it allow people to face the impossibility of any meaning at all?[35]

Shifting to the perspective of bodily becoming raises new questions about ritual while offering new answers to those already in circulation. If the first rituals evolved from the lived experience of dancing as a way to enjoy and enhance the pain-transforming power of that dancing, then we can use what we know about dance from this and earlier chapters to illuminate the structure of ritual, the sources of its efficacy, and its persistence over time.[36]

· · · · ·

Given the ubiquity and diversity of ritual activity, one way to begin the task of reconceiving ritual is to reconsider the three-stage model that undergirds many analyses in the field of religious studies and read it in terms of the rhythms of bodily becoming.[37] When we do, the relationship of ritual to dance appears anew. This same approach could be taken for other theories of ritual as well.

In a three-part model a ritual begins with actions that serve to separate the time and space of the ritual from the time and space, or "structure," of ordinary life. In a second phase of the ritual, participants enter a liminal moment, or "antistructure," in which customary codes and conventions of behavior, identity, and order are suspended. In this liminal moment, people "play." They act out characters and explore roles that open up new possibilities of thinking, feeling, and acting. They experience a generic and bonding sense of humanity.[38] In a third segment of the ritual, participants pass back from the antistructure into the structure of ordinary life, folding their experiences of play and possibility into their social roles and responsibilities.[39]

As useful as it is, this frame is limited in its ability to grasp the significance of dancing for ritual and vice versa due to its allegiance to a materialist program. For one, the frame focuses on individuals who enter and exit a process that exists independent of them. Second, the frame assumes that individuals have reasons for performing ritual that are rational, even if the participants themselves are not able to think about what they are doing in rational terms. As a result, it is the role of the scholar to interpret via scientific methods why individuals are choosing to do what they are doing.[40] Finally, the frame assumes that the key to the ritual's efficacy derives from a material exchange akin to the medical models of healing described earlier. Ritual works by identifying a perceived or actual threat to the society, defusing its danger (or harnessing its power), and then restoring a renewed and righted ordering of relationships.[41]

Nevertheless, if we align this ritual process with the lived experience of dance, rename the stages as movement patterns, and add a fourth, we suddenly have answers for why and how ritual effects transformation that honor what participants themselves claim. We also open ways to evaluate the range of possible effects rituals carry, from disruptive to empowering, disciplinary to symbolic, as a function of how the act of making the movements they prescribe guides people to participate consciously and creatively in the rhythms of bodily becoming.

. . . . .

What if we were to conceive ritual action in terms of four arcs derived from the three elements of our dance vision: creating patterns of sensation and response, cultivating sensory awareness of our movement making, and participating consciously in this rhythm of bodily becoming? What if we conceived of ritual as a cycle consisting of warm-up, practice, play, and cool down—a cycle that is designed to exercise and enhance our capacity to *dance*?

WARM-UP

In the opening moments of a ritual, participants make movements that stir their energies, quicken their sensory awareness, and focus their attention on issues or challenges that are rendered additionally important by this attention accorded to them. Participants chant, sing, or clap in time. They bow, kneel, and confess. They circle an altar, breathe deeply, clear their hearts and minds. They make movements that invoke and invite the presence of powers and spirits greater than themselves. They come together.

Such movements, when made, serve to awaken the senses of those who are making them. The rhythms and melodies, the shapes and colors, the objects and clothing call participants to make specific movements of sensory perception in the present—to see, smell, hear. The movements train participants' senses to a fuller awareness of where they are, who they are, and what they are feeling. The movements encourage participants to notice other movements being made within, among, or beyond them. In these ways, the opening movement patterns of a ritual serve less to separate a person from ordinary life and more to deepen their experience of the moment in which they are embedded.

So too, the opening movements of a ritual not only activate and orient a person's sensory awareness; they guide her to feel whatever she is feeling as something the ritual can transform—as a reason to give herself to the ritual movements. Her pain may be named as sin, error, or ignorance; it may be cast in the shape of a demon, a stranger, or familiar menace. It may be blamed on the stubbornness or selfishness of human persons or attributed to divine or natural action. Regardless, these sensations invited and evoked by the ritual's opening movements comprise the "material" or movement patterns that the ritual will work to transform. In this way the ritual warm-up serves to bring into sharper focus whatever experiences of pain or distress the ritual is poised to address.

PRACTICE

In a second and often overlapping arc, ritual participants rehearse movement patterns that others before them have discovered, remembered, and passed on for their efficacy in transforming experience. The ritual has a form, however simple, that is represented by the bodily movements its participants repeat. Participants recreate in themselves patterns of sensory movement rendered in the shape of stories, songs, or textual passages—or in bodily movement identified with animals, ancestors, gods, or spirits. Sometimes those movements guide participants in role reversals and ludic play. Sometimes the movements-made guide participants to stage a battle or share a meal. Sometimes they enact steps on a journey into worlds above or below. Participants repeat these patterns, perfect them, and become them. They give themselves to the patterns, allowing themselves to be organized and aligned by the actions of the bull or goddess or messiah.

In so doing, participants run through a spectrum of pain-altering tools. The act of repeating these familiar movements teaches participants about what has worked in the past to release stuck energies and facilitate transitions within that environment, that culture, with those people and their traditions. The options educate the sensory awareness of those making the movements, expanding and orienting their perception of and response to their current experience.[42]

PLAY

In a third phase of a ritual, the movements the participants have been rehearsing increase in intensity until a moment when those their forms yield to movements of the participants' own making. In these moments of possession or private prayer, communal ecstasy or focused meditation, participants welcome impulses to move arising singularly in them. They are launched into a time of play. They allow themselves to be moved by powers that their culturally informed movements have stirred in them and bent them to perceive. This arc of a ritual is often described as a time of communion with the spirit world. It is a time of releasing the possibility for transcendence immanent in the rhythms of bodily becoming.

The movements that arise through this play inevitably recombine basic elements of the movements that participants have been practicing. Their movement patterns form individualized complex combinations that answer to their particular situations. In this way the movement patterns that rituals require and enable serve to open in participants a sensory locus where they can tap and release their kinetic creativity—a space in which to experience themselves as connecting with the ongoing creation of what is. As healing and being healed. In this way the movements that participants make effect a transformation of their being in the world—a *visceral* transformation that occurs in and through and as a result of the bodily movements that are happening through them. They participate in the healing of themselves and their community. They know (themselves as one with) spirit.

COOL DOWN

In a fourth arc of ritual, participants make slower, softer movements that allow them to cool down physically, emotionally, and spiritually. The level of intensity drops. Yet the participants do not simply return to the social "structure." Rather, they dwell in the steady glow that persists after a burst of flame. Often, they abide in their own renewed sense of resilience and resourcefulness. They feel their own flexibility and creativity, alive in their fingertips.

At every surface of sensibility that their culturally informed improvisations have opened, participants are more vulnerable. They are more vulnerable to impulses to move arising within them that resonate with the patterns of perception and possibility they have been practicing. They are more likely to be moved by others who are similarly engaged. Insofar as they are members of a community, they are more invested members of that community. Insofar as they are individual humans, they are more singular in the contributions they make, the movements they produce, and the gifts they have to give.

In sum, ritual, conceived via the perspective of bodily becoming, is effective insofar as its movements guide participants in cultivating a sensory awareness with which they can participate effectively in the rhythms of bodily becoming, creating and becoming patterns of sensation and response that relate them successfully to the sources and resources that sustain their lives. Ritual is effective insofar as it guides participants to perceive wisdom in their pain—in sofar as it awakens the sensory awareness they need to discern whether the shapes of their living align with the requirements of their ongoing movement in a given environment. Participants are primed to discern whether and how the movements they are making are "good," not only for their own bodily selves nor even for the community, but for the wide range of forces and flows, elemental caregivers, on whose existence (their) humanity depends.

$$\bullet \quad \bullet \quad \bullet \quad \bullet \quad \bullet$$

I return for more physical therapy. The therapist tells me that I do not need the tape any more. It is time to make a different move. My rhomboid is still tender. It will not lift anything. But I can wake up and sit up in less than a couple of minutes. The tape has helped me turn a corner. Healing has taken hold, and I am in line with it.

I am working on my center. I try practicing the exercises the physical therapist gave me. I do not like them. I cannot relate to them. They do not engage my kinetic imagination. The act of lifting my head while manually holding my stomach muscles together feels awkward. Curt and abrupt. I feel resistance immediately. Self-judgment clamps my heart.

I decide to find my own way. I am still running, but not just running. It occurs to me how much of a ritual this act has become for me—how much of a dance.

When I run, I begin slowly, warming up, waking up to myself, feeling what I am feeling, making familiar moves. I call upon my self, my world, the powers that be, to move me along. I release into the earth. As my sensory awareness comes to life, I practice my best stride, making the patterns that I have learned work well in propelling me through space. I think about what I have read about running and the mechanics of our bodily selves. I think about the dance training I have received and the advice from my teachers. I practice—chin lifted, chest light, shoulders relaxed, energy streaming through my fingers, hips released, legs flowing.

The running rhythm quickens me, and soon I find myself experimenting. Must I drop my pelvis? What will happen if I don't? What happens when I land on the ball of my foot? Or the heel? The inside or out? What if I twist my upper body with each stride, rather than bulldozing straight ahead? I scan my sensory awareness for new impulses to move. They bubble forth. My gait lengthens and shrinks again. My feet leap and hop and zigzag side to side. My hands stretch up and fall down; my torso spins gently left and right. I feel grateful for these deserted dirt roads.

With arms and legs churning, I consciously explore ways of pressing and sinking into my lower belly. As I do, I realize something that shakes me to the core. *This running is helping me find a reality beyond my fear.* The rhythmic thrum of feet on the ground, the left-right cadence, the breeze on my cheek, the air in my lungs, the thud of my heart are comforting me, enabling me to reach within myself for movements that will strengthen my being in the world. I am dancing—not because I feel good, but in order to feel good. I am dancing—not in a way that anyone has taught me, but in the way my trained bodily self needs to move in order to heal itself.

Running to dance, dancing as I run, I feel the power to move, my desire to move, my desire to create, find, and make movement patterns that do not hurt. Movement patterns that heal. Running is transforming my pain into a catalyst for making dances that express a love for life.

On another visit to the physical therapist, she and I discuss theories of healing. "Sometimes a muscle is just a muscle," she remarks. I don't believe it. Or maybe I do. For what is a muscle anyway? It is movement . . . that matters.

• • • • •

This analysis of ritual in terns of bodily becoming puts forth new answers to old questions about how ritual works and why humans need it. In doing so, it illuminates how and why dancing is a "spiritual" necessity for humans, whether they are engaged in traditional religious practice or not.

For one, take the question of why rituals repeat the same actions over and again. As the logic of bodily becoming reveals, and others have noted, the repetition that characterizes rituals is not strictly speaking *repetition*. While an observer may think that a person is repeating the same movements, for the participant the visceral experience is not the same. With each "repetition" a movement becomes more firmly instilled in the movement maker, but not as a determining, inscriptive, restrictive force alone.[43] That movement made resides in a participant as a potential for moving in new directions. It becomes a stronger and more effective tool for inviting related, branching movements that may appear along the length of its sensory trajectory. With each rehearsal of a movement pattern, ritual participants may find themselves opening inward and outward at once, more willing and able to receive and follow through with *new* impulses to move, play, heal, and become bodily selves. The act of repeating ritual actions, then, is not necessarily conservative or coercive. Such repetition can actually catalyze a basic sensory creativity, releasing a person to unfold within herself possibilities for perceiving and making further movements that would not otherwise have existed in her or in the community. Repetition in this perspective is generative, at least along the lanes it defines. It heightens a sensory capacity that humans carry with them in every moment of their lives.

Second, when conceived via the perspective of bodily becoming, it is also clear that the primary power of ritual is neither symbolic nor disciplinary; it is neither cognitive nor emotional. Its primary power is *kinetic*. Its power lies in the *visceral transformation* that occurs as a person experiences the power and the effects of his own movement-making. As the repetition of the ritual taps and releases a person's sensory creativity in response to problems that the ritual has helped him name, his experience of his own self shifts. It is not just that he receives impulses to move that address the pain. Rather, a sensory awareness dawns in him of how his pain itself is a catalyst for moving in new patterns of thinking, feeling, and acting. His pain is a sign of health. Even if the pain does not completely disappear, its meaning changes. Its presence is no longer what it was. The act of making ritual movements offers relief—even if only a rekindled sense of hope—by offering a person a visceral experience of his concrete, ongoing participation in the rhythms of bodily becoming. Making the movements, he feels better.[44]

Moreover, this transformative experience of one's own movement-making power does not just work backward. It also can exert a powerful protective effect moving forward. The transformative experience helps participants further along in the process of cultivating a sensory awareness of the movements that are making them, such that they exist as a more refined instrument of discernment. With this internal resource a person is less likely to make the decision to move in ways that do not align with her health and well-being and more ready to respond proactively in moments when she does.[45] If we are able to feel what we are feeling at the outset—before the pain or problem looms overly large—then we will be better able to address it and defuse it before it becomes overwhelming.[46]

So too, this transformative experience of one's own movement-making power is, again, never simply personal. Insofar as the movements a person is making are inspired and enabled by patterns of movement shared and remembered by the group, then that experience of personal power is equally an experience of membership. By the logic of bodily becoming, a person experiences the kinetic agency of his singular self to the degree that he gives himself, his attention and devotion and energy, to the task of recreating the shared patterns of ritual action. The efficacy of the ritual, in other words, is not a function of whether or not a person *believes* in the ritual—except insofar as "belief" is a sign for his willingness to invest his sensory self in the act of making the ritual's patterns. Nor it is a function of whether or not he makes the movements—he could imitate them without investing his attention. Nor is it a function of the group gathering together per se. What matters to the ongoing efficacy of ritual is the degree to which a person allows his bodily self to be moved by the movement patterns of a ritual to move differently.[47] He need not believe in God in order to experience healing effects of congregational singing; but once that healing happens, he will have a harder time denying it.[48]

Third, from the perspective of bodily becoming, participant accounts of climactic moments of a ritual in which they describe themselves as becoming something other than they are—moments characterized by trance, possession, ecstasy, battle, or communion—are not superstitious, delusional, or even misguided. People *are* becoming something other than they were. The movements they are making *are* changing them in ways that make them more aware, at a sensory visceral level, of the movements—whether cosmic, natural, human, or divine—that are making them. They are more vulnerable to being moved by the particular movement patterns that others in their culture have discovered and repeated for their apparent efficacy in transforming pain.[49]

When a ritual participant moves like a goddess, she makes that goddess real by the fact of her movements as the enabling condition of her dance. Her movements give that recognizable movement pattern power and reality as an enactment of what is and as a mark of her self. By dancing, she is becoming the ongoing reality of that goddess power, that pattern of movement, in the world. She is bearing witness to the movement of life itself, participating in its onward, streaming flow into new forms of her movement.[50]

Fourth, these movement-enabled reflections help make sense as well of the dualistic structure of many rituals that involve characters, a narrative, or dramatic enactment. Nearly every ritual (as nearly all children's play) packs an emotional charge sparked by the rubbing together of opposing forces. What is repeated is often a clash between "good guys" and "bad guys," forces of light and dark, knowledge and ignorance. The clash may occur between spiritual entities, between humans and an external threat, between order and disorder, or as a drama unfolding within the mind and heart of an individual human. The threat may come from illness or injury, natural events, competing bands, perceived pollution, or the overwhelming challenge of finding food. Often the good guys win. Yet the bad guys are rarely vanquished. They may lose power and territory; they may even beat a retreat. But they come back. The ritual happens again. Why the conflict? Why its return?

Bodily becoming directs our attention to the choreography. These rituals exist as sequences of movement interactions. Good and evil thrust and parry; stab and block; engage and retreat. Each force or character has a style recognized by all in the culture—a way of moving that designates and identifies that force as a potential for pleasure or pain. Making their signature moves, combatants draw close enough to one another to be moved to engage and respond.

Watching and making the movements of the "good," ritual participants learn how to move in response to those who would cause pain. We develop an attitude or attack that allows us to negotiate hostile energies in culturally approved and appropriate ways. Making moves in response to those who would cause us pain strengthens us along every trajectory of physical, emotional, and intellectual movement that the battle depicts. It strengthens in us a sense of our own spirit as a willingness to surrender to this healing dance. We learn that creating and becoming such movement patterns *is* the path to transforming the pain that "bad guys" represent. The ritual works, then, by training our senses to recognize and recreate the movements of whatever force or entity will protect us from those threatening to rob us of whatever the ritual helps us name as life-giving.

In turn, ritual movements also encourage us to identify with the forces of evil or suffering, ignorance or indifference that the ritual also invokes. As we recreate and make these movements or watch others do so—movements that are often rendered as jerky, violent, heavy, asymmetrical—we recognize those movements viscerally as our own. We know that we too are capable of making them. We too are capable of feeling anger, jealousy, hatred, or revenge when our movements are blocked, arrested, or otherwise compromised. We begin to acknowledge our complicity, our responsibility, and thus our potential power in making movements that will not reproduce our physical and emotional pain.

Moving through the movements of such a ritual, we learn that the key in determining whether or not good guys persist hangs on how well we dance. If we dance well, if we dial up the emotional energy we need to recreate exemplary patterns of sensation and response, we will find and make movements that allow us to live on, to heal and be healed. If not, we will not.

When the ritual ends, then, the pleasure we feel is not a relief and elation from having won. No one wins. The pleasure is the pleasure of having energized our capacity to create and become patterns of sensation and response. The pleasure is the pleasure of having grown stronger in our center and sense of ourselves. The pleasure is a *spiritual* pleasure of having danced and been danced by forces greater than ourselves into something greater than we were. We breathe more easily. We move more freely and fluidly. We have help. We have resources. We heal. And this pleasure often settles in us as a desire for more.[49]

Fifth, if the efficacy of ritual lies in its ability to engage and animate participants' rhythms of bodily becoming, then it follows that any ritual, even when emptied of dance or performed in stillness, still depends for its form and efficacy on participants' lived experience of dancing. As we have seen, every infant and child has visceral memories of participating consciously in the rhythms of bodily becoming. Every living human must create and become patterns of sensation and response that connect her with some caregiver in life-enabling ways. Every person who lives has learned to play, to some degree, with sensations, kinetic images, objects, and emotions. And it is this movement-making ability that ritual accesses and exercises. A ritual will not work, people will not repeat it, if it cannot transform physical/ emotional/ spiritual pain, and it will not succeed in doing so unless it engages, focuses, and releases the inherent creativity of a rhythmically moving bodily self. Rituals exist insofar as they guide, encourage, and enable us to give birth to ourselves as pain-transforming movement makers.

A final implication of this approach merits a brief mention, as it awaits further exploration. Ritual, as evoked here, still provides the structure for all modalities of healing in the modern world, regardless of how matter-based those modalities pretend and aspire to be. The so-called split between religion and science occurs on a continuum the two realms of life share. Not only do the two share a passion for an abstract truth defined over and against the material world; they both covertly rely upon the rhythms of bodily becoming for authorizing their version of it. To make this point is not to dismiss Western medicine or religion, but rather to appreciate their efficacy and endurance in a new way.

Nearly every aspect of our medical system—including the physical therapy I sought out—guides us to act in ways that reinforce our belief in the materialist model as real, as the way things simply are. Sometimes it works. The patterns of movement medical professionals have evolved for manipulating matter are exceptionally effective for a range of illnesses and injuries that happen to conform to a materialist model—ruptures and rhomboid pulls, bone breaks and bacterial infections.

Yet it is readily acknowledged by experts in the field that medicine is as much art as science; and that future research will produce evidence that half of our current best practices are ineffective. We also know that half of all people who visit the doctor are not found to have anything obviously "wrong" with them. Many cases of pain go undiagnosed and untreated, lumped in the category of "chronic." The usual response is to treat the symptoms by prescribing narcotics and analgesics. Painkillers are addictive. They are addictive because they do not heal. Painkillers mask the very signs that could point the way to different movement making. In some cases, painkillers can help open up a space of sensibility within which the dance of healing can happen. But often the pain returns.

From the perspective of bodily becoming, the glaring problem with the medical model is that it fails to understand the sources of its own effectiveness as ritual dance. By encouraging providers and patients to perceive a body as a material object, medical science artificially narrows the range of sources and resources it is willing to consider. It flat out rejects explanations that do not conform to a materialist model, even when their healing effects have been demonstrated. In the eyes of modern medicine, the healing efficacy of a placebo or of a doctor's white coat is a curiosity—not a key to unleashing the healing potential of bodily becoming.

Once we acknowledge that medicine operates on a ritual structure, however, we have resources to explain why the act of manipulating matter *as well as* the act of going to the doctor's office can both be effective instruments of healing. Healing happens in both cases when doctor and patient make movements in relation to one another that cause the patient to tap and release her own capacity to create pain-transforming patterns of sensation and response.

For example, by going to the office and detailing his complaints, a patient *warms up*. He makes movements that bring his senses to life. He is invited to feel and share what he is feeling. He identifies that pain as a problem. As the doctor *rehearses* patterns of possible causes, the patient learns about the cultural forms that pain often assumes—what his movements as a member of this culture are creating. As the visit enters its most intense moments, doctor and patient improvise or *play* to arrive at a singular, culturally informed account of what is happening. As the patient *cools down* and leaves, he does so with instructions for moving differently, in ways that will allow him to participate more fully in his healing. In the best cases he leaves energized, hopeful, with a renewed sense of his imminent health.

By moving through this ritual, then, a patient kindles her faith in the medical profession. She gives herself to its forms and techniques; she gives her vital signs. Insofar as she does, the process of being weighed and measured, poked, prodded, and squeezed stirs and feeds her hope and courage. It allows her to release fear and anger. Yet the efficacy of the encounter lies elsewhere. It works when it opens her to receive and follow through with impulses to move arising in herself that align with her own health—impulses she would not have been able to find on her own. Like the use of tape to hold me together. Healing happens, and whatever catalyzes and nourishes our conscious participating in the rhythms of bodily becoming helps it along.

• • • • •

Of course, rituals do not always work. We do not always learn what we need to learn in order to release our pain or discover new ways to move. Healing does not always happen. The pleasure of success is not guaranteed. The pain

continues, unabated, perhaps most of the time. Yet the rhythm of bodily becoming illuminates such moments as well. For, whether or not healing happens, it definitely will not happen if the person needing to be healed does not
learn to move differently. Drugs will not work unless they give a person's healing energies an edge. Exercise will not work unless it awakens a person's own
desire to move. Ritual dancing will not work if its movement patterns deaden
sensory awareness of the movements that are making us. When it comes to
addressing pain, matter is not real. Patterns of movement make it so.

Thus ritual succeeds when it guides a person to make or discover the patterns of movement that she needs in order to transform her experience in the
ways she desires. It does not succeed when the patterns of movement it guides
participants to make do not put them in touch with their kinetic creativity.
And the reasons for that success or failure do not lie within either the person
or the ritual (as if they were material things). Rather, the efficacy of a ritual lies
in how the respective movement patterns that each is come together or not.

So too, even when a ritual does not work to relieve pain, participants may
still continue to perform it. Rituals often contain explanations for their own
failure, which encourage a person to try again, to surrender to its patterns
anew, with more intention or focus. Rituals may encourage participants to
trust in a process of becoming whose results manifest over time, through repetition. In such cases participants continue to repeat the ritual because the act
of trying again offers more promise and pleasure than the pain of admitting
defeat or than the emptiness of not knowing which move to make. Thus even
rituals that are not themselves effective in healing can be effective in perpetu-
ating a belief in themselves as effective in healing inasmuch as they, at some
level, enable a participant's own process of bodily becoming to continue. If
they do not, then the rituals will die.

In the end, from the perspective of bodily becoming, ritual actions and
their ongoing importance in human life bear witness to the fundamental importance of *dancing* to human being. Ritual remains a primary activity in
which humans cultivate the sensory awareness needed to participate consciously in creating and becoming pain-transforming, spirit-engendering relational patterns of sensation and response. Ritual works if and when and to the
extent that coaxes our capacity to dance into action as an enabling condition
of our health and well-being. In ritual, dance stands revealed as a spiritual
necessity.

• • • • •

On my next visit to the physical therapist, we trace the path of the receding rhomboid pain beyond my abdominal wall to a soreness in my lower right back, clamped around a sacroiliac joint that was tightening to do the leg-lifting work that my center was not. The physical therapist works on the joint, releasing potentials for movement frozen in patterns of effort made. I tell her about the right hamstring I pulled twenty-five years ago and how some of the pain settled in my sacroiliac joint. She pauses. "Some things you just need to live with."

After that visit I don't return. She helped me immensely. The tape she and her partner applied guided me in making movements that would not recreate the pain. The information and exercises she provided put me in touch with my ability to receive impulses to move that would align with the healing, recreating movement in me. She got me dancing again, on my own terms, in my own way. And because of how she helped me heal, I cannot believe that the pain circling my sacroiliac is forever.

So, when the physical therapist says that no healing can happen here, I know it is time for me to leave. In my resistance to her words I know that healing can happen, that it is happening, that it is time to let it happen in me.

I will keep dancing down the edge of the pain—stepping my way into the stream of healing that I know is flowing through me. It is my ritual. Overcoming myself. Every day. Until I move no more.

To Dance Is to Love

Whatever one generation learns from another, no generation learns the essentially human from a previous one. In this respect, each generation begins primitively, has no other task than what the previous generation had, nor does it advance further, insofar as the previous generations did not betray the task and deceive themselves. The essentially human is passion, in which one generation perfectly understands another and understands itself. . . . Each generation begins all over again.

—KIERKEGAARD, *FEAR AND TREMBLING*

I wind my way along the edge of the pasture into the woods. The path is narrow, nearly choked with brambles. I have not been here for a few days to beat them back. Thorns pierce my thighs. I plow through.

A clearing opens around me. I stand in the center of a ring of red pine and locust trunks whose vertical reach I lengthen to match. I breathe up with their branches and sink my toes as deeply into the ground as I imagine their roots can go. I move with an earth breath, allowing my exhalation to root me too in this shady spot. Here, the earth is bare, strewn with dry leaves. The trees' foliage catches most of the plant-feeding sun before it falls.

I shuffle in a circle, bending my knees and focusing my attention on the earth, on my relationship to the earth, on how the ground beneath my feet holds me up, pushes me up, lifts me up. Memories of African dances I have done and Native American circles I have trod move my bodily self in patterns new and old. I pound and press, stamp and spin, knowing. Without the unrelenting resistance of the earth, I would fall through space and not be at all. To be is to be on the earth. Of the earth. For the earth. Wherever and whomever you are.

The thought of the earth, its press upon my soles, shifts my weight to one side and back again. I become a pendulum, pulled by the tides. My knees bend further, bringing the bulk of my body closer to the earth. I want to be as close as I can be and still stand upright, ready and able to be moved. Rocks, bushes, and broken leaves; ferns and fallen limbs prod my limbs into movements I have made before in this same spirited spot. A chant pulses through my lungs with a heartbeat rhythm. I undulate my torso with the flickering leaves, suddenly conscious of similar moves I made performing Haitian dances years ago.

As I continue to dance, inspiration flashes white within me, illuminating new kinetic pathways. Blasts of direction alight and align my arms and legs with felt images of what surrounds me, expressing feelings within me. My sense of self rears and mingles. I become bark and trunk, rock and moss, pine needles and brown dirt.

The pleasure of making these movements—of receiving and being made by these movements—pulls my full-bodied sensory self into a smile. Lips follow. As the experience dawns, ideas form and float lightly in my consciousness, accompanying my movement without interrupting its flow. I am aware of how the movements that I am making as a bodily self, dancing and thinking, are *expressing* my relationship to the earth—not representing it, but continuing it and pushing it into form, like a tree expresses its cherry. These movements are making my relationship to the earth cherry-red real as the condition that is enabling me to make these movements at all. I feel the earth and know the earth *as* an inspiration to move; I feel and know the earth through the movements that come through me as I dance.

Because of the dancing that is happening to me here, I can think about "it" as some *thing* that I can perceive, honor, and value as real—a *place* to which I will return again and again for the pleasure of being moved, felt, thought into being. As I surrender to the impulses received by my practiced, opened bodily self, earth comes alive for me as an object of intense gratitude to which I owe my life.

My movements crest and stretch and subside, sinking me into a moment of stillness. The earth calls to me, to listen through me, to voices beyond me. Am "I" dancing? Or is earth dancing in the shape of me? Either way, my dancing is making real for me a sense of earth to whose ongoing existence I am accountable—an earth I want and need to nurture for the enabling pleasure of it. The task feels urgent.

How do I let these woods live?

• • • • •

Within a materialist model where matter is real, minds rule, bodies follow, texts authorize knowledge, and individuals come first, the distinction between culture and nature is often called upon to delineate the identity of human beings vis-à-vis other forms of life. Within a materialist perspective humans have and create culture because humans have minds that can operate free from matter, over and against matter, as masters of it. They make culture; they live by culture. Animals, plants, and protozoa; fungi, rocks, rivers, and wind do not. They are simply bodies. Whatever "thoughts" other-than-human organisms have, whatever decisions they make, whatever "dances" they do, are guided by instinct and the drive to survive.

A self-reinforcing logic ensues: humans are different from nature because they have the ability to distinguish themselves from nature as makers of what distinguishes them, i.e., culture. Frequently, it is some version of this logic that pops up in the justifications given for why humans can kill, consume, and otherwise use nature as they please. Culture rules.

Like the conceptual threads of a materialist model discussed in earlier chapters, this idea of culture as operating over and against nature proves equally effective in hamstringing attempts to acknowledge dancing as a vital art.[1] For one, this understanding of culture carries with it implications for the task of becoming human that buttress those associated with a mind-over-matter sense of self. In this view, to become human is to overcome (one's own) nature. To become human is to establish a difference over and against the natural world figured in terms of *control*.[2] A human is one who can control natural desires, natural resources, and natural phenomena and thus protect himself from the pain of want. A human is one who can forgo the pull of the practical and pursue the purity of a disembodied spiritual. The task for human beings is to insulate themselves from the shocks and vicissitudes, the dangers and diseases, of nature and so transform the world into what it can be—a better place, with humans on top.[3]

In relation to such an aspiration, dancing, not surprisingly, poses a problem. As the act of dancing is both bodily and conscious, instinctual and learned, it can appear from a materialist perspective to moor our mental selves in earthen bodies and thus compromise our ascending progress toward increasingly abstract and spiritual goals. For those abiding by this view, dance is what "primitive," less highly evolved, peoples do. Dance is what people who have lost their minds, or not yet grown a mind, do. Dance is what animals do. Dance is not what civilized adults do. Civilized adults may watch dance or even sponsor dance; they may tolerate dance in small amounts during carefully scripted events (like weddings, rock concerts, or evenings out), provided that the superiority of cultural ideas and forms over natural impulses is assured. With few exceptions, however, they do not usually spend time studying or practicing it. The fact that human adults can survive without dancing is taken as proof of their maturity, their intelligence, and their difference from the rest of nature: humans are free.

For those who want to acknowledge dancing as a vital art, then, the task is clear. We must revalue the distinction between culture and nature from the perspective of bodily becoming such that this distinction can no longer justify the marginalization of dancing in the modern West, its scholarship, its religions, or its global exports. Repeating the same movement-enabled overcoming as in earlier chapters, we must consider the idea that culture—even in its most spiritualized forms—is the movement of nature seeking its own becoming in human form.

In this endeavor, it will not be enough to erase the distinction between culture and nature by claiming that "we," as cultural beings, can never access a "pure nature."[4] It would be equally (il)logical to state that there is no "culture" that is not shot through with a "nature" whose movement exceeds, interrupts, dislocates, and inhabits attempts to know, use, or otherwise control it. Instead, we will need to find a way of honoring a nature that exceeds and enables human culture, even as we acknowledge the necessity of culture to that nature's ongoing survival in the human species.[5]

This chapter begins by reconceiving the distinction between culture and nature from the perspective of bodily becoming. The discussion then returns to the theme of chapter 6, attending to ritual dance as an emergent form of human culture. The chapter proceeds to enrich this account of dance by telling a movement-enabled tale about the originary moments, developmental dynamics, and contemporary forms of human culture.

In the process this chapter reveals dancing as a practice humans evolved to do so as to ensure that the cultural moves they make when birthing, connecting, and healing themselves (chapters 4 through 6)—including and especially those made in the realm of religion—remain accountable to the natural forces and resources, elements and ecosystems, on whose ongoing vitality humans' creative action depends. Dancing, as this chapter avers, provides humans with a medium and a means for acquiring an *ecokinetic* knowledge they cannot acquire any other way. On these grounds I conclude that dancing is an ecological necessity.

The Nature of Culture

The seeds for revaluing a materialist distinction between culture and nature, as for those in previous chapters, lie within the distinction itself. As those using a materialist model (begrudgingly) admit, humans are (part of) nature too. They are conceived and born with a human nature, even if the end of that "nature" is to establish culture over and against the "nature" of their bodily selves.

Implied in this admission is the fact that the conceptual distinction between culture and nature, as with the distinctions between mind and body or matter and movement, is not given. Its cast is not inevitable. This distinction is one that must be made and remade person to person, community to community, culture to culture, era to era. It is a distinction, in other words, that depends for its clarity on the *bodily movements* that human beings are making in relation to one another and to their contexts as they think, feel, and act. Bodily movements are what give the distinction between nature and culture its meaning.

Once we admit that bodily movements make and reinforce this distinction, the perspective of bodily becoming ushers in a host of implications that prove relevant to our understanding of dance as vital art and ecological necessity.

For one, when seen in light of bodily becoming, culture no longer appears as a mark of superiority that qualifies humans to lord themselves over the rest of creation. All elements of the natural world also move. Cliff, coral, or koala—the patterns of movement that distinguish one from the other represent the characteristic trajectory of bodily becoming that each entity is. It is fair to say that every moment of nature—and not just other animals—is a trajectory through which life is making itself over and against what has been. Every moment of nature has, in this sense, some degree of its own "culture."[6]

Accordingly the trajectory of movement potential that human culture represents, while unique, is not so because it exceeds nature. In fact, as we have seen, humans, to a degree unmatched in the animal or plant world, are born *lacking in nature*. As noted in chapter 4, newborn humans, sent forth into the world without basic instincts, must learn how to eat, connect, sense, think, and act from watching and learning from the movements of human others on whom we depend—and we must begin doing so long before we can think or act as an "I." More than any other creature, humans must grow our own nature from its infant shape into something more mature.

Further, the fact that humans need to complete their own natures is evidence that humans, contrary to what is generally believed, are historically and potentially *closer* to the "nature" of their environments than creatures who are born adapted to a given ecosystem. Because humans can and must grow our own natures after we are born, the natures we grow are thickly informed by the immediate field of forces in which we find ourselves. Humans cannot not grow their natures in intensive, ongoing interaction with the given nexus of variables in which they find themselves.[7]

From the perspective of bodily becoming, then, *culture emerges as what humans create as they learn from nature how to move in relation to nature in ways that will enable their movement through nature to sustain the ongoing movement of nature in human form.*

Human culture, in other words, is not the result of a mind-over-matter process. It emerges as a collection of movement patterns—as stories, songs, and dances; as rituals, tools, and symbols—that support humans in becoming, connecting, and healing in ways that are sensitive and responsive to the challenges and opportunities of their bodily selves and their living environments. From the perspective of bodily becoming, culture, for humans, represents an attempt to achieve the same sort of life-enabling ecological adaptability—the same precision of interdependent cooperation—that other living creatures enjoy naturally in their natural habitat. The fact that humans must create and become themselves through culture is a sign of our utmost, absolute dependence on currents of movement happening in and around and through our own movements, over which our mental, material, individual selves have little control.

Culture is what nature—as the movement of life—makes in and through human beings as an expression and elaboration of itself.[8]

• • • • •

As earlier chapters attest, most scholars believe that ritual dancing was not only one of the earliest manifestations of a distinctively human culture, but an enabling mother matrix for all other forms of human culture.[9] This revalued understanding of culture (as expressing the movement of nature in human form) sheds further light on the role that ritual dancing plays in its genesis and development.

As already established, ritual dancing is an activity humans evolved to tap, exercise, and put to work a singular capacity to notice, recreate, and become patterns of movement made by others. Dancing is also the activity in which humans acquire knowledge—the sensory awareness of our own movement making—we need in order to ensure that those patterns of sensation and response we notice, recreate, and become actually serve to birth, connect, and heal our bodily selves. Dancing is the activity through whose practice humans have evolved into the biological, ethical, and spiritual creatures that we are.

Here we push forward. The movement of "others" that humans are vulnerable to perceiving as they become, connect, and heal their bodily selves is not simply the movement of other humans or even impulses spit forth from their own sensations of pain. What humans are able to perceive—and train our sensory selves to perceive—are movement patterns occurring anywhere and everywhere around us that are relevant to our own moving potential. Through most of human history, up until the last two centuries, the basic genetic, sensory, and kinetic patterns with which most humans have regularly interacted have been the natural forces acting through us, the natural resources available to us, and the natural challenges suffered by us. Humans are as vulnerable to the movements of animals and trees, sunrays and windstorms, rocks and raindrops as they are to smiles and frowns.

From the movements of talons, hooves, teeth, and claws, early humans learned to make tools that do likewise. From the movement patterns used by animals to weave nests, furnish caves, and dig dugouts, we learned to build homes. From the movements of gathering and eating that other animals were making, we learned to catch, dig, scavenge, and pluck. From the movement of fur-thickened animals in winter, we learned to don their skins. From the sparking of wild fires, we learned to kindle and keep our own. Moved by the movements of animals and plants, hills and deserts, early humans learned to move like them, with them, and so find paths to survival. As they did, shapes of human culture emerged.

From the perspective of bodily becoming, then, culture develops as humans exercise their nascent ability to dance, creating and becoming movement patterns that relate them to their environments in life-enabling ways. Ritual dancing, by implication, would have taken shape not only as a forum for guiding humans to access their kinetic creativity in relation to one another and their own bodily selves. It would have also guided humans to access and express their kinetic creativity in relation to *nature*. Ritual dancing would have helped participants cultivate a sensory awareness with which they could discern which *cultural* movements available to them would best honor and sustain the *elemental* conditions of their ongoing movement.

In this sense ritual dance engendered a sense of earth within—an ecokinetic knowledge—representing the largest possible eco-whole that humans were able and willing to conceive.[10] This ecokinetic knowledge was, again, at least at first, not a way of thinking or feeling about nature or the earth. It was kinetic. It existed as a potential for making movement. It carried with it a *responsibility* for making movements that enable the ongoing lives of all of those from whose movements we have something to learn—that is, mutually life-enabling movements.

By the logic of bodily becoming, because humans are born so lacking in nature—because we can be and must become *dancers*—we are uniquely responsible for the lives of fish, fowl, and forager; for the health of the air, water, and soil; and for the ongoing health of the infinite living web of which we are one moving moment. We are responsible not due to abstract principles having to do with virtue or goodness or the inherent worth of the earth. We are responsible to the more-than-human matrix of life because we are dependent upon its myriad moments to teach us how to move in ways that will enable our own survival. Humans alone, given our extreme reliance on moving others, are responsible for completing our own natures—and creating culture—in ways that let those others live.

From the perspective of bodily becoming, the telos of human nature appears anew. Our task in creating culture is not to escape from nature, but to become a life-enabling moment of it; not to dominate the movements of nature, but to discipline ourselves to those movements; not to become culture-bound minds, but rather fully animated bodily selves. It is a telos that is antiteleological, for its end and arc unfold from whatever the movements of the moment are creating in response to sensations of pleasure and pain as the horizon of possibility. Our task, in all, is to receive, register, and recreate kinetic images of the nature in us and around us so that the movements we make in becoming, connecting, and healing nurture the elemental conditions for our ongoing movement making. Earth. Air. Water. Fire. Our task, in short, is to practice dancing. Dancing is an ecological necessity.[11]

Humans educated in a materialist paradigm, for the most part, are species snobs. Given our sensory education, we cannot help it. From the perspective of bodily becoming, we should not. For this conviction of our own distinctive nature and purpose holds the key to our submission and, hopefully, our survival. What distinguishes us from other forms of life is the degree to which we can and must learn from them how to dance (our own) nature into being.

$$\bullet \quad \bullet \quad \bullet \quad \bullet \quad \bullet$$

I leave the clearing in the woods and walk out onto a peninsula of land that rises above our hayfields like the head of a sperm whale. I walk its length, tail to blowhole, and pause at the prow. Birds are flying beneath me, skimming and scooping in search of bugs. The breeze plays over the contours of land and tree, creating a rustling around me. The clouds are big; the blue is bigger. The sky opens like a lid above my head.

Breathing in and out, a pulse of desire swells in me. I want to move. I want to move like those birds, that breeze, those stately clouds. I want to feel those movement patterns unfolding in me like a bloom-becoming bud. I cue my sensory awareness to that sensation of unfolding. I imagine it, imagine feeling it, and feel the pleasure of it. My arms, on their own accord, begin to flutter like fledgling wings.

Closing my eyes, I see nothing. I feel nothing—nothing is holding me down or holding me in. It is as if I might suddenly be absorbed into space, leaving the wind blowing and bunching behind me, a funnel of dust. Impressions of whirling dervishes percolate through my kinetic imagination. I slip back in time to that workshop I took in Sufi dance and the performance that followed. I feel the movements I made then moving me now. Spinning slowly, I merge into nothing at the heart of matter. *I am the movement that never ends.*

I stop spinning, walk up to Moon Rock, the highest point of our property, and release my sensory awareness into space.. The wind reaches for me, lightly, kindly, inspiring response. Arms I call mine curve and churn, rise and fall, ceding to an incoming arc of inspiration. The movements this wind is moving me to make make me one with the waves billowing, riding, circling the earth—like Isadora Duncan sensing her divine continuity—revealing that One to be what it is in the patterns of my bodily self. I am reborn as an airborne sprite, cavorting in tall grass, sucking in gallons of oxygen, alone on my hilltop.

Thoughts spin with abandon. I am not trying to be the wind or to imitate the wind. I am open to the possibility of being moved by movements I perceive as wind—movements capable of moving me. As I do, I am not only me, becoming a wind-flapped self, I am also nature, becoming what it is. The movement of air—of breezes breathing, of oxygen osmoting—is becoming what it has the capacity to be as a force moving me. Burning and combusting, discovering and dispersing, I am nature, creating and becoming the human it has the potential to be.

Descending from the peak, blown open, breathed out, light and airy within, I feel and know and move as if nothing matters. Nothing at all.

The Birth of Culture

While scientists have regularly endeavored to locate the origins of human culture in some identifiable difference distinguishing humans from other animal species, that project is proving increasingly difficult. The more researchers learn about these animal species, the less obvious our differences are. Here the perspective of bodily becoming helps affirm a human difference along a spectrum of culture that we as animals share—a difference that nonetheless binds us ever more strongly to our animal kin.

By one account, if culture is defined in terms of *tool use*, *intraspecies communication*, and *complex social structure*, then animals (at least) have culture too.[12] Examples are endless, and those known are only the cases that humans have been able to observe to date within their limited sensory span. Corvids regularly use sticks when fishing for insects. Whales and dolphins, songbirds and wolves have sophisticated sound patterns for relaying information.

Jellyfish comprising a Portuguese man-of-war move in relation to one another with such coordinated, choreographed precision that they seem more like a single organism than individual bodies. Moreover, rats reason their way around traps and through mazes; squirrels store and retrieve food in multiple far-flung locations after many months; chimpanzees learn patterns of behavior from humans and from one another including gestures and practices of food washing.

Nevertheless, despite these commonalities, within each category of culture the perspective of bodily becoming allows us to grasp a remarkable difference that humans demonstrate. Humans not only make and use tools, they make and use durable tools that are passed from generation to generation and found millennia later, such as cutting edges and axes, bowls and utensils. Humans make tools whose use demands practice and the mastery of precise movement patterns.

So too, humans not only communicate with one another, they create forms of communication in stone, on wood, or plant fibers that are similarly durable. These forms of communication can last in time, across space as pictures or symbols or letters, and their use, once again, demands practice and the mastery of precise movement patterns.

In the realm of social relations, humans not only abide by complex social systems, they allocate roles and responsibilities to different individuals via ritual actions such as baptisms, coming-of-age ceremonies, marriages, and funerals that mark passageways from one stage of life to the next. The performance of these role-defining rituals, regardless of whether the dancing is explicit or implicit, once again demands practice and the mastery of precise movement patterns.

With respect to these three markers of culture, then, humans not only create and become patterns of sensation and response—as animals also do—they teach movement patterns that they have discovered to other humans. A piece of stone is only a flint knife if and when another human learns to make those knapping and cutting movements for herself. A tablet carved with marks is only a message when another human learns to make the movements of shaping, forming, and arranging symbols that deciphering it requires. Any position within a community, whether cook or king, carries the power that it does only when another person learns to stand, bow, or yield as the position demands. As such, the capacity for learning, making, and transmitting patterns of bodily movement to others must exist before the durable cultural forms shared by humans have any use or meaning at all.

In this perspective, humans, as they participate in any and all dimensions of culture, extend the kinds of thinking, feeling, and acting that other animals also do along trajectories of bodily movement-making that the act of ritual dancing exercises.

· · · · ·

One theory that seeks to explain the cognitive abilities that participating in human culture requires focuses on the difference between imitative rather than emulation learning.[13] According to this theory, humans have a unique capacity to recognize the *intention* of another human actor.[14] Insofar as human young discern intention, they can infer what another person is trying to do and imitate observed patterns of movement as a means to that end.

By contrast, experiments with other-than-human primates suggest that primates learn from one another—they gather information from one another about their environment—but not by imitating intention. For example, a baby chimpanzee sees its mother roll over a log to find succulent ants to eat and does likewise. In doing so, he is taking in information about the world (there are ants under logs) that guides him in applying movements he already knows how to do (rolling logs). He is not imitating her intention; he is emulating her actions. Human youth, on the other hand, will imitate the movements that another human makes regardless of how effective that movement is for accomplishing the task at hand. Humans, scientists infer, can and do imitate *intention*.[15]

Given this observation, the perspective of bodily becoming suggests a complementary interpretation: what humans are able to discern in the actions of others is not intention per se, but kinetic images, patterns of bodily movement. Humans can and do perceive actions as trajectories of bodily becoming, unfolding in time. Humans can perceive a temporal frame in which "intention" emerges as one description of why a given bodily movement happens. This capacity, then, is not a question of empathy or mind reading. It is not a matter of recognizing cause and effect. It is about having created and become patterns of moving and being moved.

What grabs a human perceiver is bodily movement itself. Humans can foresee the trajectory and anticipate results—we can imitate intention—because we ourselves have already moved and been moved in our own explorations of the world, even if not in the exact same patterns. This so-called imitative learning is, as with mirror neuron activity, not, strictly speaking, imitative. It is mediated through whatever degree of sensory awareness our own movement-making has opened in us.

So too, humans repeat those movements that interest us not (just) for the practical ends we anticipate but for the *pleasure* of making new movements—the pleasure of discovering what we ourselves are capable of doing. It is a play that humans never outgrow, unless it is hammered out of us. Movements of any and all kinds, human, animal, or elemental, move us to respond by recreating what appears to us, and the more humans "learn" from the movement of others, the more we bring to life a spectrum of possible movements to be seen, recreated, and made. Movement continues in and as emerging forms of culture.

From a perspective of bodily becoming, then, dancing is not only the medium in which human culture persists, it is also the means by which given shapes of culture appear. Culture—its tools, roles, and modes of communication—are what humans create as they mobilize the sensory awareness of themselves as movement that the practice of ritual dancing brings to life. Dancing exercises the capacity that is required to use any tool, word, or power in a *human* manner.[16]

Moreover, as particular forms of ritual dance crystallized as culture, these forms would have continued to feed and guide the ongoing process of culture creation. In practicing movement patterns that promised to birth, connect, and heal, humans created and became a wider array of movement patterns along the trajectories their practice opened up. There were new births to facilitate, new social connections to cultivate, and new pains to heal. In response, new forms of dancing would have appeared, which educated human senses to receive impulses to move further along in creating new tools, symbols, and social roles.

· · · · ·

Once we perceive ritual dancing and culture in terms of bodily becoming, we are in a position to reconsider the role ritual dancing plays not only in relation to nature or to culture's origins but also in relation to *culture's* emerging forms. In this account, ritual dancing is not only embryo, engine, and expression of culture, it is that moment of culture that roots the process of culture creation in a sensory awareness of the ongoing evolution of nature itself. Ritual dancing *earths* culture. By creating a space in which people practice sensing and responding to pain and pleasure, ritual dancing acts as a check upon all cultural developments—including and especially religion—to ensure that the patterns of thought, feeling, and value that humans are creating and becoming serve the ongoing health and well-being of the *earth* in and around its members.[17]

Evidence for this reading of ritual dance abounds. Rituals, as we have seen, are often recognized by the elemental opposites they animate: light and dark, birth and death, sun and rain, antelope and lion. Most rituals surveyed by scholars feature natural forces and celestial bodies, animal and plant energies, often identified as ancestors, spirits, goddesses, and gods.[18] Rituals frequently relate to these figures as sources of transformative power. The figures represent the cast of characters that *warm-up* calls into presence; the models for movement patterns that participants *practice*; the terms with which participants *play*, and the ones whose retreat marks the final *cool down*. In ritual, the movement of bodily becoming comes to life in shapes with whom and to whom people can relate.

Reasons for why ritual movements conjure a sense of earth vary. In the study of early agricultural societies, for example, scholars describe ritual dancing as a kind of talisman or good luck charm—an activity intended to appease and placate powers perceived as responsible for fertile soil, clement weather, and abundant yield. In a contrasting account, scholars claim that these allusions to nature mark these rituals as practical means for coordinating a community's schedule of plowing, planting, and harvest.[19] In either of these readings, rituals represent technologies for managing natural resources out of which later cultural forms eventually grow.

The perspective of bodily becoming locates the efficacy of these rituals elsewhere—in the act of creating and becoming relational patterns of sensation and response. Ritual dancing serves as a means for acquiring and disseminating ekokinetic knowledge—that is, a visceral appreciation of nature *itself as* and *in terms of* bodily movement.[20] Ritual dancing does so by training the senses of those participating to movement patterns—the cycles, seasons, and migrations of nature; the life cycles of plant, animal, and storm—that the form of the dance recreates.[21] It is effective for the ways in which it cultivates in participants a sensory awareness of earth within.

As the ritual warms up, the movements evoke the matrix of natural forces in which participants live and the specific challenges those forces pose to their ongoing movement. The movement patterns they rehearse train participants to imagine the actions they want to have happen in relation to those elemental forces. Intervals of play allow participants to invite and receive impulses to move that align with the outcomes desired. As a result, when critical moments arise, participants will already have become, in their bodily selves, capable of sensing and responding to forces of danger and destruction in life-enabling ways. Hunting, planting, and mating; birthing, bonding, and healing, all enjoy the benefits of being danced. Success is far more likely, because the humans involved will be primed and quickened to create and become patterns of movement that align their actions with the life-supporting movements of nature in them and around them.

Through the action of dancing, then, a ritual participant would have cultivated a sensory awareness of the elemental, natural movements that was able to guide him in participating more effectively in the rhythms of bodily becoming.[22] Said otherwise, ritual dancing made "nature" into what it was in relation to "us" as something that our own movements continue, complete, and create, even as it made "us" into creatures who could do so fruitfully. It created creatures who could make the movements that render tools useful, gestures meaningful, and social roles significant *within* a given ecosystem. Ritual dancing cultivated the ability and the desire to ensure that our cultural creations of all kinds honored, cared for, aligned with, and, in a word, *worshipped* the enabling elemental conditions of human movement making.[23]

This skill in fielding environmentally responsive movement patterns that ritual dancing exercised did not require an ability to use language. It did not entail stepping outside a situation, analyzing it, and concocting a response. It involved exercising, extending, and elaborating the dance that humans are always already doing.

This account of culture's originary moments suggests a role for ritual dancing that has not and cannot be replaced. By practicing dance humans earth culture. We grow a sense of earth within that finds expression in the thoughts and feelings and actions we are thus able to receive. We cultivate within ourselves an ecokinetic knowledge of our unique responsibility in giving birth to ourselves as those who let others live.[24]

· · · · ·

I wind my way down from the top of Moon Rock through grasses that grab at my feet. Milkweed sways in the breeze I feel moving (through) me. I find my third dancing spot, tucked around the shoulder of the hill. It is a cradle of sorts, a scooped-out, sun-catching dip in the earth. Standing in its bowl, I see and feel and know the pond below me to my left, the meadows stretching to the base of the hill in front of me, the sky cupping my head. A rock appears, my rock. The rock with whom I dance. It calls to me as I approach.

Pulled to move, my bodily self falls into the patterns it has been making in the previous two stops—earth patterns, air patterns—that here mix and cross and ignite a spark in my belly. The fire of desire. I breathe into the resistance the earth gives me to generate energy along the trajectory of my own breathing down into the cave of myself, deep into the darkness, where light begins. Where life begins.

I breathe my arms up and in and go deep again, taking the swirling wind-whirls inward, pressing against the earth. The fire grows. I blow on it. My movements blow on it. The flame catches and begins to pulse like the sun this cup cradles, like the core of the earth far beneath my feet. I feel myself making the movements I have made in so many Graham classes and seen in countless performances. Deep contractions, pulling in, only to rebound in ecstatic release.

It is hot here. The desire I am fanning takes shape, welling within me as the ferocious whirl of me. Strong enough, it could explode me apart, distributing me far across space. Here in this crux of land, it flows round. It is a fire, burning in me because earth and air are moving me, because these movements are making me into a cluster of patterns that turns on itself, replicates itself, becomes itself—that wants to move and keep moving and so overcome myself.

I breathe in and let the fire out slowly, gently, in a warm stream of light that circles around me before spiraling outward and dissolving in the blue beyond.

This dancing brings to life in me an earth that lets me live. It calls me to move in ways that let the earth live as the enabling condition of my best becoming. It seems silly to say it, yet I must. Without this earth, I would not dance. There would be no dance. Earth is dancing through me.

The Development of Culture

With a shift to the perspective of bodily becoming, dancing not only appears as origin, engine, and moral compass of culture, it also describes the logic by which a particular culture—as interactive, relational patterns of sensation and response—develops in and through a community of people. Making this connection not only provides us with a template for analyzing changes over time, it carries implications for understanding the fate of dancing within culture itself.

As we have seen, movement is contagious. Humans are primed to notice it and recreate it in spite of themselves. As soon as a person makes a movement, that movement exists as one possibility not only for the person who made that movement but for others as well who have seen it or felt its effects. Any movement made becomes an occasion for others to find and unfold additional movements that travel along the trajectory of effort and attention the initial movement requires. One child jumps, a second jumps higher, a third jumps over a log, a fourth jumps to touch a tree branch, and the variations explode. A jumping culture takes root and grows. Each subsequent movement is not only guided by earlier movements made but by memories of what happened as a result of those movements—the emotional tags and explanatory ideas that organize movement patterns and predict their repeat use. The joy. The sense of accomplishment. The sprained ankle. "Culture" comes to refer to a shared collection of movement patterns that belong to, identify, and constitute as a group the people who rehearse and play with them.

As the movements that humans make leapfrog each other into being, a culture matures in ways that express the rhythms of bodily becoming observed earlier in relation to birthing, connecting, healing, and earthing, now manifest at the level of a community itself. Here, movement patterns that characterize a culture's distinctive orientation in nature *accumulate* in number, *concentrate* along certain trajectories of human possibility, *stratify* in hierarchies of specialized skill and ability, and are increasingly *abstracted* from the natural world. At some extreme the tension between culture and nature *collapses*, and the process begins again.

These five arcs of cultural development are neither linear nor chronological. They occur and reoccur in the formative moments of any group, family, couple, or clan. Once we understand these dynamics as expressions of bodily becoming, we will have the resources we need to complete the task of this chapter: affirming dance as an ecological necessity whose practice is critical to ensuring that our ongoing cultural creations express love for the earth. We will also be able to explain why dancing has lost value in modern Western culture and its religions in ways that herald its imminent return as a vital art.[25]

ACCUMULATION

In any given group of people, as humans are moved by one another to exercise their ability to create and become relational patterns of sensation and response, movement patterns accumulate. By the logic of bodily becoming, no movement is ever repeated exactly, even by the same person. Each repetition adds to the collection of elaborations and refinements known to and by the group. Movements made encourage and inspire, pull and push, opening new horizons of possibility for making further movements. To any one person in the community, this "culture" exists as an array of movement possibilities from which to borrow, apply, and improve upon as needed. Ritual options branch. Tools and symbols proliferate. Social roles expand. As generations pass, any new person born enters into a world whose proximate movement patterns are given not only by natural phenomena but by human others and human-made phenomena as well.

CONSOLIDATION

As movement patterns accumulate within a group's collective bodily memory, people moved by those patterns, as with infants, gravitate to making the movements that best align with their unique bodily potential, that best connect them with their preferred sources of nurture and nourishment, or that best transform what they suffer. Certain individuals develop a given cluster of movement variations into a skill, a specialty.

Within the group as a whole, different intensities of attention or pockets of ability form around movement patterns found most effective in helping the group navigate the challenges and exploit the resources specific to their social and natural settings. As skilled individuals raised by the culture spend time learning and practicing and sharing with one another, a culture develops areas of expertise in boatbuilding or knife making, in constructing wooden furniture or manufacturing computer electronics. Any young person born into the culture is now not only met with an extensive range of movement options, but with tracks along which to develop those possibilities. Standards of value or need within the community give preference to some movement patterns over others, and expectations endure for movements that ought to be made and mastered for use in common situations.

A person born into a culture whose movement patterns are consolidating, then, is not wholly free in relation to the possible movements of his own bodily self. Patterns of culturally preferred movement prime and shape his choices, acting with nearly as much force as the angle of a knee joint, the fall of the rain, or the turn of a day. Movement patterns define the reality in cooperation with which a person discovers how who he is can best adapt and contribute to the larger whole.

STRATIFICATION/SPECIALIZATION

As movement patterns accumulate and consolidate, they also become more efficient along certain lines of application. The movements made using stones as hooves to shape flint give rise to flint knives that spur further movements in slicing and scraping hides and then in heating and hammering harder substances for making more effective cutting tools. The tools that humans invent and use, as well as the symbols they exchange and the roles and responsibilities they define, all develop into technologies that both exert powerful effects along trajectories of desire and require more and more practice to master.

As a result, differences within a group open among those individuals who move faster along the movement-pattern learning curve of tool use or role-play than others. Differences open between those who have been practicing for a long time and those new to the task. A situation arises in which longer periods of study are beneficial and in which certain individuals pop out over and against the rest of the community as better able to teach others how to do what they have learned to do. Skills and strengths begin to concentrate in a few persons who thereby appear to others in the group as having greater value for their common survival.

With that value comes power within the group and even power over others. Individual humans who emerge as experts and teachers have the potential to wield tremendous influence. They acquire a certain rank in regards to important decisions. Their movements matter more. They also assume a responsibility to give to the community what they have to offer as the condition of their ongoing power. When they give what they have to give, the community acknowledges their value and acts to support their well-being. The concentration of skill and knowledge and power continues.

ABSTRACTION

With these cultural developments of accumulation, consolidation, and stratification, a shift happens in the task of becoming human. The task is no longer one of developing a life-enabling connection with the natural world, but rather one of navigating a cultural one. The task is no longer to find berry bushes and water holes, but to handle a bow, address an elder, or communicate with spirits. Rather than learn to hunt and skin and cook a rabbit, a human learns how to create the relationships with other humans that will help him gain access to the meat that some skilled and experienced other has already snared and prepared. In other words, the tasks that a child must learn in order to survive in a culture whose movement patterns have accumulated, consolidated, and stratified are less directly related to how he engages the natural world and more oriented to how he negotiates the tools, symbols, roles, and requirements of his cultural one. The skills a human must practice become more abstract.

These increasingly abstract movements that humans learn to make begin to circulate as currency. These skills, expressed in tools made, symbols used, and marks of power—apparently material objects or qualities—acquire a value for which others are willing to trade. This value is a function of the bodily movements that those who wield them are able to make—movements that guide those who master them to best align their efforts with the forces and challenges, cultural and natural, at hand.

Soon certain people in the community can accumulate a wealth that is separable from their own bodily movements, their own skill and expertise—a wealth that is durable—simply by accumulating what the bodily movements of others have made. And that wealth, that power, whether measured in golden blocks or gilded books, must be protected.

Collapse

Eventually, the consolidation of power in the hands of a few reaches its limit. In culture after culture, religious institution after political party, when the highest abstractions of wealth and knowledge no longer represent (in all senses) the health and well-being of the majority of people, change is imminent. Some person or group rebels or breaks away to create something new, to move differently, seeking to learn from the patterns of pain and poverty how not to recreate them. The cycle begins again.

• • • • •

This dynamic of accumulation, consolidation, specialization, abstraction, and collapse carries implications for the fate of the ritual dancing that impels it as well as for the relationship between dancing and religion that forms within it. In brief, at some point, as "culture" assumes an increasingly more important influence than "nature" on movements made by its members, "religion" loses its anchor in dancing and assumes an orientation that is increasingly focused on another world—a human-imagined, god-inhabited, desire-free world. The role of dancing in earthing ideals is increasingly devalued and disregarded.[26]

How does this process occur? As already suggested, early in the life of a culture, the ritual dancing that humans do creates in them a palpable sense of earth within that guides them in inventing movements that support and align with the movement trajectories they perceive as life-giving. Their dancing cultivates enhanced relations with the natural world as the enabling condition of their becoming, connecting, and healing. Dancing, humans complete their nature in ways that remain informed by the sensory awareness of what the natural world has to offer them in learning how to move.[27]

As movement patterns proliferate, this array of dance movements become the defining context within which the ongoing action of dancing occurs. Persons who dance invent movement forms that prove effective in transforming pain, ignorance, or confusion. Others watch and learn and build on these dances to invent others. The number and physiological range of typical dance movements increases with a branching logic along whose arms patterns converge.

With this accumulation, members of the community practice making similar dance movements in distinctive ways. The dancing of a given group consolidates into a characteristic form. Members develop a turned out leg, a bent knee, an extended arm, or patterns of interaction and then expand upon those capabilities. They invent rhythms and images, costumes and coloring designed to enhance the efficacy of the dancing forms they have discovered. Persons begin to recognize one another as friend or foe, in or out, by their style of dancing. They recognize themselves. *What do you dance?*

As people turn to these forms and rhythms again and again for pleasure, healing, or under duress, their ability to make these particular movements improves. They explore further extremes of mobility, flexibility, and agility. The range of existing dances grows more difficult to learn, more difficult to master. Certain individuals pop out, distinguishing themselves as "dancers."

As ritual dance forms accumulate and consolidate, "religion" emerges as the gathering of feelings and ideas, beliefs and practices that guide people in learning to make the movements of dancing that will best accomplish their birthing, connecting, and healing in a mutually enabling relationship with the natural-cultural world.[28] As humans engaged in ritual dancing experience its transforming effects, their experiences register in them as a desire for more of that experience, as feelings or emotions tagged to that experience, and, eventually, as ideas that describe it.[29] The first ideas about religion, the first forms of religious belief in any new community are records about the bodily movements that people are making and how those movements are making them.[30] Religion begins in the shadowy, unreachable moments when dancing takes shape of its own accord within humans as an animating, healing force. The movements humans go on to make make "religion" real as the locus of ecokinetic knowledge for whose acquisition the *act* of dancing is essential.[31]

From the perspective of bodily becoming, then, the kinetic images that appear in and as religion express what the lived experience of dancing enables people to perceive. In and through the act of dancing, earth, air, wind; fire, sun, moon; planets, animals, and plants, as well as mothers, fathers, and allo-parents, all appear as powerful, enabling *movements*. They appear as the "intentions" that move humans in combative and supportive ways—as forces, spirits, gods. We know the mountain by virtue of the heroic movements it demands we make in order to climb it, cross it, match its height and heft. The mountain lives in and through these movements as a powerful, intimidating, inspiring entity. At least initially, these religious images and ideas serve the ongoing practice of discovering movement patterns, calling attention to their efficacy, amplifying their reach, and supporting the process of transmission and learning from one generation to the next.[32]

The systems of shared beliefs and practices that scholars recognize as comprising a "religion" thus come into existence as an enabling condition of ritual dancing.[33] In this view, there is no essence of religion that abides in a feeling and intuition of the universe,[34] an ultimate concern,[35] or an encounter with a "wholly other."[36] Rather, every religion represents a unique collection of movement patterns that people have discovered and remembered for the ability of those patterns to connect them with the pain-transforming power of their own movement-making capacity. Religion emerges as the set of ideas and actions that keeps dance alive in humans by explaining, justifying, and requiring conscious participation in it. Religion arises to keep the movement of creation moving in the scale and shape of human beings.[37]

As dance movements accumulate and consolidate into shapes of religion, the arcs of abstraction and stratification come into play. The lived experience of being brought to life in dance—of having senses awakened to powerful forces sustaining us—finds expression in ideas about this feeling and a desire for a place where it could last forever. A place where there is no pain, no death, no interruption to the bliss that dancing can yield. Paradise or heaven, nirvana or enlightenment. The home of goddesses and gods. These imagined worlds are frequently rendered as gardens whose order serves as an ideal and guide for the kind of movements humans should make. Humans want to move through nature as if they were dancing—that is, in a way that enables them to find in "it" all of the nourishment and protection, warmth and fertility, they could want.

As humans allow themselves to be moved toward and by the increasingly abstract ideals engendered by their dance experience, the action of dancing assumes new meaning. Less a medium and means for humans to connect in life-enabling ways with one another and the natural world, dancing now appears as a means to access to this imagined gardenlike place. Ritual action is no longer about birthing, connecting, and healing here on earth; it is about leaving the earth to be born, connect, and heal in a better world—*one in which dancing will no longer be necessary.* "Nature" begins to appear as a flawed and finite realm from which we long to dance ourselves free.

A difference cracks open between the world as it is being received and the world as humans dancing imagine it to be, all following the logic of bodily becoming itself. Still, as long as dancing remains integral to the practice of religion, any realm of gods and goddesses or ideas about enlightenment remain accountable to the experience of becoming a human bodily self on earth, in earth, and of the earth.[38] The tension is generative.

Meanwhile, as movement patterns continue to proliferate and consolidate in increasingly abstract ritual forms, certain individuals who demonstrate a capacity for learning to create and become these patterns of sensation and response begin to rise above the others in rank as those with enhanced access to dance-enabled experiences. They gain recognition and attention as as shamans and religious leaders to whom we owe a certain respect. They appear as forces in their own right on whom we depend and with whom we must connect if we are to survive. They are the ones who move between earth and sky, between human existing and other worldly power. They open, by spanning, a difference between nature and the supernatural.[39] In their movement making the spiritual world comes to life as real.

So connected, these dancers assume the primary responsibility for inventing new dance forms in response to emerging patterns of pain in the community and its environment. Lead dancers discover and enact forms of movement ritual that guide them to the edge of what is known, what has been tried, learned, and discerned. They travel to the edge of power, where they can receive impulses to move that will carry them and the people they serve along the trajectories of human possibility that a given culture is realizing. The scope of communal creatives shrinks.

As this arc of specialization and stratification continues, not only does the role and meaning of dancing change, so does the task of learning to do it. No longer is learning to dance primarily a process of cultivating sensory awareness. Rather, it is about learning to make the specific movement patterns that those best at dancing are demonstrating. Dancing becomes something we learn from those around us who have been practicing for longer than we have. Ritual dances offer less of an opportunity to invent patterns of sensation and response and more of an occasion to recreate shared, uniform patterns that identify us with others making the same movements.[40]

No longer are young dancers training their senses to animal, vegetable, and elemental movement patterns, they are learning to arrange their bodily selves in proper forms that will assure them of their eventual, eternal liberation. Religion itself—its history, practices, and traditions; its buildings, art pieces, and music—comes to define the "world" or "ecosystem" within which people must to learn to adapt and thrive.

As culture matures, then, the act of dancing loses its role in ensuring that the movement forms humans are creating and becoming in all areas of their lives—including and especially their ideal images of what might be—remain faithful to the movement of nature in them and around them. Religious worldviews lose the awareness of their efficacy as rooted in the lived experience of dancing. They compete with one another to offer the best promises for the most comprehensive and pain-free world—the most womb-like heaven. The tradition, the hierarchy, and the gods themselves take credit as sources and instruments of power. Religious beliefs, rather than explaining the healing efficacy of dancing, begin to justify their own existence. Religious leaders stop dancing.

In such moments—and they recur periodically throughout history—dancing may survive for a while as a symbol of status, or even the activity of a sanctified religious elite. However, dancing soon drops to the lower classes as a last remaining form of recreation, distraction, and comfort. Dancing is no longer perceived as something humans need to do or learn or even watch.[41] We may dance in the garden, as an expression of our freedom and joy, but we need not. Just as we rely on others to grow our food and make our shoes, we can rely on others to dance our dances too. While there may be a time to dance, that time is not now.

At some point this development reaches a crucial moment, and an ironic reversal occurs. The nexus of movement patterns that once emerged as "religion" to name, nurture, and enhance the healing efficacy of dancing, evolves into a primary agent for expelling dance from human life. The vision of a better world that once derived from the lived experience of dancing and encouraged dancing as a means to it, now takes shape in opposition to "nature," and works to control and suppress the sensory realm, the realm of body, animal, natural, female, and dancing in the name of "spiritual" progress.[42] In religions with global aspirations, it is often true that their vision of what the world is and should be authorizes the destruction of cultures, religions, and dances other than their own.

Religion, without dance, loses its moral compass. It loses its line on nature. Again, this dynamic of dance's demise is neither linear nor chronological. It recurs cyclically as cultures emerge and grow. It follows a pattern of bodily becoming that appears in every institutional context, with the eruption of every culture-born hierarchy to greater and lesser extents.[43] It is most often catalyzed by an increasing reliance on texts and books, on reading and writing, as the media through which authority is granted and administered.[44] Those who rule the (political, religious, scholarly) roost believe that they no longer need to negotiate the paradox of their participation in the natural world. They believe that their rank does or at least should protect them from its violence and vicissitudes. They find comfort in visions of eternity, unconditional love, omnipotent divinity, their own power, or the mastery of matter itself. They succumb to the illusion that culture is more important than nature, marks our human difference from nature, and justifies our consumption and use of nature on the path to spiritual or scientific bliss. They define a human self and spirit over and against the materiality of nature as one that need not dance.[45]

Insofar as such persons believe that their ideals of a better world extend to include all humanity, they dare to preach a universality that claims its freedom from the downward pull of dancing bodies. Actions such as ascending the hierarchy, studying texts, obeying the law, and adhering to prescribed practices—all initially, implicitly expressions of our human ability to dance—appear as more important to human becoming than the act of moving our bodily selves or cultivating sensory awareness.[46] To those with their senses so educated, our relationship to the divine or to Truth matters more than our relationship with the earth in us and around us.

The evidence of history, when paired with the perspective of bodily becoming, leads to a provocative conclusion: values, beliefs, and practices, religious or otherwise, that are not grounded in the lived experience of dancing inevitably prove hostile to the very lives they claim to save. They guide humans in making movements that destroy the ability of those humans to participate consciously and creatively in the rhythms of their bodily becoming. They guide humans to ignore their responsibility for letting others live.

The implication haunts. If we do not dance, if we do not cultivate a sensory awareness of earth within, then the cultures we create will loom as passive, pallid renderings of our weakened, emptied selves.

As long as humans walk the earth, dancing remains the practice by which humans acquire the ecokinetic knowledge needed in order to participate consciously in creating culture that honors, abides by, and upholds the movement of earth in us and around us.[47]

Contemporary Cultures

Culture in the contemporary world is extremely complex and hardly singular. The contexts in which we find ourselves, in which we grow and interact, and to which we adapt are comprised of movement patterns that have been accumulating, consolidating, stratifying, becoming more abstract, and then collapsing and cross-pollinating over thousands of years. While the path that this evolution has taken is unique, the dynamics described in this chapter provide a flexible template for understanding the patterns of pain we in the modern West are currently experiencing as expressions of an impulse to move differently.

In the past five hundred years the invention of the printing press has given Western culture's preoccupation with reading and writing a turbo boost. As books have become increasingly easy to make and distribute, words have emerged as the preferred and dominant media for representing and transmitting knowledge (chapter 3). The movements we make in using these tools—given the hours we spend mastering them—have been reducing our lived experience of bodily movement and the natural world to a negligible part of human life. Books have served as powerful tools for making and disseminating (dance-enabled) visions of a virtual world—whether scientific or religious—in which dancing itself is no longer vital.[48]

This book-bound, matter-based worldview gives rise to a notion of "religion" that isolates it from culture and frames it as an object—a system of symbols—that can be studied like any other object. For many in the modern West, scholars included, "religion" is a matter of personal choice. It describes a set of beliefs and practices that a person may enter and adopt or exit and reject. Religion is assumed to provide a gloss on reality—a way of narrating, interpreting, or valuing reality; it is not reality itself. Religion comforts, explains, and exhorts; it does not create what is. Reality, by contrast, is defined by the world of forces, objects, and energies that scientific methods are able to measure. A materialist paradigm is the matrix within which an idea of religion as a private enterprise makes sense.

As the study of religion, seeking status as a science, took hold in the twentieth century, one effect was further to marginalize the place accorded to dance in religious life. Assuming that religion is not reality, scholars, in their attempts to study it, have tended to deny what participants who dance claim about what their dancing is and does.[49] Scholars tend to privilege the sensory education that reading and writing have given them; they interpret dancing in text-oriented, matter-based terms, as earlier chapters describe.

Moreover, in the modern world, this matter-based scholarly view of religion has pervaded traditions of religion themselves. Religious traditions have styled themselves in ways that will enable them to compete with science: they define themselves according to the values that science privileges, emphasizing their rational (and liberal) aspects, or aspire to reject science and define themselves in opposition to its values, stressing their charismatic, ecstatic (and conservative) aspects. In either option (or their multiple variations), the Book rules; practices of reading and writing prevail as the standard, the means, and the model for a spiritual life. Dancing loses ground. In a world where matter is real and evolves, texts rank, and individuals come first, dancing remains a liability.

Nevertheless, the expulsion of dancing from the practice of religion backfires. Without an ongoing practice of dance, religion loses its overarching relevance to "culture" as the place where a society holds its ideals and practices accountable to the movements of the earth. When a materialist bent prevails, and religion loses its connection to dance, religion cannot be what it claims— *real*. In its attempt to imitate or dismiss a scientific worldview, religion marginalizes itself. The separation of religion from dance and the devaluation of both in relation to science work in tandem as a mutually reinforcing spiral to distance human persons from their earthly lives and earthen selves.

The sensory effects of this development are now catching up with us. As religion splits from dance and both are demoted vis-à-vis science, the humans living in this environment are feeling indicative patterns of pain. The traumas that afflict us collectively and individually in this day and age can nearly all be traced to a lack of dance-enabled ecokinetic knowledge.[50] The movements we have been making are gradually reducing us to shadows of our potential selves, isolated and insulated from the rhythms and cycles in us and around us that bring sense to life.[51] Whether the issue is obesity or climate change, heart disease or water pollution, cancer or asthma, the use of fossil fuel or industrial fertilizers, we cannot even *conceive* what is wrong. We cannot conceive of our pain as anything other than a call for more of the same—that is, more controlling distance from the whims and vagaries of the natural world. Genetic modification, geoengineering, cloning, bariatric surgery, pharmaceuticals, and other technological fixes do produce effects, but they will help us heal only if and when we employ them knowing that the source of their efficacy lies in the lived experience of dancing.

Without a dance-enabled ecokinetic knowledge, we do not know and cannot learn from the infinite wealth of the natural world (in us and around us) how to complete our own natures in life-enabling ways.[52] Instead, we imbibe the abstract forms given to us by culture and pretend to find our freedom in choosing one pattern over the next. Few humans dance regularly; and those who do frequently dwell within a self-enclosed, self-protecting "dance world."

Nevertheless, the story is far from over. Given my analysis, it is also evident that the logic of dance—its dynamic emerging action in our bodily selves—can never be fully eradicated from human life. Dancing is a potential born again with the beat of each new human heart. Even movements made to exclude dance rely for their efficacy on the very human capacity that irrevocably gives rise to dancing: the ability to create and become and share relational patterns of sensation and response. As such, dance can never be fully extinguished by imperial powers who desire nothing less. The very act of imposing movement patterns on others catalyzes the movement-making ability that human beings are. Humans cannot *not* move in response in and with their bodily selves. Dance regularly appears among those who resist "the system"—including those oppressed as a result of race, gender, class, or ethnicity—as an expression of the human desire to move in life-enabling ways.[53]

We humans can create cultures that malign dance because we are able to learn how to make movements that produce this outcome. We can train our senses away from dancing because our senses are inherently vulnerable to being moved. We can learn not to dance because we are first and foremost dancers. The combinations are endless. The presence of dancing in a given culture need not coincide with values that affirm bodily selves—its techniques may have hardened into forms imposed on bodily selves to the near exclusion of bodily creativity.[54] Nor does the apparent absence of dancing signal a hostility toward the earth—there may be forms of cultural movement that support people in cultivating a sensory awareness of themselves as participants in rhythms of bodily becoming. In the creation of earth-friendly culture, what matters are the patterns of bodily movement being made and the possibilities for human becoming those movements are creating. What matters is whether or not people are cultivating the sensory awareness they need in order to discern what kind of lives those possibilities are enabling.

It is time to dance, and not only. It is a time to draw upon the lived experience of the dancing in which we are all to some extent engaged so as to engender a reality in which we honor movement as the source and telos of life. We need to encourage the flow of our creativity along the trajectories dug by matter-based values, respond thoughtfully to the pain they are creating in our hearts and minds and bodily selves, and land differently, in a new place, from which we can see a new perspective on where we have been and where we can go.

The loss of dancing heralds its imminent return as a critical, generative, nature-friendly force—an expression of a materialist culture overcoming itself in an affirmation of bodily life.

· · · · ·

To dance is to love. Our work with bodily becoming has shown us why. Love is movement. It is a willingness to move toward another, with another, and be moved by that other as the path of our best becoming, connecting, healing, and earthing. It is this love for the earth in us and around us that our bodily movement creates in us when we dance.[55]

This love is not naive. Nature is not nice. Floods and fires, earthquakes and avalanches, viruses and parasites destroy our bodily selves, our homes, and our best laid plans. Nature is indifferent to our most cherished desires, our cultural masterpieces, and our most civilized retreats. Mold ruins food and artwork; cockroaches and rats infest city dwellings; hurricanes and heat waves stress our urban centers. Then again, this nature is equally destructive and indifferent to the plans and desires of those who would cancel ours. The power coursing in and through and as us is equally ferocious, capable of great good and great harm.

Dancing, we know this power of life in ourselves. We know how vital it is for us to move in ways that align our power with the powers of which we are a part, in which we dwell, and by which we are sustained.

We cannot resist the power that is. Nor can we master it. Neither can it master us. It is us. There is no will outside ourselves to whom we must answer. There is no will outside ourselves who can control us or what is. What there is is an ongoing dance—a rhythm of bodily becoming. And when we allow ourselves to dance every day—to invite the experience shift that empties our minds into our bodily selves—we cultivate a receptivity to movement impulses—a freedom to be and become uniquely in a moment. *A freedom that I only know and realize as I move.* We surrender to the infinite pulse of nature throbbing through us, pulling at our edges, calling us, impelling us actively to recreate ourselves and our world in line with our best, relational, bodily becoming. We grow more and more adept at approaching everything we do and every act we take as an occasion to make more love.

We are born to love as the enabling condition of our best bodily becoming. Dancing is the art, the action, and the practice that teaches us how. Dancing we learn to be the nature that creates through us, and to do so in ways that are responsive to the challenges we face in our personal, social, cultural, natural environments. In all realms dancing teaches us, as much as we can, to let others live as the enabling condition of our best bodily becoming.

Dancing is thus an ecological necessity.

· · · · ·

I arrive at the fourth and final dancing place in my ritual circuit. I am now by the pond, fifteen feet from it, touching a young tree that grows beside it. The tree is about three inches in diameter—the perfect size for ringing both hands around. I do. I pull back, arching my back and turning my face to the sun. Then I curve my head down and lengthen out through my shoulders, aiming my gaze at the ground. A rush of movement surges through me; my arms tug me close and whip me around the tree, until my fingers are all that is holding me up.

There is no doubt about it. I love this tree. I love dancing with this tree. I love the way I can surrender to it, lean upon it, wrap around it. I love the way it calls to the very movements I have been opening up in relation to earth, air, and fire and sends them flowing through my sensory veins. It is my favorite dancing moment—when I am the freest. When I feel my creativity most acutely. It is the most inspiring, the most enlivening, but I also know. I could never come here first. I could not just go to the tree and actually get to the tree.

First, I had to go around—I had to bring my senses to life, be reborn to the instant, find the currents whose movements are making me. I had to warm up; I had to practice. Only then—present to myself, to the world my movements are creating, to the life I want to be living, to the self I am becoming, to the relationships I am cultivating—then, and only then, could I dance with this tree in such a way that I know love: a love that moves me to move even closer to it in a spiral of willingness.

Love for a tree? It sounds crazy. But what else is a tree than a call to dance? Dancing with this tree, because of this tree makes me into someone who knows that her living depends on its living. Pulling and twisting, arching and rounding, the movements this tree draws from me become me, transform me, opening in me a sensory awareness willing and able to make changes in my life that will honor and protect the matrix of elemental movements that enables us both.

Earth Within

The brain is an introjected earth.

—DAVID ABRAM, *BECOMING ANIMAL*

I walk down to the pond and pause in a clearing along its edge where we keep our canoe. The smooth face of a big rock beckons. I crouch upon it, eyes skimming the water. One duck and then another burst into and out of my view in a frenzy of splashes. As the excited waves in me and before me settle toward a flat horizon, one large round of ripples does not. It persists.

I don't recognize the pattern. What movement is making that shape? Is it a school of fish? A beaver? I attend more closely. The ripple-round is not singular. It is made up of many ripples bent in half. At the arrow tip of each, a lone black beetle chugs along, pulsing to a silent chant: burst and glide, burst and glide, burst and glide. My jagged surprise settles into awe. A moment ago, gazing at the same section of surface, I saw nothing. Suddenly I see hundreds of things—hundreds of movements in the making.

I am hooked, stirred, and drawn in. With each chug, a bug pushes up a rib of water that wraps around it. The rib catches the bug in its crook, yet never breaks. As the bug thrusts again, sometimes in a straight line, sometimes in circles, the wake of each wrapping ripple pushes other bugs away. There are no crashes; no beetles bash. There is only one massive teeming, a dynamic array of trajectories crossing and recrossing each other's tails and trails.

As if pulled by a magnetic force, my eyes follow one bug and then jump to another. I yield to the pull and then forcibly yank my focus back, wanting to take in the whole watery patch. As I do, the patterns of movement I am seeing trace themselves in the watery depths of my own sensory world. I move with the waves, because of the waves, rippling with delight.

Why? Why do I even notice this bevy of bugs? Why do I care? Why do I find their patterns of movement beautiful, even enlivening? I wouldn't want to eat these bugs. I can't use them for clothing or tools. Nor do I fear them as predators. They have no obvious use or value to me. With a pass of my hand, they would be gone. Yet I am so vulnerable to being moved by them. Why?

Because I am human born, with an acute capacity to move and be moved by any movement around me, coursing through me, happening to me, with or without me. Who my bodily self is pays attention to rhythms of coming and going and consciously and unconsciously seeks to recreate them. This responsiveness has little to do with rational thought or with a desire to control, measure, or test. It has everything to do with the fact that I cultivate it. It has everything to do with my need to dance the earth to life within me as a guide to letting others live.

• • • • •

The shift in the value humans accord to bodily movement in general, and to dance in particular, that I envision in these pages is already happening. If it were not, I would not be writing this book. As we have also seen, movement as an idea is already making its way into the theoretical bulwarks of nearly all disciplines. Thinkers and researchers across the board are reconfiguring basic notions of being, becoming, and knowing so as to privilege bodily movement as the medium of human existence. Myriad humans around the world are already reshaping their actions in response to the patterns of pain that are occurring as nature flows and overflows current cultural situations.

Meanwhile, dance on concert stages, on screen, and on the streets thrives as an ideal to which we aspire, a source of pleasure to which we turn, a sign of hope that springs eternal. Dance is appearing in TED talks and alternative Christian liturgies; Buddhist ceremonies and new age raves; in proliferating movement practices such as 5Rhythms, Nia, Zumba, TheGroove, Continuum, not to mention classes in yoga, tai chi, or aikido. Once we look we see it nearly everywhere else—in the cracks, at the margins, at the bottom. We see it in music videos and reality television; in rediscovered rituals and folk events. We see it in political movements and in the persistence of dance schools and companies, even when financing is hard to secure.

Why We Dance aims to speed along this imminent shift by helping people to perceive these nascent movements, from the philosophic to the personal, as necessarily related. *Why We Dance* is itself a branching of movement patterns. It enacts possibilities for thinking about dancing that are intended to stimulate more thinking along the trajectories they describe. Its movement patterns exercise the kinetic-sensory-conceptual muscles scholars and researchers will need to design projects whose driving questions allow the significance of dance to emerge—questions that presuppose and seek to illuminate the rhythms of bodily becoming and their vital, constitutive importance for human life.

These directions for the future emerge out of each chapter. The first three chapters delineate the principles with which such projects should begin in order not to foreclose desired understanding from the outset. These chapters lay out loops of critical self-reflection so that a researcher can check that her approach remains open to being moved by the appearance of new movement patterns and new clutches of meaning. Any attempt to do justice to the experience of dancing must shake loose models and methods based on the assumptions that matter is real, matter evolves, and knowledge about what matters can be written down. While the philosophy of bodily becoming presented here represents one way to find this freedom, there will and must be others that arise and remain accountable to other trends in philosophy, theology, and theory.

The final four chapters, in turn, sketch flexible arcs along which specific questions concerning various facets of human existence can unfurl. Here we need projects that target the role of bodily movement in the development of our brains and bodies in utero and throughout our lives. We need projects that do not just map the motor cortex or plot the neural patterns associated with particular emotions, nor assess the effects of exercise on regenerating brain cells. While this work is important and informative, in order to get at the important of dance we need to ask how and why the action of making a movement trains our sensory awareness to possibilities of making movements we have not yet made. We have to embrace the idea of our bodily selves as inherently creative and seek to match some of that dynamism in our thinking about them.

So too we need projects that focus on the role of bodily movement in cultivating the ingredients of empathy and mutual understanding among human young as they mature—projects that acknowledge how the work of recreating (and not just imitating) the movement patterns of others is itself transformative for the one making the movements. We need ways of gauging how various movement patterns serve to cultivate a sensory awareness and what kinds of responsiveness to others that sensory awareness yields.

Further, within the fields of religious studies, theology, and the philosophy of religion, we need projects that attend to the bodily movement extant in all religious traditions as an enabling condition of meaning. We need projects that call us to identify the patterns of movement being made and map the opportunities for experience, belief, and knowledge that the act of making those patterns engenders. We need to develop resources for evaluating the impact of these movement patterns on the ongoing ability of humans to participate consciously in the work of bodily becoming.[1] We need gods who dance and gods who dance through us.[2] For, unless our highest ideals and values acknowledge dancing as itself an irreplaceable, vital art, there will always be some other criterion to which dancing must account.

Finally, we need scholarly projects that assess the degree to which a lived sensibility of one's own movement making feeds a willingness and ability to move with the earth in mutually life-enabling ways. Here the terrain is vast and wide open. There are extensive connections to make between the sensory education we receive at the hands of our technological inventions and our capacity for resisting obvious patterns of self-destruction. My deep conviction is that massive cultural change will not and cannot occur until humans cultivate within themselves the knowledge of their own bodily becoming that they need in order to see, imagine, and act differently. Only when we cultivate this ecokinetic knowledge will we be able to understand the persistence, the universality, and the recurring eruptions of dance in human history as a force for change. We will be able to participate in that history going forward.

In addition to scholarly work, there is work to be done by artists of all kinds, dancers in particular. Each of the projects described in the chapters of this book is not only a call for understanding, it is also a call for enactment. In the case of dance the world of intellectual endeavor is dependent for its success on ongoing, in-depth engagement with dancers and their dancing. Scholars will not understand dance unless they participate, in some way, in the process by which others create and perform dance. Scholars need to see dance, study dance, and participate in dance in order to cultivate the sensory awareness of their own bodily becoming that can support them in understanding dance. Dancers, on the other hand, need to know how relevant the dances that they create are to the cultural process of generating values and ideas. We thus need to encourage collaboration among intellectuals and artists for the mutual enrichment of both.

So too, there is work to be done by all of us—as individuals, families, and communities—in making space for dance in our lives. We not only need to reconceive of dancing as a vital art, a biological, ethical, spiritual, and ecological necessity—we need to give ourselves permission to explore our fundamental sensory creativity, with the support of others, in ways that attune our senses to the enabling earth in us and around us.

In this respect, again, *Why We Dance* seeks to make the moves that demonstrate how. In our thoughts and acts, dancing must be reborn as a practice to which we turn when we are confused, stressed, or depressed as a means of cultivating peace and calm, flexibility and flow; as a strategy of discernment, an instrument of divination, and the movement that completes our nature in human-enabling ways. Dancing must be reborn as a transformative power, ever latent in the moment-to-moment rhythms of bodily becoming. Dance must be reborn as the activity through which we learn to love the life and lives that nurture ours.

We must ask. What would it be like to live in a society where dancing—the act of creating and becoming patterns of sensation and response—were nurtured in every child, integral to every educational system, and expected of every competent adult? What if learning to cultivate a sensory awareness of ourselves as movement and participate consciously in the rhythms of bodily becoming were considered a fundamental human right? What if people grew up believing in the practice of dancing as necessary for their best becoming?

What if this dance was taught as a resource for solving problems, reconciling conflicts, and building relationships? What if people learned to dance as a practice for clearing their minds, opening their hearts, and mending their bodily selves? What if people learned to dance as a means to personal, interpersonal, and social health—as a vital resource for moving in relation to one another so as to catalyze the next generation of new ideas?

What would it be like if there were spaces and places to dance in houses and hospitals, in churches and office buildings, in airports and bus stations, beaches and parks? What would it be like if people everywhere danced alone and with others, for themselves or for others, on the field or along the sidewalk, waiting for a plane or bus or bank machine, as a way to relax, recoup, or rev up? What if we fed ourselves a daily diet of inspiring movement patterns—putting ourselves in situations where we could move and be moved by the dancing of others?

What would it be like to live in a society where people of all ages dance everywhere and anywhere for the pleasure of it, the health of it, the healing, pain-transforming power of it? What kind of humans would we be? How would we think and feel? What would we want? How would we relate to the earth in us and around us? What kind of worlds would we bring into reality?

It is worth finding out.

· · · · ·

In a world according to dance, where movement is perceived as the source and telos of life, the great drama of existence entails learning how to discern and align our bodily selves with this movement's ongoing pulse.

While every culture provides some inspiration, no one is an exclusive model. What dance can become has not yet been realized. Even so, there are resources for imagining that future everywhere. The need for dance reaches forward along every trajectory of unmet human desire. Just as our biological form harbors genetic patterns whose lineage reaches back through every human act and every creaturely move to the first inklings of life, so too do our cultural forms of dance. We will move to where we need to go by being where we are.

We will not fix the world simply by devising rational responses to perceived problems. We will not achieve peace by imposing our ways on others. We will not end climate change by adhering to goals of energy use and conservation. However, I firmly believe that we will make progress on all registers if we can cultivate a sense of bodily selves as earth, as related to earth, as the continuing life and presence of earth, fully responsible for every move we make.

If we practice dance, we may come to love the earth as who we are. And if we are willing and able to fall in love with a more-than-human world, then we will orient ourselves within it differently. We will want and need to let others live for our own good. We will lose our desire for activities that dull our senses or destroy the patterns of nature that might educate them to their acuity. In all settings we will work to ensure that others receive the support they need to participate consciously in their own bodily becoming. We will cultivate a sense of the pain that our movements are creating—the destruction and waste—as a guide to moving differently. We will advocate for the ongoing health and fertility of the earth, in all its aspects and dimensions, as best as we can imagine. For it is only when movement comes to life as fully as possible in moments that sustain our human lives that the movement of life will continue to express itself in human form. As long as we are living, nature is creating through us.

Of course, we humans kill to live. We must. Yet, once we cultivate a sensory awareness of ourselves as dancers, we do so differently. We can reject any killing that fails to preserve the ongoing integrity of the myriad interlocked and overlapping ecosystems in which we live and from which we have so much to learn. We will ask, regularly and insistently: what are we creating?

Humans need not survive on this plant. There is no guarantee that we will.[3] We may become one more species that dwindles only to make room for others who can move in a world that our movements have rendered inhospitable to us. Regardless of whether or not humans endure, movement will.

• • • • •

I walk down toward the pond where, months ago, I first saw that bevy of bugs. I fan my mind open to the infinite movement around me. Cloud tufts dot the bright blue sky. Grass blades cross and hum in the late summer breeze. The ground beneath my feet springs back at every toe touch. Everything today is soft, feels soft, smells and sounds and tastes soft. Everything is urging me to move freely, joyfully, as I stride along.

The opening to the pond appears. I slip in between the trees, over the rocks, and make my way to the edge. Six feet from it I pause. The surface of the pond is as still and flat and clear as a mirror, yet something is moving. I know it, but I cannot yet see it. The rays of my gaze pierce the glare. Feet below, a dark stripe flickers. As I wait, the shape of a fish comes into view around its black band. Twenty inches long, the bass is wary, waiting, softly undulating. The feathers of its fins twist and pulse. I adjust my weight. A twig snaps. Instantly the fish disappears. Moments later it is back, waiting. For what? To hook me?

It does, with the movement of its delicate fins. Kinetic images of movements I have made and seen vibrate within me—the torso undulations in

Haitian dances for the serpent god, Yanvalou; the serpentine hands of the goddess dancing Bharata Natyam; the sinuous pulses of break-dance masters on the street. I muse. We humans think we are so original. Every move we humans make has been made before. To practice dancing is to cultivate the sensory awareness that enables me to move like a fish, feel like a fish, even become a fish—a sensory awareness that distinguishes me as human. Dancing, I hone my ability to move with cloud, bug, or blade of grass and so learn from it secrets of my own movement-making potential. Dancing funds my desire to let these moving others live as the enabling condition for my best becoming.

As I turn from the fish and walk back up the hill toward home, it comes with me, swimming in my sensory awareness. I feel its patterns within me, waving as I walk. I feel its calm, cool, floating, hovering being. I am its pond, its nature, its enabling condition. And it is mine.

May the dance continue.

Notes

Why Dance?

1. Any process of definition is circular. It moves between particular phenomena and an account of what distinguishes those phenomena as alike in search of a statement that is helpful for producing knowledge concerning those particulars and their relationships. In describing my account of dance as "visionary," I acknowledge my intention to pull into view aspects of "dance" that have not yet received much attention while placing less emphasis on other aspects that have. I do not distinguish between "dancing" as action and "dance" as its codified form, as Sam Gill does in his book *Dancing Culture Religion*. I hold that there is no "dancing" apart from the form by which that dancing is discovered, animated, and manifest.

2. In *Between Dancing and Writing* I set the stage for this project by examining works by René Descartes, Immanuel Kant, G. W. F. Hegel, Friedrich Schleiermacher, and Gerardus van der Leeuw that have proven to be formative moments in the development of the academic study of religion, and assessing the implications of their ideas for considering dance as a medium of religious experience and expression. In *Nietzsche's Dancers* I introduce a philosophy of bodily becoming via careful readings of both the dance imagery in Friedrich Nietzsche's work and the Nietzsche references in the writing and dancing of American modern dancers Isadora Duncan and Martha Graham. *Why We Dance* continues to develop this philosophy of bodily becoming as a way to break open our study and understanding of dance in relation to human health and well-being.

3. The closest description I have found to the sensory awareness I am imagining here is what Alan Fogel calls "embodied self-awareness" or ESA. In his definition,

ESA is "the ability to pay attention to ourselves, to feel our sensations, emotions, and movements, online, in the present moment, without the mediating influence of judgmental thought" (*The Psychophysiology of Self-Awareness*, 1). What distinguishes my position from ESA and related accounts, such as "mindfulness," "felt sense," or the "lived experience" of existential phenomenology, is the focus on *movement*. Sensory awareness as I am using it is not just an awareness of the movements that we are making (i.e., proprioception). Rather, it is an awareness that *we are* the movements we are making. It is a circular knowledge that *I am the movement that is making me*. It is a sensory self-awareness of how "we," as animate bodily selves, participate in our own bodily becoming.

Contrast this sensory awareness with the kind of "mindfulness" described by Ellen Langer as a "soft awareness marked by an absence of mindless attention to any specific part of the body (or of anything else for that matter) that prevents us from experiencing our fuller selves" (*Counterclockwise*, 29). The "fuller self" to which I wish to call attention is no "thing," but a dynamic, open-ended process of bodily becoming.

4. For recent approaches to defining dance, see dance scholar Sondra Horton Fraleigh, *Dance and the Lived Body*; anthropologist Judith Lynne Hanna, *To Dance Is Human*; philosopher Francis Sparshott, *Off the Ground*; dance scholar Susan Foster, *Reading Dancing*; and scholar of religion Sam Gill, *Dancing Culture Religion*.

5. As Hanna writes, "To dance is human, and humanity almost universally expresses itself in dance. Dance interweaves with other aspects of human life, such as communication and learning, belief systems, social relations and political dynamics, loving and fighting, and urbanization and change. It may even have been significant in the biological and evolutionary development of the species" (*To Dance Is Human*, 3). I take on the challenge implied by the last sentence in this quotation.

6. McNeill, *Keeping Together in Time*, 39.

7. The image is painted on Fulton's Rock, Drackensberg Mountains, KwaZulu-Natal and discussed in Chris Knight's book, *Blood Relations*, 333.

8. Based on his analysis of objects found at village community sites dating from the eighth to the fourth century BCE, Josef Garfinkel concludes: "Dancing is the oldest and one of the most persistent themes in Near Eastern prehistoric art, and this theme spreads with agriculture into surrounding regions of Europe and Africa" (*Dancing at the Dawn of Agriculture*, 3).

Garfinkel counters critics who question whether these images represent actual "dancing." Describing one of the most commonly represented figures on early village art—a stick figure with arms and legs drawn as bent at right angles—he writes: "Some scholars have interpreted this body position as indicating adoration or prayer . . . but the position of the legs would be too uncomfortable to maintain for long. It is a dynamic posture maintained for short intervals while dancing . . . [that] becomes a code symbol for dance" (33–34).

American dancer Isadora Duncan makes a similar case for the images on Greek pottery: "There is not one which in its movement does not presuppose another movement. This is because the Greeks were the greatest students of the laws of nature, wherein all is the expression of unending, ever-increasing evolution, wherein are no ends and no stops" (*Art of the Dance*, 57).

9. Bill McKibben, in *The End of Nature*, argues that "nature," meaning "a certain set of human ideas about the world and our place in it," has died (7). Given that the by-products and pollutants of human living have become the most powerful force for change on the planet, "We have deprived nature of its independence, and that is fatal to its meaning" (50). "We can no longer imagine that we are part of something larger than ourselves," and the result is guilt, sadness, and a feeling of loneliness (71).

10. McKibben, along with Wendell Berry and others, argues for a "biocentric vision of people as part of the world" (*The End of Nature*, 14), and "a voluntary simplification of our lifestyles" (164). Contemporary dancers are taking up this call, arguing that dance can and should play a role in cultivating the desire to shift our perspectives and practices. For example, see Olsen, *Body and Earth*. See chapter 7 for further discussion of dance as an ecological necessity.

11. Ecopsychologist Theodore Roszak describes a "materialist program" within which all "things" are made of matter and arranged by chance in time (*The Voice of the Earth*, 103). It is a program, he admits, that endures even though its principles have all been disproved.

In charting the scope of this paradigm, my work parallels philosopher Teresa Brennan's account of the "foundational fantasy" that she sees infiltrating Western culture. This fantasy, she confirms, works at personal, interpersonal, and economic levels to reinforce fixed points of energy that deplete human persons and the natural world of their ability to reproduce. It is a fantasy that prefigures "a deeper dualism between mind and body in which direction or agency is seen as mental and mindful, while activity, paradoxically, is viewed as something that lacks intelligence" (*Exhausting Modernity*, 28). What is "depleted" by fixed points of energy, I qualify, is the ability to participate consciously in the rhythms of bodily becoming—i.e., the ability to dance.

12. In challenging this materialist paradigm, I align with and depart from the "new materialism" of contemporary scholarship. I seek not only to reimagine matter as dynamic, animate, and moving, but to privilege movement itself as the currency of life. The new materialists are still held back in their ability to appreciate dance as a vital art by the references to "matter" as the locus of "the real." See the edited volumes *New Materialisms* (Coole and Frost) and *New Materialism* (Dolphijn and van der Tuin).

13. Carolyn Merchant, in *The Death of Nature*, documents the change that occurred between 1500 and 1700 CE when the dominant metaphor "binding together the cosmos, society, and the self" shifted from living organism to machine (xxi). In

this mechanical model, she reveals, nature, once imagined as animate and enspirited, is now perceived as passive and inert—a "mindless, submissive body" (190).

14. A fact recorded by dance scholars and historians, including E. Louis Backman in his classic *Religious Dances in the Christian Church and in Popular Medicine*. Up until the Reformation, for example, dancing remained a feature of religious holidays and festival days in honor of saints. After the Reformation, dancing occurred, with a few notable exceptions, in millennial, marginal, often "heretical" movements, such as the Quakers, Shakers, the African American shout, and the Native American Ghost Dance.

15. As we shall see, despite their renewed attention to materiality and bodily life, even post-postmodern theories of reality and knowledge can neither comprehend nor appreciate dance as much more than optional bodily action capable of serving some functional, aesthetic, or symbolic role.

16. St. Denis, "Credo."

17. This method is indebted to the "physiological" or "genealogical" approach demonstrated by Friedrich Nietzsche in his project of revaluing what he perceived as life-denying Christian values. Rather than mount a rational argument against these values, or propose alternatives to them, he identifies the source of these values' power in bodily practices—our sensory education—and then seeks to engage and redirect the trajectories of human creativity those values express. For guidance in what that new direction might be, he begins with the physical, emotional, spiritual pain he himself feels in trying to live those Christian ideals, intent on "thinking through his senses" for values that will not recreate the pain. Through this process he arrives at a notion of radical affirmation—a love for life, all of it—whose signature mark is dance. One who loves life is a dancer. For further discussion, see Nietzsche, *Genealogy of Morals*, and LaMothe, *Nietzsche's Dancers*, chapters 2–3.

18. Karen Barbour discusses this writing strategy in her own enactment of it, *Dancing Across the Page*, drawing comparisons with ethnoanthropology, as well as feminist theory and dance studies. As she recounts, scholars from these fields are all seeking ways to honor and represent the "embodiment" of knowledge (*Dancing Across the Page*, chapter 3).

19. Brian Massumi describes a method of providing examples that are distinguished by a "singularity" or "belonging to itself" that is "simultaneously an extendability to everything else with which it might be connected." As he affirms of this method, "Every detail is essential to the case" (*Parables of the Virtual*, 18), as it is for each chapter frame I provide.

20. Jane Bennett is one who notes the importance of sensory education for perceiving the vitality of matter when she writes: "The capacity to detect the presence of impersonal affect requires that one is caught up in it" (*Vibrant Matter*, xv). She praises craftspeople and scientists who attend to nonhuman matter, discern life in it, and thus

collaborate more fruitfully with it (60). Yet she stops short of praising dancers and urging the same sensory attention to the vital materiality of a human bodily self.

1. To Dance Is to Matter

1. Alan Fogel describes a shift that can occur between conceptual self-awareness (CSA), such as involved in the continuous stream of conscious thought, and embodied self-awareness (ESA), which involves feeling our sensations, emotions, and movements (*The Psychophysiology of Self-Awareness*, 98–99). For me, this sensory awareness is not simply *of* movement (proprioception), as if movement were one thing alongside sensations and emotions of which I can be aware. It is a movement-enabled awareness of my self in all respects and degrees—physical, emotional, spiritual—as *being* movement.

2. I owe this notion of "communicating participation" to Martha Graham. For her, dancing communicates participation in the movement of life. As she writes of her art: "It only demands that the dance be a moment of passionate, completely disciplined action, that it communicate participation to the nerves, the skin, the structure of the spectator" (Armitage, *Martha Graham*, 86).

3. With the use of this term *paradigm*, I am alluding to Thomas Kuhn's classic work, *The Structure of Scientific Revolutions*.

4. Terrence Deacon contrasts the defining property of matter as "a resistance to change" with the defining property of energy as "that which is required to overcome resistance to change" (*Incomplete Nature*, 225).

5. The dualism between matter and mind is generally considered a primary axis of Western thought, at least since Descartes, even though it occurs in a matrix of entangled statements that subsequent chapters address. For a deconstructive critique of metaphysical dualisms deemed fundamental to and by Western theology and philosophy, see Mark Taylor, *Erring*.

6. As Carolyn Merchant confirms, "our Western commonsense reality is the world of classical physics," a world characterized by a dualism between the passivity of matter and the externality of force and activity (*The Death of Nature*, 276). In the words of Maxine Sheets-Johnstone, this Cartesian orientation is "our cultural disease" (*Giving the Body Its Due*, 15).

7. As Deacon explains, "In Newton's mechanics . . . all causes were defined in external terms" with the implication that "persistent linear motion" was a "spontaneous tendency" that has no cause (*Incomplete Nature*, 211).

8. As Brian Massumi affirms, "When positioning of any kind comes a determining first, movement comes a problematic second. . . . Movement is entirely subordinated to the positions it connects. . . . Adding movement like this adds nothing at

all" (*Parables of the Virtual*, 3). What is missing from such accounts, he insists, is a notion of movement as a "qualitative transformation" (3). My account of this transformation—and it is not merely qualitative—follows.

9. Merchant describes three "root traditions" of such "organic" alternatives and notes their modern lineages (*The Death of Nature*, 106ff).

10. For example, as Rosi Braidotti affirms, the new materialists propose a monistic appreciation of Being or "single matter" that "positions difference as a verb or process of becoming at the heart of that matter" (Dolphijn and van der Tuin, *New Materialism*). Note, however, that "matter" is still given priority as that in which movement resides as its "heart." As Manuel DeLanda confirms: "Any materialist philosophy must take as its point of departure the existence of a material world that is independent of our mind" (Dolphijn and van der Tuin).

11. For one discussion of the materialist basis of modern science, see Deacon, *Incomplete Nature*, 3–8 (chapter 1). As Deacon affirms, this attention to explaining physical objects "that are materially and energetically present" produces a "persistent dualism" between matter and meaning, the natural and human sciences (3, 6).

12. When physicists at the 1927 Copenhagen Interpretation of Quantum Mechanics admitted that nature at the subatomic level cannot be "understood in terms of elementary space-time realities," they also affirmed that their theories still had value—not as representations of reality, but as the best explanations for "all possible experimental situations" (Zukav, *The Dancing Wu Li Masters*, 42). As one physicist affirms, science remains "anchored in concrete sense realities that form the basis of social life" (Henry Pierce Stapp, quoted ibid.). Science cannot move beyond this sensory reality. In other words, for physicists at least, "matter" as we experience it through our senses, remains the measure of what is "real," even when what is being studied is not (matter). I would argue that the same enabling limitation holds for all human endeavors, shifting the question of knowledge acquisition from "what is?" to "what are our movements training our senses to see?"

13. Writing about the scientific study of nature, Massumi affirms, "Measurement stops the movement in thought" (*Parables of the Virtual*, 10). Measurement makes "matter" what we want it to be: an object, first and foremost, that moves.

14. As critiques of "old materialism" spread through contemporary theory and philosophy, many agree that there is a need for creativity and invention alongside this criticism. As Braidotti affirms, "The creation of concepts is itself experience or experimentation . . . artistic and scientific practices have their role to play as well . . . experimenting with thinking is what we all need to learn" (Dolphijn and van der Tuin, *New Materialism*). The conviction that animates this book is that "dance" provides a valuable catalyst and practical resource for such creative thinking.

15. One of infinite examples is a book whose theme is relevant to this chapter, *The Dancing Wu Li Masters*, introduced in note 12. In the first chapter, Zukav explains the

meaning of "Wu Li" and of "Masters," but does not say a word about "dancing." He simply affirms that dancing—rather than "explaining"—is what Wu Li Masters do with the world (9).

16. Nietzsche blazes the trail here with his embrace of dance as an effective symbol for the kind of moral-spiritual practice that is needed to overcome the insidious effects of the ascetic ideal—itself an expression of dualist mind-over-matter thinking. As Nietzsche explains, the ascetic ideal lives in our bodily selves, and so the task of revaluing it must involve relearning our basic patterns of relating to ourselves, others, and the world. See discussion in LaMothe, *Nietzsche's Dancers*, chapters 2–3.

17. Of course, the debate over whether movement or matter is primary dates to the ancient Greeks, with Heraclitus and Aristotle, respectively. Aristotle won. Since then, movement advocates have remained a minority voice, and dance, by association, has appeared as having lesser value as art, religion, or science than more seemingly fixed media of expression such as those associated with words and images. However, the balance is tipping, with good reason and even better results. As Maxine Sheets-Johnstone argues, even Aristotle himself was more of an advocate for the primacy of movement than has been allowed in offering a "process metaphysics" rather than a "metaphysics of matter" (*The Primacy of Movement*, xxii, chapter 2, part 2).

18. Describing physics in a way that is applicable across fields, Zukav writes: "The search for the ultimate stuff of the universe ends with the discovery that there *isn't any*" (*The Dancing Wu Li Masters*, 216). Or, in the prophetic words of Nietzsche, with allusions to Plato: "God is dead; but given the way of men, there may still be caves for thousands of years in which his shadow will be shown. —And we—we still have to vanquish his shadow, too" (*The Gay Science*, #108, 167). The belief that matter is real is a shadow of God. It is the principle of faith on which science rests (#344, 280–81).

19. Zukav describes two paths in particle physics, one taken by those who are continuing the (elusive) search for the smallest particle, and the other taken by those who are focusing on interactions and energy exchanges as the medium in which matter is constantly being created and destroyed. At this level, as he describes, there is no dancer; "there is only the dance" (*The Dancing Wu Li Masters*, 278). See also Capra, *The Tao of Physics*; Roszak, *The Voice of the Earth*, part 2: Cosmology.

20. Thanks to David Abram for the term *more-than-human*, in all its appearances from this mention forth (*The Spell of the Sensuous, Becoming Animal*).

21. For example, "new materialists" intend to expose human bodily selves as enmeshed within relations of power that circumscribe their ability to act. See two recent collections: Coole and Frost, *New Materialisms* and Dolphijn and van der Tuin, *New Materialism*. Another group of scholars across multiple disciplines is working with "affects" and "emotions," intent on affirming the bodily nature of all thinking and acting. See for example, Teresa Brennan, *The Transmission of Affect*; Massumi, *Parables of*

the Virtual; and, for a collection of essays, Gregg and Seigworth, *The Affect Theory Reader*.

22. Jane Bennett, for example, intent on sparking an ecological consciousness, envisions a "fabulously vital materiality" (*Vibrant Matter*, 63). She conjures a "picture of the universe in which becoming continually vies with being" (93), in which "there is no point of pure stillness, no indivisible atom that is not itself aquiver with vital force" (57). She uses the term *actant* to mean a "source of action" that is not necessarily agential (3).

23. See for example, Deleuze and Guattari in a passage quoted by Bennett and others: "there is a pure plane of immanence, univocality, composition, upon which everything is given, upon which unformed elements and materials dance that are distinguished from one another only by their speed and that enter into this or that individuated assemblage depending on their connections, their relations of movement" (*One Thousand Plateaus*, 255, my emphasis).

24. "We need an account of the material world in which it isn't absurd to claim that it produced us" (Ilya Prigogine and Isabelle Stengers, quoted in Deacon, *Incomplete Nature*, 143).

25. Deacon argues that there are "absences that matter" (*Incomplete Nature*, 8), that is, constraints that are not specifically present but still permeate and organize "what is physically present" (9).

26. Rodolfo Llinás makes a compelling case, described more fully in chapter 4, that, "The central generation of movement and the generation of mindness are deeply related; they are in fact different parts of the same process. In my view, from its very evolutionary inception, mindness is the internalization of movement" (*I of the Vortex*, 5).

27. Daniel Wolpert makes the point that we have designed computers that can beat the best humans in chess; but we have not designed a computer than can move around the pieces of a chessboard with the agility of a five year old. See his TED talk, "The Real Reason for Brains."

28. Sheets-Johnstone's magisterial work on *The Primacy of Movement* is critical to anyone involved in this project. She carefully reads through a range of scientific and philosophical debates demonstrating how researchers working in materialist models both assume and ignore the primacy of movement to matters of consciousness and cognition. As Sheets-Johnstone argues, humans, along with all other animals, "think in movement" (chapter 12).

29. Here I push new materialists and proponents of affect theory beyond accounts of matter as relational, self-creating, and ever in the process of becoming. We need not only to animate matter, we need to embrace fully the movement of our bodily, sensory, relational selves as constitutive and generative of matter. Closer to my work is the proposal by Luce Irigaray for a "process metaphysics" that conceptu-

alizes being as fluid, in which "movement and energy is [*sic*] ontologically prior to thingness and the nature of things takes its being from the organic context in which they are embedded" (discussed in Young, *On Female Body Experience*, 80–81). However, I don't want to dissolve a bodily self; I want to affirm the unique patterns of its/our rhythmic bodily becoming. See Irigaray, "Mechanics of Fluids" in *This Sex Which Is Not One*.

30. Take Michel Serres in his book *Genesis*. Serres writes in search of the multiple, the noise, aiming to evoke it as the enabling cause of all things and subjects. In his project, dance serves as a mirror and model for a kind of thinking that is marked by the erasure of the self in a field of possibilities. However, the identity Serres draws between dancing and thinking obscures the differences in sensory education the two practices afford. His dancing body is a romantic, feminized "whore," who is naked, blank, and mute: "The dancer has nothing; he is nothing" (46). The impulse to embrace dance as the medium in and through which we become is a good one. However, in order to dislodge the implicit materialism, the difference between thinking and dancing as self-creating bodily practices must be acknowledged and overcome.

31. Among contemporary thinkers, Massumi comes close when he affirms: "The real is a snowballing process that makes a certainty of change" (*Parables of the Virtual*, 214). Yet even those who affirm the processual nature of reality have yet to take account of its rhythms of becoming as they occur in and through a human bodily self's own movements or of dance as a mode of participating consciously in that process. See LaMothe, "Can They Dance?"

32. As Zukav, Massumi, and others affirm, our ordinary sense of matter and energy as a dualism does not exist at the quantum level. As Einstein asserted, energy is mass and mass is energy. "Energy has mass and mass represents energy" (quoted in Zukav, *The Dancing Wu Li Masters*, 173). What binds matter and energy in a tensive, generative interplay is movement.

33. Zukav confirms that if we are to move beyond Newtonian materialism we need to move beyond its "by-product," namely, the "idea that we do not understand something until we have a picture of it in our heads" (*The Dancing Wu Li Masters*, 22).

34. In my attempt to evoke (rather than define) movement, I am inspired by G. W. F. Hegel—or at least by my reading of him. As Hegel writes in *Phenomenology of Spirit*, Spirit is movement, and the movement that Spirit is is the movement of becoming itself. Spirit is both substance and subject, and in such a way that the two cannot be separated. Spirit is not a substance that moves; spirit is the movement that is making it what it is, in every shape and form that appears, including the shape and form of a human bodily self. Further, I find in his *Lectures on the Philosophy of Religion* a qualifying moment to his apparent idealism. It is only in the *cultus*—that is, in the practice of bodily movements—that humans come to know as true for themselves that they are the moving moment wherein Spirit becomes conscious of itself. See

discussion of Reason and Religion in Hegel in LaMothe, "Reason, Religion, and Sexual Difference."

35. "What is it all for. . . . Nothing, I think, except to continue. That is the testimony in the marsh: Life directs all its powers to one end, and that is to continue to be. A marsh at nightfall is life loving itself. Nothing more. But nothing less, either" (Moore, *Holdfast,* 22–23). "To continue to be," I would add, is to continue not only to become, but to move.

36. The difference of this understanding from proprioception is subtle and significant. Proprioception is defined as a felt sense of my body as moving in space. Massumi elaborates: "Proprioception translates the exertions and ease of the body's encounters with objects into a muscular memory of relationality. This is the cumulative memory of skill, habit, and posture. At the same time as proprioception folds tactility in, it draws out the subject's reactions to the qualities of the objects it perceives through all five senses, bringing them into the motor realm of externalizable response" (*Parables of the Virtual,* 59). Here Massumi describes a movement pattern that represents both a capacity to perceive and to respond. Yet, proprioception limits this dynamic to sensations of physical movement. The idea of a sensory awareness of the movement making me is both inclusive and specific; it illuminates the constitutive importance of bodily movement to every aspect of our becoming, emotional, intellectual, and spiritual as well. There is no perception of movement possible outside the workings of movement itself.

37. In using these words, *sensation* and *response,* to refer to nonhuman movement patterns, I beg the question of whether all things that appear to us as material—such as rocks and clouds—have some kind of "self" or nervous system that is capable of sensing and responding. I would argue that everything we can perceive is capable of sensing and responding to us in ways that we have not yet imagined. We may not know yet how rocks sense and respond to our presence as we walk on them, but they do.

38. Isadora Duncan claimed to have learned this truth from her study of Greek art and their appreciation of nature: "In the thousands and thousands of figures which I have studied on these vases, I have always found an undulating line as the point of departure. Every movement, even in repose, contains the quality of fecundity, possesses the power to give birth to another movement" (*Art of the Dance,* 90). She was able to perceive this quality of Greek art, I would add, because she was already training her sensory awareness to movement impulses arising within her.

39. Note that I do not use the word *body* to describe a material dimension of human being. As is now evident, I do not believe there is such a material dimension. I use the term *bodily self* or *bodily becoming.* Along with Barbour, Braidotti, Grosz, Young, and others, I too want to affirm the "embodiment" of the subject, as a way to honor the

biological, symbolic, and sociological, as well as the spiritual, artistic, intellectual, and emotional dimensions of human subjectivity (Barbour, *Dancing Across the Page*, 69). However, I want to tip the balance and affirm that that *embodiment* is itself, across all registers, a function of rhythmic, relational movement and that there are shapes and forms of specifically human movement that matter to who we are.

40. Sheets-Johnstone goes further than others in elucidating the constitutive role that movement plays in our sense of self and world. As she writes, "Movement is at the root of our sense of agency and . . . the generative source of our notions of space and time. . . . Self-movement structures knowledge of the world" (*The Primacy of Movement*, xvii).

41. Massumi writes that "The one-ness of the body is a back-flow . . . a back-formation" that arises as a function of a body's own movements in relation to other objects (*Parables of the Virtual*, 150). However, a sense of one-ness is not merely back-flow. That apparent stability also precedes, invites, funds, and is capable of receiving impulses to move that would not otherwise exist.

42. Neil Shubin, paleontologist, professor of anatomy, and author of *Your Inner Fish*, describes our human body plan as "a time capsule" telling of critical moments in the history of life. He writes: "we are simply a mosaic of bits and pieces found in virtually everything else on the planet" (149), including the first "fish with hands" whose fossil he discovered, Tiktaalik.

43. Shubin, for example, explains that 90 percent of the proteins in the human body appear in the form of collagen, a connective tissue that is tense when stretched and hard when compressed. Collagen requires a "relatively large amount of oxygen" (*Your Inner Fish*, 137), thus, was not a possible expression of life energy until one billion years ago, when levels of oxygen increased and "bodies appeared everywhere" (138). More poetically, Abram describes air as an "elixir generated by the soils, the oceans, and the numberless organisms that inhabit this world, each creature exchanging certain ingredients for others" (*Becoming Animal*, 101).

44. Shubin defines a body as a division of labor among component parts that are able to stick together, communicate with one another, and replicate themselves (*Your Inner Fish*, 112–18). He claims that creatures formed bodies one billion years ago due to actions of predation: to eat and not be eaten (138). Implicit in this explanation is the idea that bodies evolved as a function of movements that microbes were already making in order to extend their capacity to do so.

45. Nietzsche describes the process by which a nerve-stimulus becomes a percept as a primary level of metaphor making: "When we talk about trees, colors, snow, and flowers, we believe we know something about the things in themselves, and yet we only possess metaphors of the things, and these metaphors do not in the least correspond to the original essentials" ("On Truth and Falsity," 178).

46. Alan Fogel affirms the essential relation of movement to sensation when he writes, "In order to attend to anything, there must be a movement, and therefore an activation of muscles" (*The Psychophysiology of Self-Awareness*, 30)

47. While Massumi, drawing on William James, affirms that "Participation precedes recognition" (*Parables of the Virtual*, 232), we also must take account of the nature of that participation. It is conscious and unconscious, but not simply so. The degree of our conscious participation is a function, I will argue, of how we dance. Of course, this statement is also a formulation of the Heisenberg uncertainty principle, again with an emphasis on movement.

48. Implicit here is a notion developed by Benedict Spinoza and picked up by Bennett, Deleuze and Guattari, and others concerning the notion of sensation as a function of differing relations of speed. I would add, however, that the difference that makes matter real for us is not just a function of relative and relational speeds (as if there were some thing that was speeding), but of patterns of movement—human bodily movement—distinguishable by a host of qualities in addition to speed, including direction, shape, effort, range, trajectory, etc. Compare Bennett, *Vibrant Matter*, 57–58.

49. "All obedience to law which impresses us so forcibly in the orbits of stars and in chemical processes coincides at the bottom with those qualities which we ourselves attach to those things, so that it is we who thereby make the impression upon ourselves" (Nietzsche, "On Truth and Falsity," 187). For Nietzsche, what we are able to perceive occurs through a process of "active construction" in which we are constantly guided by movements we have already made. As Sandra and Matthew Blakeslee write: "Your understanding of reality is constructed in large part according to your expectations and beliefs, which are based on all your past [i.e., movement] experiences, which are held in the cortex as predictive memory" (*The Body Has a Mind of Its Own*, 41).

50. David Abram concurs, describing a human body as "an open unfinished entity utterly entwined with the soils, waters, and winds that move through it—a wild creature whose life is contingent upon the multiple other lives that surround it, and the shifting flows that surge through it" (*Becoming Animal*, 110)—and, I would add, the infinite movement potentials enfolded in its bodily self. There is no "entity" other than that which a bodily self's own movement pulls into being as real.

51. Martha Graham famously made this comment. However, she did not claim that everyone has the capacity to discern the truth of movement. Such discernment, for Graham, emerges after long years of practice (*Blood Memory*, 4).

52. As Nietzsche avers: "Alas, all this delusion and all these mistakes still dwell in our body: they have there become body and will.... Indeed, an experiment was man. Alas, much ignorance and error have become body within us" ("Thus Spoke Zarathustra," in *The Portable Nietzsche*, 188–89).

53. Teresa Brennan calls for people to extend their consciousness into the "body"—to practice a "living attention" to how a body receives and interprets affects (*The Transmission of Affect*, 53)—and thus free the energy that has been bound by illusions of mind/matter dualism. However, the attention to movement she prescribes does not extend to a bodily self's own movements and thus falls short of appreciating the sensory source of human creativity.

54. This movement pattern is derived from the first exercise of the Duncan technique.

2. To Dance Is to Evolve

1. Affirming the usefulness of evolution as an explanatory theory, Robin Dunbar credits Darwin for establishing that evolutionary change is driven by "animals' need to adapt to changing circumstances," that the basic unit of evolution is the individual, and that every change has both cost and benefit (*Grooming, Gossip, and the Evolution of Language*, 31–32).

2. This tendency finds expression and reinforcement in the metaphors scientists use to describe evolution. Recall Neil Shubin's description in chapter 1, note 42, of a body plan as a "time capsule" or "mosaic" (*Your Inner Fish*, 149).

3. While Richard Dawkins's critics disagree on whether or not genes are "selfish," they rarely challenge the idea that some material unit—whether organism or collective—is. What was bold about Dawkins's assertion was the implication that genes (as material bits) themselves have a kind of agency—not that materiality and selfishness go hand in hand. See Dawkins, *The Selfish Gene*, for the extreme view.

4. Theodore Roszak criticizes the reliance on chance as a way to explain evolution. Describing the "real problem" with a materialist program, he writes that there is "no place to locate mind in the cosmos except inside a human skull" (*The Voice of the Earth*, 151).

5. This issue is especially relevant when it comes to explaining human capacities that require a coordination of multiple genetic developments, such as language use. Dunbar, for example, argues that language evolved as an extension of grooming practices—not as the mode of communication for which we now use it. While grooming likely evolved in monkeys and apes as a form of hygiene, he argues that the strong hormonal responses that such actions created were then "recruited" by early hominids to solve problems of predation (*Grooming, Gossip, and the Evolution of Language*, 38). As hominid groups grew too large for their members to groom one another, they appropriated practices of vocalization already evident in Old World monkeys and apes for a new purpose: to trigger the same relationship-building responses that grooming does, but at a distance (115, 192).

6. Against those who insist upon the essential selfishness of human individuals, E. O. Wilson argues that humans evolved as creatures who exploited the reproductive advantage given by a well-defended nest (*The Social Conquest of the Earth*). See also Tomasello, *Why We Cooperate*.

7. It is now thought that mutations in HOX genes, so-called master switches present in all animals that turn on sequences of genes responsible for determining bodily structures and their placement, may be responsible for dramatic, instant genetic mutations in physiology (such as upright walking in humans), thus lending support for Stephen Jay Gould's theory of "punctuated equilibrium" (Walter, *Thumbs, Toes, and Tears*, 20).

8. As defined by William McNeill, community dancing occurs when an "indefinite number of individuals start to move their muscles rhythmically, establish a regular beat, and continue doing so for long enough to arouse euphoric excitement shared by all participants, and (more faintly) by onlookers as well" (*Keeping Together in Time*, 13).

9. Gilbert Rouget defined trance as "transcendence of one's normal self, as a liberation resulting from the intensification of a mental or physical disposition, in short, as an exaltation—sometimes a self-mutilating one—of the self" (Wade, *The Faith Instinct*, 91). Erica Bourguignon found that, among the five hundred small-scale tribal societies she studied, 90 percent performed some form of regular dance/trance ritual, in which a person lost sensory awareness and retained little memory of what had occurred (ibid.).

10. McNeill distinguishes between a trance state and warm emotional affect, both of which rhythmic movement in groups can induce (*Keeping Together in Time*, 8).

11. Barbara Ehrenreich, in *Dancing in the Streets*, describes dance as a "biotechnology of group formation" (24). Wade describes ritual dancing as a "social binding mechanism" (*The Faith Instinct*, 275).

12. McNeill writes: "Group consolidation through dance was, perhaps, critical in separating our remote ancestors from other protohomind species" (*Keeping Together in Time*, 11). See further discussion in chapter 5.

13. Wade, for example, argues that ritual dancing solves what he calls the problem of human society: "how to make selfish individuals place society's needs above their own" (*The Faith Instinct*, 39).

14. Wade draws on three criteria proposed by Stephen Pinker to argue that the capacity for communal, ritual dancing did not evolve as an accidental by-product of some other development, but is itself adaptive. It is a capacity that is innate, that improved individuals' chances for survival, and that functioned to engineer social relations (*The Faith Instinct*, 62–66).

15. The assertion that dance is first and foremost communal is inevitably accompanied by the assertion that it is "religious." This line of thought is present in the earliest

2. To Dance Is to Evolve

Western scholars of religion and dance, such as W. E. Oesterley, who wrote that "all dancing was originally religious and was performed for religious purposes" (quoted in Paul Halmos, "The Decline of Choral Dancing," 173). See chapters 6 and 7 for further discussions of religion and dance.

16. Even McNeill, who concedes that "keeping together in time" "remains the most powerful way to create and sustain community that we have at our demand" (*Keeping Together in Time*, 150), admits that there are forms other than dance in which humans can enjoy this benefit, including parades and military exercises, pilgrimage or coordinated ritual prayer. Wade describes ritual dancing as "raw religion, before it was tamed by the busy life and cooler tastes of cities" (*The Faith Instinct*, 106).

17. Ehrenreich does affirm that we need to do something with our bodily selves in order to accomplish our goals of happy and healthy social relations. As she asks, "Why not reclaim our distinctively human heritage as creatures who can generate their own ecstatic pleasures out of music, color, feasting, and dance?" (*Dancing in the Streets*, 260). Dance, in this instance, remains one possible means to a desirable end.

18. This position finds many advocates in the twentieth century, including Osterley and the philosopher Suzanne Langer in her book *Feeling and Form*. As Ehrenreich, summarizing her account of modern European disgust with dance, concludes, "the essence of the Western mind . . . was its ability to resist the contagious rhythm of the drums, to wall itself up in a fortress of ego and rationality against the seductive wildness of the world" (*Dancing in the Streets*, 9). See chapters 4 and 7 for further discussion of the mind/matter and nature/culture distinctions operative in materialist resistance to dance.

19. David Abram confirms: "the enfolding biosphere is the very matrix within which our organism came to acquire its current form. Our senses have coevolved with the chemistry of these waters and this air, shaping themselves to the particular patterns of the animate earth. Our human eyes have evolved in subtle interaction with other, non-human eyes—as our ears are now tuned, by their very structure, to the howling of wolves and the thrumming of frogs" (*Becoming Animal*, 78).

20. Abram describes this dynamic in terms of "reciprocity": "Whenever we touch any entity, we are ourselves being touched by that entity. . . . Such reciprocity is the very structure of perception. We experience the sensuous world only by rendering ourselves vulnerable to that world." He continues, "the terrain enters into us only to the extent that we allow ourselves to be taken up within that terrain" (*Becoming Animal*, 58). I would qualify that the terrain "enters into us" in accord with how we *move* in relation to it and with whether and how we allow ourselves to be moved by it.

21. Roszak calculates the time it would take for the universe to evolve through chance, given the range of variables and permutations. Assuming the relatively short life of the universe, he deems it impossible. "Chance may be the factor that has to be

225

eliminated if the evolutionary explanation of life is to retain its cogency" (*The Voice of the Earth*, 116).

22. Katherine Harmon, "'Junk' DNA Holds Clues to Common Diseases," *Scientific American*, September 5, 2012. This point is relevant in the work of new materialists as well who interpret the significance of this fact in terms of interaction among different levels of matter (Coole and Frost, *New Materialisms*, 17).

23. Of course, it is well established that movement is necessary in order for certain sensory capacities and brain functions to manifest themselves. In an oft-cited experiment, kittens who were not able to spend their first weeks of life moving their own bodily selves did not learn to see—even if they were moved on little carts (Blakeslee and Blakeslee, *The Body Has a Mind of Its Own*, 12–14). My point here goes further. Genes do not even exist as potentials for becoming without the movements that pull them into existence as possible extensions of the movements that made them.

24. I use the term *overcoming* with Friedrich Nietzsche (and Zarathustra) in mind: "Man is something that shall be overcome" ("Thus Spoke Zarathustra," in *The Portable Nietzsche*, 124).

25. I would argue that even minerals, while they are not "bodies" with the ability to renew and reform themselves, still participate in the movement of life. The movements of rocks—how they form, harden, melt, crack, fall—are what make them what they are.

26. Here I agree with Zukav's depiction of the physicists for whom "The distinction between organic and inorganic is a conceptual prejudice" (*The Dancing Wu Li Masters*, 51), especially from the point of view of evolution. The organic/inorganic dualism reinforces a mind/matter dualism as well as a culture/nature prejudice; see chapter 7.

27. Rodolfo Llinás, in analyzing the evolution of eyes, affirms that there is no teleological path to an eye, but that different eyes arose along the evolutionary path via the use and exploitation of "emergent properties"—that is, by "exploring and exploiting the properties [or, movement potentials enabled by] light" (*I of the Vortex*, 105). "Eyes are neurons that embed geometrices of bouncing light" (109).

28. I am deliberately setting aside questions about the role of "culture" in this process, leaving them to chapter 7. While there is no human "nature" without "culture," it also makes sense to consider human bodily selves as members of a life medium that includes, subtends, and exceeds any human or cultural formulation.

29. Do animals dance? Honey bees and sand cranes, for example, are two species who engage in rhythmic, patterned bodily movement seemingly as a way to communicate. Yet Abram writes that animal dances "remain within the sphere of felt bodily expression" (*The Spell of the Sensuous*, 79), whereas for humans the meaning is "abstract." The notion of bodily becoming offers resources for thinking about this

"abstraction" in terms of the range of movement patterns humans are able to perceive and make. See chapter 7 for further discussion.

30. Daniel Heller-Roazen reads Aristotle as designating sensation, or aisthesis, "a kind of being moved upon and acted upon," as the enabling core of cognition. As Heller-Roazen describes, "Sensible life comes into being with the presence of the power of touch, and inevitably ends, with perfect symmetry, with its absence" (*The Inner Touch*, 27). I would qualify that the key to our intelligence lies in our responsivity to movement—a responsivity that includes but is not limited to the skin's sensitivity.

31. Abram argues that the invention of the alphabet marks the first and decisive step in the human alienation from the natural world—an alienation from which we now suffer. With an alphabet, a "written character no longer refers us to any sensible phenomenon out in the world, or even to the name of such a phenomenon . . . but solely to a gesture to be made by the human mouth" (*The Spell of the Sensuous*, 100).

32. Chip Walter, for example, in *Toes, Thumbs, and Tears*; or Daniel Lieberman in *The Evolution of the Human Head*.

33. A fact that proves especially true for humans leading a sedentary existence. As Neil Shubin writes: "If the legs are not used much, the muscles will not pump the blood up the veins" (*Your Inner Fish*, 188). Yet the problem, here, is less the repurposing, I would argue, and more that humans have evolved cultural practices at odds with their inherited movement potential.

34. Dennis Bramble and Daniel Lieberman argue that "the demands of endurance running" or ER, possibly used to hunt or scavenge, may have been a "major contributing factor to the human body form" ("Endurance Running and the Evolution of Homo," 351). While a few features that enable ER are present in earlier members of the hominid line, most of the features, with the exception of an Achilles tendon, have been found in fossils of Homo erectus. See also Bernd Heinrich, *Why We Run;* and Christopher McDougall, *Born to Run*.

35. As of 1.8 million years ago, Richard Wrangham claims, Homo erectus emerged as a new species, "tied to the use of fire by our biological needs, relying on cooking food to supply enough energy to our bodies" (*Catching Fire*, 17). Cooked food, he argues, and improvements in cooking technology, explain the gradual increase in proportional brain size between Homo erectus and Homo sapiens.

36. About 250,000 years ago, and perhaps as early as 500,000 years ago, "Homo sapiens was marked by the appearance of language" (Dunbar, *Grooming, Gossip, and the Evolution of Language*, 112).

37. Sarah Blaffer Hrdy argues that, at some point in the Pleistocene (1.8 million to 10,000 years ago), coextensive with Homo erectus and other hominids, a line of apes began to practice cooperative breeding. In so doing they created the occasion for infants and caregivers to develop the ability to create intimate relationships with

2. To Dance Is to Evolve

one another. This intersubjectivity, she argues, explains the desire for language as well as the press toward a relatively larger Homo sapiens brain (*Mothers and Others*, 31). As she affirms, "Without alloparents, there never would have been a human species" (109).

38. For example, Lieberman writes, "the way the head is integrated during development—from different structures sharing the same walls, from functional effects on regional growth, and from shared developmental pathways—permits the head to be highly functional, adaptable, and changeable over evolutionary time" (*The Evolution of the Human Head*, x).

3. To Dance Is to Know

1. For examples of this logic related to our desires for food, sex, and spirit, see LaMothe, *What a Body Knows*.

2. In evoking this view of knowledge, I am not forgetting its many critics, with whom I sympathize. I am merely reminding readers of its tenets, eager to continue the process of their overcoming by revealing how they still operate in relation to dancing. For the classic critique of knowledge as an expression of power rather than of the truth it claims to be, see Foucault, *Power/Knowledge* and *The Order of Things*.

3. Mark C Taylor names "the book" as one of four nodes that uphold the Western theological tradition and its dualistic metaphysics. The other three nodes are God, Self, and History. See Taylor, *Erring*, chapter 4.

4. As Maxine Sheets-Johnstone confirms, the West "pedestals human language, and silences the human body" (*The Roots of Power*, 10).

5. Michel Serres offers a relevant critique of this mode of establishing knowledge in an extended comparison between a writer and a mountain climber. I quote, with a dose of irony: "Because writing is no more forgiving than the mountain, most walker-writers have themselves preceded [*sic*] by guides and surrounded by ropes: citations-belays, notes-mountain huts, references-pitons. The sham craft consists in the multiplication of proper names; the genuine writer's craft demands a solitary engagement from the entire body and its sole singularity" (*Variations on the Body*, 12).

6. For example, the social constructivism and linguistic turn of postmodern theory in the 1990s not only deny "the living body," they protect the privilege accorded to language over matter, claiming that meaning is a function of power relations that work through cultural forms. By contrast, Sheets-Johnstone is one who draws on Maurice Merleau-Ponty's notion of an "I can" to seek alternate sources of corporeal power in lived experience rather than linguistic play (*The Roots of Power*, 11).

3. To Dance Is to Know

7. Dance, for one, is what Michel Foucault would call a "subjugated knowledge" in both senses of the word. Its historical contents "have been buried and disguised" by assumptions to "functionalist and systematising theory," and it has been "disqualified as inadequate . . . or insufficiently elaborated" as a "naive knowledge . . . located low down on the hierarchy, beneath the required level of cognition or scientificity" (*Power/ Knowledge*, 81–82).

8. Citing the example of Martha Graham, Howard Gardener includes "kinetic intelligence" among his list in *Frames of Mind*.

9. Mark C. Taylor, for example, in his book *Altarity*, reads a number of philosophers to demonstrate how "writing *always* leaves crumbs or remains—literary remains" (328); writing cannot re-present the particular, the impossible, or absolute difference. Taylor concludes: "The only response to the writer's solicitation is to write" and rewrite some more (353).

10. A predicament deftly enacted by Søren Kierkegaard in his pseudonymous responses to Hegel's system, especially *Fear and Trembling; Concluding Unscientific Postscript*. According to Kierkegaard's pseudonyms, that which cannot be known through writing is faith, and the sign of faith is a dancer's leap. In *Fear and Trembling*, Abraham, the father of faith, is likened to a ballet dancer (41). For discussion, see LaMothe, *Between Dancing and Writing*, chapter 4.

11. For an analysis of such sightings in the work of Gilles Deleuze and Felix Guattari, Jane Bennett, and David Abram, see LaMothe, "Can They Dance?"

12. Susan Foster formulates this dilemma in the introduction to *Reading Dancing*. She then draws on nondualistic theories of language in Foucault and Barthes in order to develop a method of "reading" dancing "as a system of codes and conventions," which attends to the bodily practices and semiotic cues that enable bodies to "write" (in) dance (*Reading Dancing*, xviii).

13. For example, Sondra Horton Fraleigh writes: "the art of dance draws upon the meanings we attach to our bodily enacted existence as a whole, as these may be made to appear in movement." She continues, "The movement medium of dance is continuous with and also an enactment of our embodiment" (*Dance and the Lived Body*, xvi).

14. For example, Foster's "theory of representation" aims to "reveal how the dancing body as well as the dancing subject comes to be endowed with a symbolic significance that permeates its very existence." That symbolic significance emerges, she writes, through the creative process, as dancers choreograph, rehearse, cooperate with other artists, and perform for audiences (*Reading Dancing*, 3).

15. For the twenty-nine women she interviewed, for example, Johanna Lesho found that "dance was at least one means of connecting with the sacred" (Lesho and McMaster, *Dancing on the Earth*, 21). As the editors write, through dance, "we can

discover a connection to something larger than ourselves that has the power to carry us forward" (9).

16. For a discussion of Graham's technique in terms of the movement patterns or kinetic images it guides a dancer to create and become, see LaMothe, *Nietzsche's Dancers*, chapter 7.

17. Martha Graham, "Preface" (in Morgan, *Martha Graham*). For an analysis of Graham's use of religion language in this passage, see LaMothe, *Nietzsche's Dancers*, 177.

18. Neuroscientist Rodolfo Llinás makes this point when he writes that a "brain's understanding of anything, whether factual or abstract, arises from our manipulations of the external world, by moving within the world and thus from our sensory-derived experience of it" (*I of the Vortex*, 58–59).

19. Abram concurs. With the invention and use of the alphabet, he writes, "the animating interplay of the senses has been transferred to another medium, another locus of participation" (*The Spell of the Sensuous*, 131)—from the natural world to a world of books. For one so trained, rocks and streams no longer speak, but pages do.

20. For example, "The practice of reading and writing over long periods will subliminally reinforce the user's belief that the world is a chain-linked tessellation of events that occur in linear time" (Shlain, *The Alphabet Versus the Goddess*, 337).

21. For a discussion of writing and walking, see Solnit, *Wanderlust*.

22. Thoreau does so in his essay "Walking."

23. Friedrich Nietzsche is ever an exception. As he writes: "Only thoughts reached by walking have value" ("Twilight of the Idols," in *The Portable Nietzsche*, 471).

24. Walter Ong contrasts oral cultures with literary cultures, cataloging the different kinds of thinking and memory skills that each practice develops in his book *Orality and Literacy*.

25. As Jacques Derrida famously utters in *On Grammatology:* "There is nothing outside the text" (158).

26. As Alan Fogel notes, "The longer we stay in thought, the more difficult it becomes to shift back over to the direct experiencing of the subjective emotional present" (*The Psychophysiology of Self-Awareness*, 100). He ascribes this difficulty to a nonlinear switch in the medial prefrontal cortex that shifts between conceptual self-awareness, or thinking, and embodied self-awareness (ESA). If we don't actively stop thinking and cultivate a sensory awareness, then "thought regulation becomes substituted in awareness for embodied self-regulation. These thoughts get compounded with the imagined dangers of crossing over to the side of ESA" (101).

27. Of course, not all dance practice will encourage and afford the same kind or degree of sensory awareness. Much depends on the technique, teacher, and training methods. However, anyone seriously attempting to create and become patterns of movement will inevitably, to some extent, exercise and grow a sensory awareness of

himself as moving somehow, from somewhere, in ways that use pain and pleasure, however manifest, as guides for allowing the movement to continue.

28. This understanding of sensory awareness aligns with the notion of a "lived body" conceived in existential phenomenology and embraced by feminist and queer theorists, among others, as a hedge against disembodiment (Young, *On Female Body Experience*). Yet it is important to note that the antidote to our disembodiment is not simply "more sensation" or "more experience." As Nietzsche was aware, a surfeit of sensation is precisely what desensitized bodily selves crave (*Human, All Too Human*). The remedy, rather, is a sensory education to the rhythms and shapes of bodily becoming—to the movements that are making us—such as the action of dancing provides.

29. Note that this infinity of a bodily self does not mean that a bodily self can, in any moment, do everything or anything "it" (or "I") wants. Rather, it means that the potential of a bodily self for receiving new sensations—through which minds can reflect—is endless, and is so until a person dies. Even then, it could be argued, the movement patterns of the bodily self simply change from those that support self-enabling movement to those of decomposition and decay that were always already present and do not.

30. Here I agree with Heller-Roazen, who claims that we of the modern West have realized the Cartesian ideal. We have educated ourselves into a "common insensibility" such that we "no longer sense what [we] sense": "Consciousness, resolutely cognitive, now remains alone" (*The Inner Touch*, 287–89). In this observation, however, lies a Nietzschean hope. We can learn to participate differently in the dynamic we see enacted in the bodily becoming of our generation.

31. De Mille, *Martha Graham*, 22.

4. Dance Is to Be Born

1. For a description of this cycle of breaths and the circumstances of its discovery, see LaMothe, *What a Body Knows*, chapter 2.

2. This critique of Western birthing practices is one that I share with Young (*On Female Body Experience*, 55–60) and discuss in LaMothe, *What a Body Knows*, chapter 21.

3. While not all humans give birth, all humans are born. In narrating a "female" experience of giving birth as the experiential frame of this chapter, I align my work with feminist theorists who are critically engaging the tradition of Western and existential philosophy to "describe subjectivity and women's experience as lived and felt in the flesh" (Young, *On Female Body Experience*, 7), in order to enrich our understanding not only of "women" but of human living and, in this case, of dance. I also

affirm, along with Sarah Blaffer Hrdy, that "every female who becomes a mother does it her way" (*Mother Nature*, 79).

4. In charting the history of the modern West, scholars credit René Descartes, and his *Discourse on Method*, with shifting the locus of subjectivity from the sensation of being alive (which Heller-Roazen traces back to Aristotle) to the act of cognition (Descartes, *Discourse on Method*, 21; Heller-Roazen, *The Inner Touch*, 165–66).

5. Friedrich Nietzsche, in his critique of subjectivity, set the stage for the 1960s, in which Merleau-Ponty, Simone de Beauvoir, and other existential phenomenologists catalyzed a shift from Descartes's thinking mind to the "lived body" or "embodiment" as the locus of subjectivity and consciousness. Yet this turn toward the body and its experience was subsequently snarled in debates pitting so-called essentialists against social constructivists (for one discussion, see Young, *On Female Body Experience*, chapter 1). In line with Nietzsche, I draw upon *dance* as a critical resource for advancing an understanding of bodily becoming that affirms that the lived experience of our bodily selves, when cultivated through attention to our sensory creativity, can serve as a dynamic, responsive locus for responsibly negotiating our inevitable implication in cultural relations of power.

6. "Sperm and egg come together to make a single cell." The "genetic material" fuses and the cells begin to divide (Shubin, *Your Inner Fish*, 86).

7. This assumption provides the grounds for the pro-life argument that life begins at conception, thereby revealing the pro-life argument as more of a *materialist* argument than a spiritual one.

8. This theme of rebirth is common to religions around the world, throughout history, including the Christianity whose beliefs about Jesus's body, as baptized, crucified, and resurrected, funded the materialist notion of matter as that which was left behind for humans to study.

9. "All the genetic switches that make fingers, arm bones, and toes do their thing [turn on] during the third to eighth week after conception" (Shubin, *Your Inner Fish*, 47). In Shubin's analysis, every new development of the embryo represents a new pattern of movement potential that is itself forced into existence as a result of other movement patterns occurring earlier in time in relation to one another.

10. As Rodolfo Llinás confirms, "brains are an evolutionary prerequisite for guided movement in primitive animals . . . active movement is dangerous in the absence of an internal plan subject to sensory modulation" (*I of the Vortex*, 18). In other words, because humans move, we need a brain capable of planning and prediction. The fact that we can and must move is what makes our brain and its intentional, predictive capacities important.

11. Alan Fogel points out that these prenatal movements are not "conscious" or intentional. They are more akin to spontaneous "twitches." This twitching: "seems to be an essential mechanism to start the development of neuromotor links that intro-

duce one body part to another and serve to integrate the body schema" (*The Psycho-physiology of Self-Awareness*, 85–86). By "bodily schema," Fogel is referring to a sense of a bodily self moving in space and in relation to itself. For Fogel, such body schema comprise the formative matrix of self awareness.

12. Fogel confirms that the "the pathways in the brain for sucking, moving, and touching," which develop in the womb, "loop through neural pathways for self- and other awareness" (*The Psychophysiology of Self-Awareness*, 13).

13. Note that this shift privileges movement and participation over sensation as the enabling agent of consciousness. Any sensation presupposes movement, as noted in chapter 1. Nor is the movement that sensation presupposes simply "a kind of being moved upon and acted upon," as Heller-Roazen claims for Aristotle (*The Inner Touch*, 24). Nothing can appear to a bodily self without that bodily self activating patterns of movement potential. To live is not to perceive (Aristotle in Heller-Roazen, *The Inner Touch*, 30); to live is to *move*.

14. Llinás makes the point that a brain is a "closed system," in that it uses sensory inputs to "modulate images it is already generating" and put them in context (*I of the Vortex*, 7–8). A brain, he claims, is born with as much "a priori order" as a "body"— and as much plasticity. It can generate intrinsic images of the world independent of sense data (57), yet modify and recraft those images in response to the sense data its movements convey.

15. Llinás describes "mind" or what he calls the "mindness state" as the class of all brain states in which "sensori-motor images, including self-awareness, are generated." Each sensori-motor image is "the conjunction or binding of all relevant sensory input to produce a discrete functional state that ultimately may result in action" (*I of the Vortex*, 1). This "sensori-motor image" is what I call a kinetic image or pattern of sensation and response. Self-awareness, then, or a sense of self, is itself a kinetic image.

16. Fogel insists that this task of "expanding self-awareness is our original and primary occupation . . . the very core of our psychophysiological being" (*The Psycho-physiology of Self-Awareness*, 12).

17. It is tempting, given our materialist training, to think of a fetus as a material entity undergoing a purely biological process that, at some point in time, crosses a threshold and acquires a distinctly human mind or soul. However, in a movement perspective, the movements that find expression in a human consciousness must always already be "human" in some way from the moment of conception.

18. In nonhuman primates, for example, the birth canal is larger relative to the size of an infant's head. A primate infant is born face up and can even help pull herself out. In humans, in order to move through the birth canal, an infant must rotate from face forward to sideways as the head emerges and then turn another 90 degrees to face back as it is born in order to get its shoulders through (Walter, *Thumbs, Toes, and Tears*, 33).

19. Bramble and Lieberman, "Endurance Running and the Evolution of Homo," 346–51.

20. Dunbar, *Grooming, Gossip, and the Evolution of Language*, 108–12.

21. Of pre–Homo sapiens hominids, Walter confirms: "The same evolutionary forces that were making them more mobile and more intelligent were also making birth more difficult" (*Thumbs, Toes, and Tears*, 34).

22. Dunbar, *Grooming, Gossip, and the Evolution of Language*, 129.

23. Unlike primates, "A baby human is born when its brain is less than one-third its final size" (Dunbar, *Grooming, Gossip, and the Evolution of Language*, 128).

24. Dunbar estimates that a primate takes five to ten years to mature, compared to the fifteen to twenty years required for a human (*Grooming, Gossip, and the Evolution of Language*, 129).

25. Kangaroos provide another example of upright walkers with early births. Kangaroos, who do not have primate arms, solve the problem of overly dependent young by creating external wombs—belly pouches—within which infants can continue to develop until ready to emerge.

26. In her discussion of cooperative breeding, Hrdy describes "a self-reinforcing evolutionary process [that] produces parents and alloparents who are more sensitive to infantile signals and babies who are better at emitting them" (*Mothers and Others*, 220). See chapter 5 for further discussion.

27. In the first three years, an infant brain triples in size. In the next ten, it grows by another third (Walter, *Thumbs, Toes, and Tears*, 36).

28. As Hrdy confirms, "Unable to count on mothers to commit to them as reliably as newborn chimps and other primates can, hominid fetuses are under pressure to convince mothers to do so" (*Mother Nature*, 482).

29. Hrdy admits that it is difficult to think of an infant operating strategically in order to secure the attention of caregivers. However, she affirms that "a human child is born eager to connect with others" (*Mothers and Others*, 23). This eagerness finds expression in responsive movement making. Fogel confirms that "newborn longing is a longing for connection" (*The Psychophysiology of Self-Awareness*, 13), though not yet with any "thing."

30. Indirectly affirming this statement, Hrdy asserts that the size of the human brain could have evolved slowly, without any big initial payoff, "If mothers selected first to live long enough to get their last offspring to independence, and thereafter selected because their altruism produced increased survival of close kin" (*Mother Nature*, 285). The "payoff" was rather gradual and across the board, enhancing all aspects of bodily life. The lengthening of childhoods occurred during the span of Homo erectus as mothers grew larger.

31. McNeill suggests that Homo erectus may have been the first hominid to discover the emotional benefits of community dancing (*Keeping Together in Time*, 25–6).

This discovery, he surmises, may have catalyzed an evolutionary arc in Homo erectus that led to the emergence of Homo sapiens approximately 200–250,000 years ago. McNeill holds that this capacity to dance may also have provided the foundation for the explosion in cultural innovation, art, and tool use that occurred around 40,000 BCE (24). My point is that this discovery may have been catalyzed by the need for the community to come together to support the earlier births induced by upright walking.

Merlin Donald, in *Origins of the Modern Mind*, identifies dance with the "mimetic skill" that Homo erectus developed as part of the cognitive repertoire that enabled the emergence of language and symbolic thought. Mimesis, for Donald, is the "ability to produce conscious, self-identified, representational acts that are intentional but not linguistic" (168). Again, this mimesis may have had its enabling root in the increasingly intense relationships between parents and their earlier-born infants.

32. Daniel Chamovitz gives evidence of how plants perform the functions of seeing, smelling, feeling, hearing, remembering, and knowing where they are in relation to gravity. He compares the movement of "dancing plants" to ballet and affirms that plants have a "built-in" or endogenous behavior to oscillate in space—what Darwin called "circumnutation" (*What a Plant Knows*, 106). Chamovitz suggests that plants demonstrate a kinetic intelligence out of which later a brain-based animal dancing could develop (91–112).

33. Science writers Sandra Blakeslee and Matthew Blakeslee report: "The maps that encode your physical body are connected directly, immediately, personally to a map of every point in that [peripersonal] space and also map out your potential to perform actions in that space. Your self does not end where your flesh ends, but suffuses and blends with the world, including other beings" (*The Body Has a Mind of Its Own*, 3).

34. As the Blakeslees admit: "Your body maps the world according to what you have learned to do with your muscles" (*The Body Has a Mind of Its Own*, 170). What is recorded, then, are patterns of relational, bodily movement. Further, these kinetic images are not simply options a "mind" can choose to mobilize based on sensory input. These kinetic images are actively involved in determining how our senses move and what they can perceive.

35. As the Blakeslees report:

It turns out the sensory maps of your parietal lobe are also de facto motor centers, with massive direct interlinkage to the frontal motor system. They don't simply pass information to the motor system, they participate directly in action. They actively transform vision, sound, touch, balance, and other sensory information into motor intentions and actual movements. And by the same token, the maps of the motor system play a fundamental role in interpreting the sensations from your body. . . . Physical sensation and action are best seen as a single sense that, like a coin, has two inseparable faces with different appearance. (*The Body Has a Mind of Its Own*, 116)

36. Llinás explains that the course of organismic evolution reveals a gradual increase in the number of interneurons connecting sensation and response (*I of the Vortex*, 11). He also suggests, from an evolutionary perspective, that neurons form in a nervous system as the medium mediating sensation and response (78). A brain is not only the connecting and coordinating of sensation and response, it is also an internal space in which new combinations may be imagined and realized, that is, predicted.

37. Walter, *Thumbs, Toes, and Tears*, 103. The physiological mechanism for this connection is the pyramidal neurons, distinguished by long axons.

38. For many philosophers and scientists in the modern West, including Immanuel Kant, human reason results from a progression of increasing reflection leading from sensation through emotion to understanding and finally to a kind of thinking that is free from finite, bodily constraints. A movement paradigm calls attention to a second developmental flow leading from reason back through emotion to experience that is equally important to the veracity and value of our thinking. See LaMothe, *Between Dancing and Writing*, chapters 1–4 for a sustained analysis of the bidirectional relationship between reason and experience that appears in the juxaposition of Descartes, Kant, Schleiermacher, Hegel, and Kierkegaard.

39. Walter, *Thumbs, Toes, and Tears*, 95–100. When Walter writes, "we manipulate thoughts the way we do because our hands once learned to shape sticks, stones, and animal skins into tools," I would add, and because we danced the way we did (57). The coevolution of toolmaking, gesture, and speech he describes occurring in Homo erectus would have been happening at the same time that humans were discovering the powerful and transformative effects of rhythmic bodily movement. I would further add that this interdependent development between thought and movement is not limited to the past. It remains an ongoing human reality.

40. As Walter discusses, "our brains never stop adjusting to the world around us." Instead of reaching a fixed adult state, humans "tend to retain many of the youthful physical and behavioral traits of our species . . . well into adulthood" (*Thumbs, Toes, and Tears*, 35, 32), especially, I would add, if we practice.

41. Siegel, *The Developing Mind*, 13. As he writes: "At birth, the infant's brain is the most undifferentiated organ in the body. . . . Experiences lead to an increased activity of neurons, which enhances the creation of new synaptic connections. This experience-dependent brain growth and differentiation is thus referred to as an 'activity-dependent' process" (14).

42. Young summarizes Merleau-Ponty on this point: "By projecting an aim toward which it moves, the body brings unity to and unites itself with its surround-

ing; through the vectors of its projected possibilities it sets things in relation to one another and to itself" (*On Female Body Experience*, 37). I would emphasize that "the body" is always already moving and moved, such that these "projections" run along trajectories of movements made and remembered such that the "relations" that are thus created are not simply "set" but rather cultivated or realized. We *participate* in rhythms of bodily becoming that are ever ongoing, and any "unity" we create is itself transitory. See also Merleau-Ponty, *Phenomenology of Perception*, chapters 3–4.

43. Llinás summarizes this line of thought: "As the nervous system evolved, the constraints generated by the coordinate systems that describe the body were slowly embedded into a functional space within the nervous system. This provided a natural, activity dependent understanding that a creature would have of its own body" (*I of the Vortex*, 57)—and, I would add, of that bodily self *as* movement.

44. These senses of inner and outer are usually tagged to different kinds of neuroreceptors: the inwardly focused interoceptors and the outwardly focused exteroceptors. The interoceptors include neurons for perceiving pain and movement, while the exteroceptors pertain to our five senses. However, these neuroreceptors operate together in enabling states of self-awareness that emerge as holistic patterns of sensing and responding. As Fogel writes, "Awareness emerges as a whole systems phenomenon, a consequence of the coactivation across these and other regions of the brain and body in the interoceptive network" (*The Psychophysiology of Self-Awareness*, 58).

Llinás explains that this ability to synchronize our various perceptions into a singular awareness is a function of our brain's electrical impulses. Neuronal activity oscillates at 40hz. The synchronous activation of neuronal activity allows us to coordinate multiple sensory inputs and create a "unitary perceptual entity" out of many sensory and motor cues (*I of the Vortex*, 124)—including a sense of self.

45. Fogel designates three levels of embodied self-awareness: I, the unconscious regulation of heart and breathing; II, the limbic system and its regulation of emotion; and III, conscious self-awareness. While levels I and II can and do function without conscious intervention, he writes that "humans can add embodied self-awareness into the homeostatic self-regulation system to make it more powerful as a tool for homeostasis" (*The Psychophysiology of Self-Awareness*, 51). In other words, in my terms, we can cultivate a sensory awareness that enables us to participate consciously in a bodily self's own movement of becoming.

46. Teresa Brennan, in a different vein, writes that an "ego" forms as an otherwise fluid energy is bound up at fixed points through repetition. She describes an ego as "constructed inertia" that is "less likely to adapt and follow new pathways," rather than flowing with the "movement of life" as in utero (*Exhausting Modernity*, 61–62). By thinking about these "points" as patterns of sensation and response, however, we can

4. Dance Is to Be Born

appreciate how they also enable flow in various directions and how some of those patterns can actually support us in adapting and following new pathways, especially in
response to ranges of challenge or conflict specific to where we are.

47. For Merleau-Ponty, a self constitutes itself in and through its own movement.
That movement returns to it as a quality, a potential, a property—a sense of "I-can"
(Sheets-Johnstone, *The Roots of Thinking*, 28–29). Yet, for Merleau-Ponty, "the body" remains an immanent quality that, ideally, remains transparent to one's self-transcending
intentions and projects (see Young, *On Female Body Experience*, for critique). In my
account, a bodily self is the movement of its own transcendence, where that transcendence appears as a potential for novelty inherent in the ongoing rhythm of bodily
becoming—a novelty that arises in the discontinuity of electrical activity animating
muscles twitches and brain synapses.

48. This crucial point is indebted to Nietzsche's *On the Genealogy of Morals*. The
materialist paradigm is as much an expression of our capacity to participate consciously in the rhythms of bodily becoming as is a philosophy of bodily becoming.
The difference concerns what we are creating. As a result, Nietzsche aligns his critique of Christian values as hostile to life with the trajectory of creation they represent in order to redirect that creativity in directions that affirm life instead.

49. Doidge, *The Brain That Changes Itself*, xix. Of course, the notion of "plasticity"
suggests that the brain is a subject that changes shape based on various pressures applied to it or various charges sent through it. A better metaphor might be "movability,"
signaling that the brain itself generates movement even as it suffers it.

50. Doidge acknowledges, "Neuroplasticity has the power to produce more flexible but also more rigid behaviors." He continues, "Once a particular plastic change
occurs in the brain and becomes well established, it can prevent other changes from
occurring" (*The Brain That Changes Itself*, xx). This "plastic paradox," as he calls it,
suggests why resistance to dance can prove so entrenched and why practice is needed to
exercise the flexibility and creativity of our movability. In a paper published on effects of various activities on dementia, only dancing scored as high as or higher than
"mental activities" for its ability to sustain healthy brain activity (Verghese et al.,
"Leisure Activities and the Risk of Dementia in the Elderly"). See discussion by
Stanford dance instructor Richard Powers.

51. Fogel confirms that embodied self-awareness, especially in a technological
culture, must be actively maintained, cultivated, taught, and renewed (*The Psychophysiology of Self-Awareness*, 13). Or, as he says, "You have to practice finding yourself
again and again" (101).

52. Duncan preferred to work with children, claiming that adults were too far immersed in mind over body ways of being to remember their ability to dance. "If we
are to bring about a renaissance of the art of dancing, it will not spring from the head

238

of any learned professor, but will rather bud forth from the joyous movements of children's bodies" (*Art of the Dance*, 76).

53. Duncan agreed that the practices of reading and writing impact our practices of dance: "very soon the movement is imposed from without by wrong theories of education, and the child soon loses its natural spontaneous life, and its power of expressing that in movement" (*Art of the Dance*, 77).

54. Nietzsche describes this phenomenon as "decadence": "The instincts are weakened. What one ought to shun is found attractive. One puts to one's lips what drives one yet faster into the abyss" (*The Birth of Tragedy and the Case of Wagner*, 165).

55. Brennan's call for extending consciousness into the body so as to cultivate a knowledge of how negative affects feed on and frustrate our living energy, freezing us into patterns of anxiety, anger, and conquest (*The Transmission of Affect*, 154), is one half of this task. The other consists in discerning how the movements we are making participate in those patterns of feeding and frustration in such a way that we remember our own our sensory creativity. At that point knowledge of how to move differently will emerge spontaneously in and through our bodily selves, rather than from—or at least alongside of—a process of analysis.

56. As Llinás affirms, even though a brain may function as a closed system, it is not "solipsistic," because it was built in the first place "by internalizing properties of the outside world" (*I of the Vortex*, 109). By cultivating a sensory awareness of our own movement making, then, we can create the situation in which our ever forming intrinsic kinetic images coordinate more fully and completely with the worlds in which we move.

57. Of course, its classic expression is Freud, in *Civilization and Its Discontents* (11), who takes this longing for granted as human.

58. Integral to Brennan's "foundational fantasy" is a repressed longing for the mother's breast expressed as a desire for instant gratification, for being nurtured, and for control over her as the source of comfort (*Exhausting Modernity*, 36).

Kristeva also describes this longing for the mother and its instrumental role, for example, in the evolution of Marian symbology. See her essay "Stabat Mater" (in *The Kristeva Reader*, 160–86).

5. To Dance Is to Connect

1. I introduced the term *impulse to connect* in an earlier work as a way to access the paradoxical dynamics of love in family relationships. In *Family Planting* I demonstrate how this idea formed in response to conflicts arising in my relationships with my parents, my partner, and our children as a guide to moving differently. Here I offer

the theoretical discussion of how and why dancing helps us exercise and educate this impulse to connect in life-enabling ways.

2. After analyzing the ratios representing the relationship of neocortex to overall brain size for a range of mammals, Robin Dunbar concludes that the human ration of 4:1 suggests that 150 "seems to represent the maximum number of individuals with whom we can have a genuinely social relationship" (*Grooming, Gossip, and the Evolution of Language*, 68–77).

3. As Dunbar writes, "Sociality is the very core of primate existence; it is their principal evolutionary strategy, the thing that marks them different from all other species. . . . It is based on intense bonds" (*Grooming, Gossip, and the Evolution of Language*, 18). To be human is to be born wanting and needing to belong to a community "that will treat them like kin" (Hrdy, *Mother Nature*, 531).

4. A question raised most pointedly by Søren Kierkegaard, in *Fear and Trembling* who insists that it is not. We may think we are individuals, but not until we make a choice—or take a leap of faith—do we distinguish ourselves. The guiding idea of this chapter is that we are individual and relational, and not simply or immediately either. We must become both as a function of how we dance.

5. Hrdy describes "interconnected, environmentally sensitive feedback loops" in which relational patterns linking mother and infant develop. While potentials for mutual nursing pleasure, for example, are latent in human bodily selves, individual mothers and infants learn what to feel and how to respond in relation to one another and their contexts (*Mother Nature*, 193–96). "Almost none of these biological responses are automatic" (378).

6. In a classic series of three books, John Bowlby sought to explain "the evolutionary origins of emotional attachment that humans forge with mothers and allomothers." For a discussion of his work and that of his associate, Mary Ainsworthy, see Hrdy, *Mother Nature*, 394–407. See also Bowlby's *Attachment* and Cassidy and Shaver's *The Handbook of Attachment Theory*. For one critique of Bowlby's work, see Hrdy, *Mothers and Others*, 82–92.

7. Siegel, *The Developing Mind*, chapter 3.

8. McNeill, *Keeping Time Together*, 23.

9. Émile Durkheim uses the term *general effervescence* to describe the phenomenon by which coordinated rhythmic movement allows participants to experience and then conceive of the power of the group as itself a "thing," a "moral power," a "god" (*The Elementary Forms of Religious Life*, 213–14).

10. Nicholas Wade argues that dance, as a form of proto-religion, exercises a genetic predisposition (seen in great apes) to empathy and reciprocity, and applies it in the service of moral restraint, social cohesion, and emotional commitment (*The Faith Instinct*, 33–39). He finds the closest analogue to ancestral religion in the dance

rituals of existing hunter-gatherer peoples whose sacred narratives convey moral and practical lessons.

Likewise, Josef Garfinkel, analyzing dance motifs from the art of agricultural societies, concludes: "Dance is thus an activity through which society instills collective discipline in its members. The participant in the dance accepts the rules of the community . . . internalizing discipline . . . through bodily activity" (*Dancing at the Dawn of Agriculture*, 80). Garfinkel notes that the success of agriculture as a means of production depended on this collective discipline (64).

11. Gerardus van der Leeuw, in *Sacred and Profane Beauty*, cites this function of dance to explain why the Christian tradition has been so hostile to dancing. It is not a fear of the body, per se, but a fear of sex. For discussion, see Hanna, *Dance, Sex, and Gender*.

12. Hrdy discusses how the cover of the paperback edition of John Bowlby's *Attachment*, published in 1971, featured an Amazonian Indian woman, nearly nude, walking with a basket on her head and a young child on her hip (*Mothers and Others*, 85). Bowlby used the example of such peoples to argue for continuous-care-and-contact for the first three or four years as the optimal form of child rearing.

13. Wade, for example, bases his argument about communal dancing as a first form of religion on studies of the Andaman Islanders, the !Kung or San people of South Africa, and the Australian aborigines (*The Faith Instinct*, chapter 5). He defends his comparison by pointing to the professed fidelity of these people to their traditions and genetic evidence of both continuity and isolation (99).

14. Durkheim is one of several exceptions in this regard. At the end of his account of religion and the rise of scientific thinking, he asks whether or not humans will still need the experience of undergoing ritual and actually feeling the feeling of collective effervescence (*The Elementary Forms of Religious Life*, 418–29). However, his notion of ritual does not explicitly entail rhythmic bodily movement or dancing. It should.

15. Hrdy affirms that human infants need more than just physical nurture. They seem to need a sense of being connected, of security or belonging (*Mothers and Others*, 115).

16. While many contemporary thinkers make the argument that humans are relational beings, few carry that analysis through to its implications for the importance of bodily movement in our sense of self. Compare Brennan: "all beings are connected energetically" (*Exhausting Modernity*, 41) and Haraway: "Beings do not pre-exist their relatings" (*The Companion Species Manifesto*, 6). Once we conceive of relationships as patterns of sensation and response, we can appreciate how important a sensory awareness of the movements making us is for tapping our sensory creativity in the service of relationships that move us to become in individual ways. For examples arising in relations with parents, partners, and progeny, see LaMothe, *Family Planting*.

17. A parallel example of this dynamic is found John Blacking's analysis of the music of the Venda, a people in South Africa. Music, Blacking writes, is "humanly organized sound" performed to produce a "soundly organized humanity by enhancing human consciousness" (*How Musical Is Man?* 100). Yet that organization is not a matter of yoking individuals in common action. Rather, by making music together people make the community real as the enabling condition of their individual selves. "When they [the Venda] share the experience of an invisible conductor in their drumming and singing and pipe playing, they become more aware of society's system of active forces, and their own consciousness is enhanced" (107). The music, in other words, enacts (both represents and exercises) the relationships that are needed for any individual musician to play. It makes those relationships real as the enabling condition for that person to become an individual who can and does contribute to the good of the whole. Speaking of *tshikona*, a traditional Venda ritual involving music and dance, he writes, "because of the quality of the relationships that must be established between people and tones whenever it is performed . . . it is an example of the production of the maximum of available human energy in a situation that generates the highest degree of individuality in the largest possible community of individuals" (51). Although Blacking focuses on music, he does mention that, in some cases at least, music is taught through "symbolic dances" that are physically strenuous and rhythmically complex (39). Thus the way is clear to make a case for dance analogous to his for music.

18. Merleau-Ponty illustrates this point in his essay, "The Child's Relation with Others" (*The Primacy of Perception,* 140).

19. The organizing structure and principal ideas for this section of the chapter took shape during hours spent caring for my fifth child, Leif, born June 14, 2009.

20. Fogel says as much when he affirms, "the body is a complex dynamic system . . . a process . . . never completely at rest" (*The Psychophysiology of Self-Awareness,* 41–42).

21. Merleau-Ponty affirms that "psychogenesis" begins and a newborn infant starts to develop consciousness "by being interoceptive"—that is, with a visceral awareness felt in the body that is not bounded by or even tied to a sense of being a body (*The Primacy of Perception,* 121). It is, as Merleau-Ponty affirms, a "question of differences" (124). That visceral awareness, as we have seen, is itself a function of movement.

22. Hrdy affirms that "the first regions of the neocortex to form in utero are those that eventually represent and control sucking actions by the mouth and tongue" (*Mothers and Others,* 40). The potential for making these womb-readied movements is thus awakened by the movement of nipple or breast toward the infant, who then, in the making of those movements, discovers new sensations.

23. Fogel identifies this process where a brain creates feeling out of sensation as a process of "rerepresentation" in which a brain communicates with itself (*The Psychophysiology of Self-Awareness*, 60). I would qualify that this "rerepresentation" acts as a layering, which is also a refining and thickening of the kinetic image any sensation is. No separate or separable feeling exists, but rather the quality or meaning of the movement itself changes.

24. In psychological parlance, this dynamic is one of "coregulating" and can occur with and without conscious participation. Coregulating with an adult via movement and touch, according to Fogel, is an infant's primary state (*The Psychophysiology of Self-Awareness*, 174). A 2013 study in *Current Biology* documents how infants, under age six months, when carried by a walking (as opposed to sitting) caregiver, immediately stop voluntary movement, cease crying, and experience a rapid decrease in heart rate (Esposito et al. "Infant Calming Responses").

25. Hrdy debunks the idea that any aspect of mothering is "natural" and discloses how lactation provides both the need and the chance for developing a peculiarly human social intelligence (*Mother Nature*, 145). Blakeslee and Blakeslee also affirm that mirror neurons kick in within minutes of birth throughout the brain (*The Body Has a Mind of Its Own*, 172), providing newborn infants with a way to process perceptions of other people's movements through their own sensory awareness.

26. This quality of a movement to give rise to another movement is one that Erin Manning describes in terms of "preacceleration": "the virtual force of movement's taking form, the feeling of movement's ingathering, a welling that propels the directionality of how movement moves." Every movement, in other words, is a "pulsion toward" (*Relationscapes*, 6). Note too that pulsion is a function of the directionality of movement itself. The "toward" is given as a forward projection of the "from," altered as it is by other forces operating in the "now." The same is true for an impulse to connect, which includes a sense of connecting with the possibilities for sensory pleasure present in the moment.

27. At this point my analysis aligns with that of Massumi, who writes: "The 'unity' of objects over their constituents is, paradoxically, borrowed from the body's movement. Objects are the way in which the body's slowness is expressed in perceptual fusion" (*Parables of the Virtual*, 149). I would add that the "constituents" of that object are itself the movement possibilities it opens for one who is willing to play; and that "slowness," an allusion to Spinoza, Deleuze, and Guattari, is only one of the movement patterns of a bodily self that enables "it" to appear.

28. As Merleau Ponty writes of a child, beginning around six months: "Our perceptions arouse in us a reorganization of motor conduct, without our already having learned the gestures in question" (*The Primacy of Perception*, 145).

29. This analysis lends support to Massumi's claim that "objects are anaesthetic specifications of the growth pain of perception's passing into and out of itself" (*Parables of the Virtual*, 161). Simply to conceive of an object, in this sense, is to know some relief from the felt pain of not actively enjoying the potential for pleasure that relationship (with it) yields. However, perception is not merely "passing into and out of itself." Rather, patterns of movements made enable a perception that is both a sensation and an inner response to that sensation.

30. Replace "body" with "bodily movement," and this sentence of Merleau Ponty's illuminates this dynamic: "The child's own body is for him a way of understanding other bodies through 'postural impregnation.' . . . The child's person . . . is in a way scattered through all the images his action gives rise to, and it is because of this that he is apt to recognize himself in everything" (*The Primacy of Perception*, 150). This "postural impregnation" is the dynamic by which our movements into the world create a deepening sense of self within, moving us to move with them.

31. Reporting on a research study, Fogel confirms that an "infant's ability to become aware of their own feelings, intentions, and emotions depended upon the adults' ability to 'recognize' that feeling in the infant and respond" (*The Psychophysiology of Self-Awareness*, 183), a recognition that manifests as a moving toward and moving with in response to an infant's sensations of pleasure and pain.

32. According to V. K. Ramachandran, mirror neurons "appear to be the evolutionary key to our attainment of full culture" for the way in which they allow us "to adopt each other's point of view and empathize with one another" (*The Tell-Tale Brain*, xv–xvi; chapter 4).

33. In *Choreographing Empathy*, dance scholar Susan Foster critiques the assumption that mirror neurons allow for a direct and unmediated visceral response to movement activity. She argues that our ability to see and sense and respond to movement patterns in others is thoroughly conditioned by cultural experiences and social relations. My reading supports her view.

34. The Blakeslees gesture in this direction when they affirm: "Your mirror neurons make dance appreciation possible" because you can have the feeling of making the movements yourself (*The Body Has a Mind of Its Own*, 170). This feature is not a fortuitous side effect, I would add. It is the reason the mirror neurons evolved in humans as they have.

35. Recounting the experiments of Hugo Critchley, the Blakeslees conclude: "The more viscerally aware, the more emotionally attuned you are" (*The Body Has a Mind of Its Own*, 181).

36. Fogel confirms that mirror neurons can "generate efferent signals to the muscles that lead us to make similar, imitative movements." He adds that, "via practice and continued observation, body schema self-awareness can expand" (*The Psychophysiology of Self-Awareness*, 207). The point here is that the capacity of mirror neurons to

respond is not given. It can be developed, with the effects of improving our ability to sense and respond to movement impulses. We can cultivate a sensory awareness of the movements making us. We can cultivate a vulnerability to the dynamic process by which our movement creates a sense of earth within.

37. Note that I am not assuming that such practice will yield a uniform ability or that one kind of practice will suffice for all. Every person has a unique potential and capacity to understand a unique set of others given the unique set of movements he or she has made and been made by. A person of a culture who is an expert in its movements may discern and understand and be moved by a given performance to a different degree than someone without that training and experience. However, even someone without that training and experience will be able to perceive and be moved by aspects of the movement that activate her training and experience.

38. Walter, *Thumbs, Toes, and Tears,* 68.

39. Walter's words about laughter resonate here: "a baby's laugh provides a powerful emotional gift that encourages her care. The more laughter, the more bonding; the more bonding, the better the chances of survival. It sparks a potent feedback loop" (*Thumbs, Toes, and Tears,* 150).

40. As Hrdy claims, "The first social bonds ever forged were between a mother and her offspring" (*Mothers and Others,* 41). She also supports the idea that those bonds consisted primarily of movement patterns. She cites developmental psychologist Andrew Meltzoff: "infants' connection to others emerges from the fact that the bodily movement patterns they see others perform are coded like the ones they themselves perform" (49).

41. Hrdy explains this fact as evidence that humans, as opposed to other contemporary primates, evolved from a line of cooperative breeders. As she affirms, in primates "early flickerings of empathic interest—what might even be termed tentative quests for intersubjective engagement—fade away instead of developing and intensifying as they do in human children" (*Mothers and Others,* 58). In conditions of cooperative breeding, that intensification was critical to a child's ability to read multiple people's faces and engage their attentions.

42. The implication here is not that dancers are "more ethical" humans, only that participation in the study of a particular dance necessarily educates our moral sensibilities to certain values. The cast of values into which a dancer is educated depends on the culture and tradition and methods of training and practice.. Here again, my aim is not to privilege one technique or tradition of dance as more or less ethical, but rather to provide ways of asking about what the practice of dance is creating and may potentially create.

6. To Dance Is to Heal

1. Exceptions prove the rule. See "Painless," *New York Times Magazine*, November 15, 2012.

2. Examples of those who do appear later in this chapter.

3. See ritual theorist Ronald Grimes: "Ritual is one of the oldest forms of human activity we know. It may have been the original multimedia performance—an archaic, unifying activity. It not only integrated storytelling, dance, and performance, but it also provided the matrix out of which other cultural activities such as art, medicine, and education gradually emerged, differentiating themselves from one another" (*Deeply Into the Bone*, 13).

4. This cast of the categories and their separation from one another again pledge allegiance to a materialist perspective, implying that a pain can be one or the other.

5. As psychologist/anthropologist Bradford Keeney affirms, the problem with much therapy is that it presumes "a material world of physical objects obeying the laws of force and energy" (*Aesthetics of Change*, 12).

6. Commenting on the power of mental factors in illness, Harvard psychologist Ellen Langer goes so far as to ask: "What would happen if we considered all illness to be psychosomatic?" (*Counterclockwise*, 189). She urges people to embrace the power of their minds over their bodies as an enabler of good bodily health (121).

7. David Jones gives an excellent example of this dynamic in his history of cardiac care in the twentieth century. He describes how bypass surgery and angioplasty were introduced and used liberally without clinical trials because "the logic of the procedure was self-evident. . . . You have a plugged vessel, you bypass the plug, you fix the problem, end of story." The trials, when eventually completed, revealed that neither procedure lengthens life. Jones summarizes: "The gap between what patients and doctors expect from these procedures, and the benefit that they actually provide, shows the profound impact of a certain kind of mechanical logic in medicine. . . . If doctors think a treatment *should* work, they come to believe that it *does* work, even when the clinical evidence isn't there" ("A Cardiac Conundrum," 26).

8. For the classic text in dance therapy, written by its modern-day "founder," see Chace et al., *Foundations of Dance/Movement Therapy*.

9. This description of dance as facilitating a coming together of body and mind pops up everywhere in contemporary culture, among scholars too. Roszak, for example, describes shamanism as a mode of healing in which "body and mind participate" (*The Voice of the Earth*, 79). See also Halprin, *Dance as a Healing Art*; Lesho and McMaster, *Dancing on the Earth*.

10. Even in cases where healing modalities call practitioners to pay attention to their sensory selves and honor their feelings as guides for action, it is generally as-

sumed that the "actor" who goes on to formulate the "plan of action" is a conscious thinking mind. Dancing, in this sense, stirs up feelings with which I can then deal. In a movement paradigm, an "I" disciplines itself to the rhythms of bodily becoming.

11. One prominent exception to this statement is the work of Alan Fogel in *The Psychophysiology of Self-Awareness*. While not focusing on dance per se, his book provides a psychophysiological rationale for why bodywork of various kinds is effective. As is evident, I rely heavily on his work in conceiving my case for dance as healing art.

12. "An emotion requires sensing the body feelings as well as whether those feelings are liked or disliked, and what those feelings make one want to do" (Fogel, *The Psychophysiology of Self-Awareness*, 40).

13. As Chip Walter confirms, the ideas we think arise out of our sensory awareness. They arise out of the feelings we feel as a reflection upon them. This reflection, in turn, is a function of movement itself, and one that serves to expand and elaborate how those emotions are and can be felt. As he writes: "Our emotional life is more complicated and enriched because of our intelligence" (*Thumbs, Toes, and Tears*, 139).

14. Fogel alludes to this complexity when he describes pain as a "state of self-awareness" (*The Psychophysiology of Self-Awareness*, 163), where that self-awareness spans thoughts, emotions, and sensations. The implication, of course, is that changes in self-awareness can produce changes in sensations of pain and even effect their disappearance, as Fogel describes in terms of bodywork and this chapter explores in terms of bodily movement or dance.

15. Roszak alludes to a similar process when he describes the pain of living in an industrial society as expressing an "impulse to change" (*The Voice of the Earth*, 47). Here the pain is both relational and itself a source of wisdom as to the kind of changes that must occur. It is, I would add, a function of the movements we are making.

16. Fogel affirms the point I am making in this section when he writes that feeling pain "activates the homeostatic recovery system of the body. . . . Feeling it with more clarity improves results" (*The Psychophysiology of Self-Awareness*, 161). Conversely, if we practice ignoring the pain, we shut down our own healing action, initiating a looping cycle of dysfunction and avoidance. Fogel writes, "the threat . . . begins to come from within the body" (144) in the form of pain itself. In other words, attempts to ignore pain generally manifest as more pain.

17. Human minds, Keeney affirms, are embodied in conversations, families, and ecosystems. Any healing must account for these "patterns of interaction" (*Aesthetics of Change*, 38). Such ecological healing, according to Keeney, happens when the therapist helps generate random possibilities that inspire people to create alternative patterns of interacting with one another (135). This chapter describes how dancing can serve such a function.

18. For example, speaking of classification-based Cognitive Functional Therapy (CB-CRT), a new patient-centered approach to managing chronic back pain, Peter O'Sullivan writes, "the solutions that 'stick' are usually found by the person themselves." In the research study of which he was a part, CB-CRT produced superior outcomes to traditional approaches of manual therapy and exercise (Vibe Fersum et al. "Efficacy of Classification-Based Cognitive Functional Therapy"). He adds: "This approach . . . requires confidence that pain is to be respected but not feared. It also requires trust and engagement on the part of the person with pain" (quotes in O'Sullivan).

19. Writing about what he has learned in the process of becoming a shaman in the oldest living culture in the world, the !Kung of the African Kalahari, Bradford Keeney affirms "the solution to a problem in life is stepping more fully into life" (*Bushman Shaman*, 40). In their dancing ritual, "Shamans first move the locus of mind to the heart and whole body rather than to the inside of the computational cerebral brain. This whole-body knowing is, in turn, a vehicle for stepping into relational mind, allowing for 'the other' to be felt in more intimate and expressive ways." Dancing thus "brings us into the mind of nature, an ecology that holds diverse ways of knowing and being." As Keeney confirms: "Then it is life that heals" (39). I offer an explanation for how and why dancing enables "life" to heal.

20. Daniel Chamovitz explains how plants have a "procedural memory" that involves storing and recalling patterns of sensation and response and is associated with "anoetic consciousness." In his view plants are conscious, but not symbolically self-conscious (*What a Plant Knows*, 132; chapter 6).

21. Note again that I am not appealing to a "pure experience" of pain, but rather, acknowledging that any experience of pain we have is always already a result of the movements we are making and of the movements that are making us. Nor am I making a claim that applies to all extant forms of dancing. Because experience is always relational, there is always the danger that our capacity for sensing can be conditioned in ways that divert us from our health—even by forms of dance. Yet our capacity for sensing is also, when carefully cultivated, our one and only source of body-wise resistance. Here I align with Elizabeth Grosz who affirms against social constructivists that, "without some acknowledgement of the formative role of experience in the establishment of knowledges, feminism has no grounds from which to dispute patriarchal [or materialist] norms" (quoted in Young, *On the Female Body Experience*, 9).

22. As noted, Donald argues that that act of dancing signals a cognitive capacity of mimesis that would have corresponded with the ability of Homo erectus to make and use tools. Hrdy, writing about the same general time period, locates the emergence of this "imitative competency" within the mother-infant relationship, thus suggesting a coevolutionary connection between dancing and the formation of intimate relations in Homo erectus (*Mothers and Others*, 58–59).

23. Grimes echoes this idea: "The ability to invent meaningful rites depends to a large degree on our ability to attend, to be fully and unreservedly present. Ritual is not just a way of acting, it is also a kind of awareness, a form of consciousness" (*Deeply Into the Bone*, 71).

24. Note that this narrative does not assume that every attempt to dance in response to pain was successful or effective. All that was necessary was for someone to feel some relief—enough to be willing to repeat the action. As Langer affirms, "only one participant is needed to prove that something is possible" (*Counterclockwise*, 17); once that possibility is established, it becomes a beacon for others to create a new reality. As Langer continues: "Too many of us believe the world is to be discovered rather than a product of our own construction and thus to be invented" (18). In the movement of dancing, humans do both—discovering what it is possible to create.

25. Comparing San Bushmen art and the art of the first agricultural village communities, Garfinkel notes that the San art tends to feature an individual—possibly the shaman of a community—and that when more than one individual is portrayed the movements are diverse, not uniform as they are in village art. While it is unclear— and always will be—whether the first dances were "individual" or "communal" in nature, the art evidence suggests that dancing became more strictly communal and formalized in the context of agricultural societies (*Dancing at the Dawn of Agriculture*, 73ff).

26. Fogel notes that whole body movements "are better at communicating emotional intensity and level of arousal" compared to the face alone; whole body movements are "more likely to activate the entire neural network for interoception, body schema, and emotion in the perceiver" (*The Psychophysiology of Self-Awareness*, 222). This finding suggests that humans evolved a capacity to move together as a way to activate within one another the sensory creativity needed to address the causes and symptoms of their own pain. Here the "coregulation" that occurs between infant and caregiver through movement and touch expands into rhythmic, kinetic, communal patterns.

27. Fraleigh explains that dancing yields an experience of freedom that grounds knowledge of ourselves as agents or subjects: "As we express our embodiment in dancing, we create it aesthetically and experience it more freely. Dance frees us from the constraints of our practical lives and utilitarian movement. In short, we experience a sheer freedom in dance as we move free of any practical outcome" (*Dance and the Lived Body*, 17). I add that a sense of self arises from a lived experience of receiving, imagining, and making movements that effect transformation not only of external environments but of our very bodily selves—of our pain.

28. McNeill, for example, in line with other notable anthropologists and scholars of religion, suggests that the lived experience of community dancing gave rise to the

idea of a "vital spirit" that is separable from the body, can leave during sleep and death, and is capable of meeting others in an alternate space and time. He calls this idea one of human's greatest "intellectual accomplishments" (*Keeping Together in Time*, 45).

29. This logic is common in an analysis of tools—of which, I argue, pain-relieving movement patterns were one kind. Once we create a movement potential, that movement potential exists within us as a need for the kind of sensory engagement or relationship that exercises it. Replace tools with "movement patterns" and the Blakeslees' point holds: "Humans have enriched their body mandalas . . . to the extent that we require—and even seek out with insatiable, instinctive hunger—rich sensorimotor interaction with tools starting in infancy" (*The Body Has a Mind of Its Own*, 145). A body mandala is "tightly integrated network of body maps" (13)—that is, of patterns of movement potential—that make up our sensory awareness of our (selves as) bodily selves.

30. Take for example, Grimes: "By *ritual* I mean *sequences of ordinary action rendered special by virtue of their condensation, elevation, or stylization*" (*Deeply Into the Bone*, 71). The emphasis here and elsewhere is on action that is distinguished by the manner in which it is done, the uses to which it is put, and/or the contexts in which it appears.

31. Catherine Bell provides an historical survey of ritual theories in part 1 of her book *Ritual*. Key to her definition is that ritual is a "complex sociocultural medium" that is chosen to invoke "ordered relationships" between human and "non-immediate sources of power, authority, and value" via a "vocabulary of gesture and word" (*Ritual*, xi). In Bell's theory, dance is one of many multisensory elements that can accompany the act of ritualizing.

32. Asad argues that scholars of religion assume the latter, while neglecting the former, to the detriment of their own understanding. As he explains, "Symbols . . . call for interpretation. . . . Disciplinary practices . . . cannot be varied so easily, because learning to develop moral capabilities is not the same thing as learning to invent representations" (*Genealogies of Religion*, 79). He further reveals a scholarly materialist motive: we want to believe ritual is a symbolic action, because, if it is, we can "capture the essence" of ritual without actually doing it: "All that is required is the attempt to understand, with 'sympathy and respect as well as openness to the sources,' what . . . rituals 'portray and symbolize'" (79).

33. Speaking of the formation of *habitus*, Bourdieu underlines the importance of people moving together for the constitution of the group as a group: "The reason why submission to the collective rhythms is so rigorously demanded is that the temporal forms or the spatial structures structure not only the group's representation of the world but the group itself, which orders itself in accordance with this representation" (*Outline of a Theory of Practice*, 163).

6. To Dance Is to Heal

34. In response to Eliade's claim that ritual serves to orient humans in time and space (*The Myth of Eternal Return*) and Turner's claim that ritual serves to solidify social structures (*The Ritual Process*), Smith (*To Take Place*) and Taylor (*After God*) who argue that religion is just as likely to dis-place and dis-order.

35. Geertz raises this possibility in his essay "Religion as a Cultural System" (*The Interpretation of Culture*, 87–125).

36. In trying to imagine and recreate the earliest forms of ritual dancing, scholars look to the examples of remaining hunter-gatherer cultures, assuming that their cultures, unaffected by practices of agriculture and literacy, have remained more or less the same since 12,000 BCE. These practices generally involve all members of the community, male and female, young and old, accompanied by music/drums, engaging in rhythmic movement around a circle as part of a periodic nighttime event, during which at least some members of the group enter a trance state (e.g., Garfinkel, *Dancing at the Dawn of Agriculture*, chapter 3). My interest is to explain the assumed "religious" character of these dances in terms of how the movement-making catalyzes conscious participation in the rhythms of bodily becoming.

37. First articulated by anthropologist Arnold van Gennep in his *The Rites of Passage*, and elaborated by Turner in *The Ritual Process*, chapter 3.

38. Turner, *The Ritual Process*, 96–97.

39. Ibid., 94–130.

40. De Certeau frames the point I am opposing in these terms. In a materialist approach to studying ritual, "The unconsciousness of the group studied was the price that had to be paid (the price it had to pay) for its coherence. A society could be a system without knowing it. Whence the corollary: an ethnologist was required to know what the society was without knowing it" (*The Practice of Everyday Life*, 56).

41. For example, the case of the Ndembu Isoma ritual that occupies the first chapter of Turner's book concerns a woman who has been unable to conceive a child. She and her husband engage in a ritual designed to help her exorcise the demonic forces that must be preventing pregnancy. The process, Turner explains, involves a clear articulation and affirmation of *communitas* (*The Ritual Process*, chapter 1, 3).

42. Speaking to this issue of how making the movements of another educates our senses, Abram writes: "Traditional, tribal magicians or medicine persons . . . seek to augment the limitations of their specifically human senses by binding their attention to the ways of another animal . . . The more studiously an apprentice magician watch the other creature . . . learning to mimic its cries and to dance its various movements, the more thoroughly his nervous system is joined to another set of senses—thereby gaining a kind of stereoscopic access to the world" (*Becoming Animal*, 217).

43. Bell demonstrates such an interpretation of repetition, or "invariance," in ritual when she describes that its significance "lies in the simple means by which precise

duplication of action subordinates the individual and the contingent to a sense of the encompassing and the enduring" (*Ritual*, 153).

44. Reginald Ray describes this idea from a Buddhist perspective: "To be awake, to be enlightened, is to be fully and completely embodied" (*Touching Enlightenment*, xv).

45. Ray, for example, describes somatic practices of Buddhist meditation whose repetition allows us to "discover that the life we need to live is actually being born, moment by moment, within the emptiness of the body . . . as the energy that arises" (53). The somatic practices he describes involve cultivating a sensory awareness of what we are feeling and finding, in the pain, an impulse to move differently. As he writes, "simply becoming aware of the discomfort means that movement has begun" (75). We reconnect with a movement of healing and compassion ever arising in ourselves—with a wilderness within us—and thus touch enlightenment.

46. Fogel confirms that the "failure or inability to consult our embodied self-awareness is one of the pathways for the emergence of physical disease in the body" (*The Psychophysiology of Self-Awareness*, 100). Insofar as ritual promotes a sensory awareness of the movement making us, it thus acts as a prophylactic against future health-depleting agents.

47. Bell implies as much when she describes how the "goal of ritualization is completely circular: the creation of a ritualized agent, an actor with a form of ritual mastery, who embodied flexible sets of cultural schemes and can deploy them effectively in multiple situations so as to restructure those situations in practical ways" (*Ritual*, 81). I would add, but it is not *merely* circular, and those "flexible sets of cultural schemes" are best conceived as *kinetic images*—patterns of potential movement.

48. Katherine Dunham, dancer and anthropologist, in *Dances of Haiti*, writes about her study of Haitian voudou, a danced religion. As a dancer, she was able to learn the dances for each loa quickly and perform them with a full physicality that the Haitians recognized as proof of her favor with the gods. She was initiated as a priestess or mambo in the community. As she recounts, the importance of what she believed paled in relation to how she danced; and in her dancing, as she discovered, the spirits became real for her.

49. For further discussion of transformation in ritual dance, see LaMothe, "Transformation."

50. The American Ruth St. Denis, inspired by classical religious dances of South East Asia and the Middle East, claimed that, when dancing as a goddess, she would *become* the goddess. While many have accused her of cultural imperialism and naive essentialism, it is also possible to affirm that St. Denis, in making movements that evoked patterns of sensation and response associated with a goddess—whether or not they were "authentic"—gave life to this kinetic image as a medium through which a

person could experience Her in the way that St. Denis did: as a catalyst to conscious participation in the rhythms of (her own sensory) creativity. See LaMothe, "Passionate Madonna."

51. Speaking of the Rosen Method, Fogel writes that "healing manifests as a reclaiming of movements" (*The Psychophysiology of Self-Awareness*, 215). The same is true for ritual dancing. When healing happens, the movements that are "reclaimed" are those that succeed in expressing mutually enabling relationships connecting an individual human and her community. I would add that movement is not simply reclaimed. As healing happens, new patterns are discovered and remembered.

52. See Grimes: "Though not a rite like an indigenous healer might perform, the interaction between patient and doctor is heavily ritualized" (*Deeply Into the Bone*, 343).

7. To Dance Is to Love

1. Zukav mirrors the connections I am drawing in this chapter between a matter-based perspective and an inability to conceive of the ecological import of dancing: "The idea that objects exist apart from event is part of the epistemological net with which we snare our particular form of experience. The idea is dear to us because we have accepted it, without question, as the basis of our reality. It profoundly influences how we see ourselves" and, as I have shown, how we value dancing. He continues, "It is the root of our inescapable sense of separateness from others and the environment" (*The Dancing Wu Li Masters*, 279).

2. Sheets-Johnstone asserts that the tendency to conceive of nature as something "out there" for us to control is based on a "corporeal archetype" given in the bipedal stance of a human male displaying an erect penis. When we conceive of nature as out there, she affirms, we miss the miraculousness of nature in us and around us (*The Roots of Power*, 333).

3. Roszak describes the "madness" of the city as a "wishful biological independence from the natural environment" (*The Voice of the Earth*, 219).

4. Many theorists across fields affirm that the distinction between nature and culture is a social, cultural construction. Haraway, for example, coins the term *natureculture* to express the inseparability of the two terms (*The Companion Species Manifesto*, chapter 1).

5. Here I am close to Massumi, who writes, "Nature and culture are in mutual movement into and through each other. Their continuum is a dynamic unity of reciprocal variation" (*Parables of the Virtual*, 11)—a dynamic unity, I would add, that is best understood and engaged via the study and practice of dance.

6. The point here is not that there is no difference between animal, vegetable, and mineral, but rather that no "thing" or "body" ever stays the same and that the way in which it "becomes" is specific to the movement patterns it inherits and exerts. Even though animals and plants can heal and rebuild their bodily selves in ways that rocks cannot, both are subject to change based on forces at work within and without. For similar discussion, see Abram, *Becoming Animal*, 46–56.

7. As Abram describes it, a bodily self "is a sort of open circuit that completes itself only in things, in others, in the encompassing earth" (*The Spell of the Sensuous*, 62). Those "things" and "others" are the natural and cultural movement patterns on which any singular life depends.

8. The logic here is familiar to those working in the wake of G. W. F. Hegel. For Hegel, human Reason is where Spirit becomes conscious of itself as Spirit. Others have elaborated on this logic, claiming that human self-consciousness or self-knowledge is where the earth becomes conscious of itself. Roszak, for example, quotes de Chardin: "the universe attains self-consciousness in the human mind" (*The Voice of the Earth*, 198). For me, that "self-knowledge" is a sensory awareness of ourselves as participating in the rhythms of bodily becoming—a knowledge realized in dance. In what follows I am most inspired by Isadora Duncan. See LaMothe, *Nietzsche's Dancers*, chapter 4.

9. Recall Wade, who argues that language, dance, music, and religion coevolved. Dancing, he adds, "being mostly just rhythmic movement, seems the most ancient" (*The Faith Instinct*, 88). In this chapter I revisit this idea of coevolution and suggest that language, music, and religion are more than "just rhythmic movement" in a way that dancing itself enables.

10. As Abram concurs: "As we reacquaint ourselves with our breathing bodies, then the perceived world itself begins to shift and transform," coaxing our breathing body into a new "dance" (*Becoming Animal*, 63): "the recuperation of the incarnate, sensorial dimension of experience brings with it a recuperation of the living landscape in which we are corporeally embedded" (65). Such reacquainting and recuperating, I add, not only coaxes us into a (metaphorical) dance, it requires it.

11. In defining this task, I draw inspiration from many sources and aim to advance the project along trajectories we share. For example, ecofeminist philosopher Warren, writing about the First Nation Peoples, observes that "prayer and dance are two familiar ways the powers of nonhuman natural beings were acknowledged and respected" (*Ecofeminist Philosophy*, 86). At the heart of Warren's ecofeminist ethic is care. Without the "ability to care," she insists, we cannot be moral (112). The implication—though she does not tease it out—is that the act of dancing can help humans learn to care about the more than human world. This chapter explains how and why that might be so.

12. Tomasello, "The Human Adaptation for Culture," 510.

13. A distinction elaborated by Tomasello to distinguish the unique features of human culture and its accumulation and transmission of movement patterns over time (ibid., 520).

14. This "theory of mind" describes an ability "to understand what another individual is thinking, to ascribe beliefs, desires, fears, and hopes to someone else, and to believe that they really do experience these feelings as mental states" (Dunbar, *Grooming, Gossip, and the Evolution of Language*, 83). Dunbar calls this ability, "beyond question, our most important asset" (101).

15. Tomasello, "The Human Adaptation for Culture," 520.

16. McNeill argues that the discovery of dancing marked a "critical transformation" in communication at emotional and symbolic levels that improved the "carrying capacity" of information networks (*Keeping Together in Time*, 33–34). I would add that the information that could be "carried" was precisely the patterns of movement that humans found life-enabling.

17. This argument aligns with one made by Carrie Noland, who affirms that "kinesthetic experience"—namely, "a body's ability to feel itself move" —can provide a site for resisting social conditioning by encouraging variations and innovations in the production of culture. As she writes, "gestures, learned techniques of the body, are the means by which cultural conditioning is simultaneously embodied and put to the test" (*Agency and Embodiment*, 2–3).

18. Indigenous cultures and hunter-gatherer cultures regularly feature gods and goddesses who bear a special relationship to the land, the local earth, in which the community lives. As Tikva Frymer-Kensky confirms of Mesopotamia's early agricultural communities, gods and goddesses "were immanent in all the forces of nature" (*In the Wake of the Goddesses*, 45).

19. Through acts of communal ritual dancing, Garfinkel writes, "Agricultural village societies . . . [were] linked in a direct bond to the forces of nature, and their awareness of nature's cycle was heightened. The uniform rhythmic movement of the figures in a circle . . . is an imitation of the most basic processes of nature: the lunar cycle, the seasonal cycle, and the growth and death cycle of plants" (*Dancing at the Dawn of Agriculture*, 64). He continues, "the community rituals, symbolized by dance, were the basic mechanism for distributing education and knowledge to the adult members of the community and from one generation to the other" (97). He further suggests that the act of ritual dancing fulfilled "the functions of writing, including the transmission of information, teaching, and documentation" (92).

20. Among his litany of reasons for why direct experience of nature matters, Richard Louv argues that "nature inspires creativity . . . by demanding visualization and the full use of the senses" (*Last Child in the Woods*, 7). Such "fully activated senses" he adds are necessary in order for us to "feel fully alive" (58). Yet simply setting oneself in "nature" is not sufficient for activating our sensory potential. Nor is there a "full"

spectrum to activate. The sensory realms we are able to activate and the spectrum we are able to perceive both depend on how we move our bodily selves.

21. While Garfinkel claims that dancing in early agricultural villages served to educate people's senses to the rhythms and cycles of the natural world, he assumes a nature "out there" such that the act of this "education" is one of "domestication." "The formalized body positions and the strictly regulated direction of movement symbolized the acceptance of the social order by the individual" (*Dancing at the Dawn of Agriculture*, 93). See complementary perspective to this position in chapter 6.

22. "The senses . . . are the primary way that the earth has of informing our thoughts and of guiding our actions" (Abram, *The Spell of the Sensuous*, 268). I would add: the senses, as awakened and brought to life through the action of dancing.

23. Here, as in ecofeminist philosophy (or shamanistic spirituality), the point is not just to conceptualize the interconnections among all beings; the point is rather to be able to act in ways "that maintain, promote, or enhance the health of relevant parties" (Warren, *Ecofeminist Philosophy*, 115).

24. Louv points out that the word *nature* comes from the word *nasci*, meaning, "to be born" (*Last Child in the Woods*, 8). This idea resonates with the discussion in chapter 4 as well. Nature is a being born. We are nature being born.

25. The following narrative about the emergence of culture is schematic. It is designed to function as a template that can be laid over contrasting theories of culture so as to illuminate the importance of dancing to and as culture. Moreover, as a schema, it is not strictly speaking historical, but represents a trajectory of becoming that occurs again and again in human history as active nodes of culture-creation take shape, mature, and wither.

26. This section is written with two historical arcs in mind: the emergence of symbolic culture in 40,000 BCE through 12,000 BCE and the first twelve thousand years of human history in the Near East, beginning with the agricultural revolution and the first urban centers around 11,000 BCE and extending to the rise of Christianity in the first centuries of the Common Era. It is generally believed that dancing was a central component of human culture from its earliest hunter/gatherer moments through the agricultural revolution, at least until the advent of alphabetic writing. At that point its significance changed in ways the following narrative suggests. Again, however, the logic of cultural development described here repeats throughout human history.

27. "The multiple ritual enactments, the initiatory ceremonies, the annual songs and dances of the hunt and the harvest—all are ways whereby indigenous peoples-of-place actively engage the rhythms of the more-than-human cosmos, and thus embed their own rhythms within those of the vaster round" (Abram, *The Spell of the Sensuous*, 187).

28. In her analysis of the songs of lamentation sung by goddesses, for example, Frymer-Kensky notes that the language of these laments describes intense bodily

movements such as clawing, tearing, smiting, and crying out. She suggests that "the people of Mesopotamia, hearing the poems, may have entered the occasion and experienced and manifested their grief by performing those same dramatic actions" (*In the Wake of the Goddesses*, 37–38). The perspective of bodily becoming explains how the performance of these actions allows people to feel what they otherwise could not in a way that releases their sensory creativity to find in that pain an impulse to move and to affirm life.

29. This logic parallels the development of an infant as described in chapters 4 and 5. Support for making this connection comes from scholars such as Donald, who suggests that the discovery and development of an ability to dance laid the cognitive groundwork for the emergence of language (*Origins of the Modern Mind*, 168–69).

30. By focusing on ideas, I sidestep the question of whether we need words in order to think ideas. It may be that words evolved in tandem with patterns of bodily movement in a dynamic that Ramachandran names "synkinesia" (*The Tell-Tale Brain*, 172–73). While making remembered, rehearsed bodily movements, a hominid may have engaged in internal movements of mouth and throat that echoed full body movements. Synkinesia describes a cross-activation of brain maps. As we have seen, in Broca's area the maps for speech making and motor movement are next to one another. If we further appreciate that what early hominids noticed about tools was the pattern of movement using it required, and confirm that movement patterns themselves were our first tools, then it may be that words and ideas form together as a resonant echo and future enabler of effective bodily movements. As Ramachandran claims: "early hominins had a built-in, preexisting mechanism for spontaneously translating gestures into words" (173).

31. In these reflections I am always aware that, in the words of Jonathan Z. Smith, "there is no data for religion. Religion is solely the creation of the scholar's study. It is created for the scholar's analytic purposes by his imaginative acts of comparison and generalization" (*Imagining Religion*, xi). While there may be no such "thing" as religion, there is a word, *religion*, that organizes individuals and institutions, paths of scholarship and careers, and that has, historically speaking, been wielded so as to exclude what appears as *dance* from the sphere of what has value as religion. Thus I engage the term as a pattern of movement whose coefficients must be recalibrated so as to enable *dance* to appear.

32. McNeill suggests that, "if dancing was already part of the repertoire of human behavior when language emerged, then words had to interpret and give meaning to the feelings aroused by keeping together in time. . . . We may surmise that such a deployment of words had the effect of elaborating and diversifying dance behavior" (*Keeping Together in Time*, 41).

33. A logic suggested by Lewis-Williams and Pearce, writing of the prehistoric rock art of the San people: "If 'dance' is the principal way of traveling to that [supernatural]

world—which it is—we must allow that many of the painted 'scenes,' even if they appear to depict, say, hunting, are in fact in some way related to 'dance'" (*Inside the Neolithic Mind,* 281). The implication is that the point of the images was to represent, remember, and communicate the range of experiences that dancing could engage and enable.

34. A claim made by Schleiermacher in response to Kant's identification of religion with "rational belief" (*On Religion,* 22).

35. Tillich's formulation of what the idea of God represents (*The Courage to Be*).

36. Otto's way of describing the nonrational essence of religious experience (*The Idea of the Holy,* 26).

37. Garfinkel, commenting on the early agricultural religions, concludes that "the most important aspect of the religious experience was the dance circle" (*Dancing at the Dawn of Agriculture,* 87). He finds linguistic evidence for this point. In Hebrew the word *haq* means both festival day and circle dance. The same is true in Aramaic and Arabic. He concludes: "The festival day is the day of the dance, when all the community gathers together in a common circle" (62). Thus the festival day serves to reinforce the importance of dancing for the community.

38. This dynamic holds for indigenous religions, such as the lifeways of First Nation Peoples. For example, the Ghost Dance of 1890, a millennial development among persecuted, displaced American tribes that was influenced by Christian ideas, retained as its central ritual a circle dance familiar to native peoples. Moving in a circle, participants affirmed their participation in the regenerative power of the Earth and her ongoing capacity to support native life. Those who practiced the dance urged nonviolence as a path to the restoration of peace and harmony. www.native-americans-online.com/native-american-ghost-dance.html.

39. Speaking of his experience in Indonesia, Abram writes that the shaman "acts as an intermediary between the human community and the larger ecological field, ensuring that there is an appropriate flow of nourishment. . . . It is only as a result of her continual engagement with the animate powers that dwell beyond the human community that the traditional magician is able to alleviate many individual illnesses that arise within that community" (*The Spell of the Sensuous,* 7). That "engagement" most often took the form of consciously performed rhythmic, patterned bodily movement.

40. Garfinkel makes the point that the dance motif he identifies in early agricultural societies depicts the synchronized movement of anonymous equals, while the culture of the time was undergoing radical consolidation and stratification of power around the new means of production. Communal dancing, he writes, may have served the function of "screening and masking" reality (*Dancing at the Dawn of Agriculture,* 90), offering participants an experience of equality belied by the codified and controlled patterns of the dance movements themselves.

41. Frymer-Kensky explains that, with the shift in Near Eastern religions from polytheism to Hebrew monotheism, not only did a single male god take over powers attributed to goddesses, but ritual participation in the act of cocreation was no longer necessary to ensure the success of the harvest or hunt. God was all-powerful; nature was under God's sole command, and the only job of humans was to act ethically, according to the law and commandments (*In the Wake of the Goddesses*, 93). Dancing, in other words, that had been central to Mesopotamian goddess rituals was no longer required.

42. In the West this situation held from the fall of Rome through the dawning of the Renaissance and the Enlightenment, when "science" and "art" pulled out of religion to operate alongside of it as its complements and competitors. Throughout this time, dancing survived among the peasants in folk forms. Only with the Renaissance, as the courts amassed power equal to the church, did dancing flourish as an art and leisure activity of the aristocracy—for a while.

43. For example, in the life of many a splinter Christian group the initial impulse to form a new community takes expression as an explosion of new bodily movements, as in eighteenth- and nineteenth-century Europe and America. The movement literally erupts in and through the bodily selves of those whose current practices are causing them intellectual, emotional, and even physical pain. The rise of the Quakers, the Shakers, and the African American Shout are three such examples. As the groups consolidated and institutionalized, their spontaneous dancing practices were first codified and then slowly replaced by verbally guided internal movements of visualization and devotion.

44. Leonard Shlain describes this dynamic in terms of the hemispheric lateralization of brain action: "when a critical mass of people within a society acquire literacy, especially alphabetic literacy, left hemispheric modes of thought are reinforced at the expense of right hemispheric ones" (*The Alphabet Versus the Goddess*, viii). The result, for Shlain, is a subtle change in neuronal development that causes most people in a culture to privilege activities associated with the left brain—including abstraction, linear thinking, and reason—over those that more fully engage the right brain, such as processing images, sensory perception, and dancing. For Shlain, in the West, at least, the necessary "critical mass" tipped the hemispheric balance between 1500 BCE and 500 BCE, prompting the demise of goddess worship, "feminine values," and women's power (7).

45. "To be able to leap from the particular and concrete to the general and abstract [as literacy trains us to do] has allowed us to create art, logic, science, and philosophy. But the skill tore us out of the rich matrix of nature. The part torn away became the ego" (Shlain, *The Alphabet Versus the Goddess*, 22).

46. Analyzing the rise of Hebrew monotheism, for example, Shlain observes how the first four of the Ten Commandments all function to reinforce the kind of abstract,

disembodied thinking that literacy both requires and exercises (*The Alphabet and the Goddess*, 87).

47. Olsen, in *Body and Earth,* is one who shares this perspective.

48. Abram writes, "Transfixed by our technologies, we short-circuit the sensorial reciprocity between our breathing bodies and the bodily terrain. Human awareness folds in upon itself" (*The Spell of the Sensuous,* 267). As Abram writes, we need to put language back in contact with the èarth, "releasing the budded earthly intelligence of our words" (273) so that they "make sense." As he writes, "To make sense is . . . to re-new and rejuvenate one's felt awareness of the world" (265). His words point toward dance.

In this intent, he is not alone. Lawrence Buell, in cataloguing the work of American nature writers, insists that writing about nature can play a role in educating our senses to a "nature-responsiveness," "teasing us toward an awareness of ourselves as environmental beings" (*The Environmental Imagination,* 251) and thus creating "culture" that runs counter to "the intractable homocentrism in terms of which one's psychological and social worlds are always to some degree mapped." For Buell, the key to a biocentric writing is "environmental mimesis" (114). His favorite example is Henry David Thoreau's *Walden.*

Yet such attempts at "environmental mimesis" or earth-friendly writing will "make sense" only if and when they express a practice of moving in, through, and as nature—a practice of dance.

49. See Grimes: "Most scholars do not pay much attention to personal narratives about ritual experience . . . some theorists consider an individual's intentions, stories, and experiences irrelevant to ritual" (*Deeply Into the Bone,* 10). Also LaMothe, "What Bodies Know About Religion and the Study of It."

50. As Halmos aptly describes it, a community without dancing suffers from "biosocial impoverishment" ("The Decline of Choral Dancing," 177).

51. Louv describes such a phenomenon as one of "cultural autism," in which our senses are so colonized by the forms of culture that we are no longer willing or able to seek out experiences of the natural world. It is a state characterized by "tunneled senses, and feelings of isolation and containment" (*Last Child in the Woods,* 64).

52. Louv, arguing for direct experience of nature, makes many points about what such experience can accomplish, including invigorating senses (*Last Child in the Woods,* 58); reducing stress (50), nurturing solitude (51), stimulating creativity with all its "loose parts" (96), allowing for experiential learning (66), providing resources for the development of an inner life (95), and, finally, restoring a capacity for direct attention (103). However, all of these effects, I argue, depend not on "direct experience" of "it" (a materialist model) but on cultivating a sensory awareness of the movement making me. They are aspects of ecokinetic knowledge—a sense of earth

within—capable of guiding us to participate responsibly in the rhythms of bodily becoming we are.

53. History is replete with examples. See Hanna, *To Dance Is Human,* chapter 6. As Barbara Ehrenreich asserts, "the aspect of 'civilization' that is most hostile to festivity is not capitalism or industrialism—both of which are fairly recent innovations—but social hierarchy. . . . When one class, or ethnic group, or gender rules over a population of subordinates, it comes to fear the empowering rituals of the subordinates as a threat to civil order" (*Dancing in the Streets,* 251).

54. Such is the critique of Western classical ballet, for example, developed by modern dancers such as Ruth St. Denis, Isadora Duncan, and Martha Graham. For these women, ballet, as practiced in the early twentieth century, served to devalue bodily life, rather than affirm it. Of course, ballet technique and training have both evolved, and much depends on how the technique is taught, to whom, at what age, and with what intention.

55. As Aldo Leopold wrote, in his deeply influential *Sand County Almanac,* we may wax poetic about environmental ethics, but we will not act accordingly unless we have love for the land (xix). As Warren affirms, the crux of morality consists in an answer to one question: "How does one develop the ability to care?" (*Ecofeminist Philosophy,* 202).

Earth Within

1. I am moving in this direction myself, introducing what I call an ecokinetic approach to the study of ritual dance. See LaMothe, "Transformation."

2. "I would only believe in a god who could dance . . . Now I am light, now I fly, now I see myself beneath myself, now a god dances through me. Thus spoke Zarathustra" (Nietzsche, "Thus Spoke Zarathustra," in *The Portable Nietzsche,* 153).

3. Roszak muses that the earth "may at some point decide that this so-clever human species is too troublesome a hazard to maintain" (*The Voice of the Earth,* 159).

Bibliography

Abram, David. *Becoming Animal: An Earthly Cosmology.* New York: Pantheon, 2010.

———. *The Spell of the Sensuous: Perception and Language in the More Than Human World.* New York: Vintage, 1996.

Armitage, Merle, ed. *Martha Graham: The Early Years.* New York: Da Capo, 1978.

Asad, Talal. *Genealogies of Religion: Discipline and Reasons of Power in Christianity and Islam.* Baltimore: Johns Hopkins University Press, 1993.

Backman, E. Louis. *Religious Dances in the Christian Church and in Popular Medicine.* Trans. E. Classen. New York: Allen and Unwin, 1952.

Barbour, Karen. *Dancing Across the Page.* Chicago: Intellect, 2011.

Begley, Sharon. *Train Your Mind, Change Your Brain: How a New Science Reveals Our Extraordinary Potential to Transform Ourselves.* New York: Ballantine, 2007.

Bell, Catherine. "Modernism and Postmodernism in the Study of Religion," *Religious Studies Review* 22, no. 3 (July 1996): 179–90.

———. *Ritual: Perspectives and Dimensions.* New York: Oxford University Press, 1997.

———. *Ritual Theory, Ritual Practice.* New York: Oxford University Press, 1992.

Bennett, Jane. *Vibrant Matter: A Political Ecology of Things.* Durham: Duke University Press, 2010.

Blacking, John. *How Musical Is Man?* Seattle: University of Washington Press, 1973.

Blakeslee, Sandra and Matthew Blakeslee. *The Body Has a Mind of Its Own: How Body Maps in Your Brain Help You Do (Almost) Everything Better.* New York: Random House, 2007.

Bourdieu, Pierre. *Outline of a Theory of Practice.* Trans. Richard Nice. New York: Cambridge University Press, 1977.

Bibliography

Bowlby, John. *Attachment.* 2d ed. New York: Basic Books, 1983.

Bramble, Dennis and Daniel Lieberman. "Endurance Running and the Evolution of Homo." *Nature* 432 (November 18, 2004): 345–52.

Brennan, Teresa. *Exhausting Modernity: Grounds for a New Economy.* New York: Routledge, 2000.

——. *History After Lacan.* New York: Routledge, 1993.

—— *The Transmission of Affect.* Ithaca: Cornell University Press, 2004.

Buber, Martin. *I and Thou.* Trans. Walter Kaufmann. New York: Touchstone, 1971.

Buell, Lawrence. *The Environmental Imagination: Thoreau, Nature Writing, and the Formation of American Culture.* Cambridge: Harvard University Press, 1995.

Capra, Fritjof. *The Tao of Physics.* Berkeley: Shambala, 1975.

Cassidy, Jude and Phillip R. Shaver. *The Handbook of Attachment: Theory, Research, and Clinical Applications.* 2d ed. New York: Guilford, 2010.

Chace, Marian, Susan Sandel, Sharon Chailkin, and Ann Lohn, eds. *Foundations of Dance/Movement Therapy: The Life and Work of Marian Chace.* American Dance Therapy Association, 1993.

Chamovitz, Daniel. *What a Plant Knows: A Field Guide to the Senses.* New York: Scientific American, Farrar, Straus and Giroux, 2012.

Coole, Diana, and Samantha Frost, eds. *New Materialisms: Ontology, Agency, and Politics.* Durham: Duke University Press, 2010.

Cozolino, Louis. *The Neuroscience of Human Relationships: Attachment and the Developing Social Brain.* New York: Norton, 2007.

Csordas, Thomas, ed. *Embodiment and Experience: The Existential Ground of Culture and Self.* Cambridge: Cambridge University Press, 1994.

Daly, Ann. *Done Into Dance: Isadora Duncan in America.* Bloomington: Indiana University Press, 1995.

Damasio, Antonio. *The Feeling of What Happens.* San Diego: Harcourt, 1999.

Dawkins, Richard. *The Selfish Gene.* Thirtieth anniversary ed. New York: Oxford University Press, 2006.

Deacon, Terrence W. *Incomplete Nature: How Mind Emerged from Matter.* New York: Norton, 2012.

De Certeau, Michel. *The Practice of Everyday Life.* Trans. Steven Rendall. Berkeley: University of California Press, 1984.

Deleuze, Gilles and Felix Guattari. *One Thousand Plateaus: Capitalism and Schizophrenia.* Trans. Brian Massumi. Minneapolis: University of Minnesota Press, 1987.

De Mille, Agnes. *Martha: The Life and Work of Martha Graham.* New York: Random House, 1991.

Derrida, Jacques. *Dissemination.* Trans. Barbara Johnson. Chicago: University of Chicago Press, 1981.

——. *Margins of Philosophy*. Trans. Alan Bass. Chicago: University of Chicago Press, 1982.

——. *Of Grammatology*. Trans. Gayatri Spivak. Baltimore: Johns Hopkins University Press, 1976.

Derrida, Jacques and Christie V. McDonald. "Choreographies," *Diacritics* 12, no. 2: 66–76.

Descartes, René. *Discourse on Method*. Trans. Laurence J. Lafleur. New York: Macmillan, 1956.

Dill, Karen. *How Fantasy Becomes Reality: Seeing Through Media Influence*. New York: Oxford University Press, 2009.

Doidge, Norman. *The Brain That Changes Itself: Stories of Personal Triumph from the Frontiers of Brain Science*. New York: Penguin, 2007.

Dolphijn, Rick and Iris van der Tuin, eds. *New Materialism: Interviews and Cartographies*. Open Humanities Press, MPublishing, University of Michigan Library, 2012.

Donald, Merlin. *Origins of the Modern Mind: Three Stages in the Evolution of Culture and Cognition*. Cambridge: Harvard University Press, 1991.

Dunbar, Robin. *Grooming, Gossip, and the Evolution of Language*. Cambridge: Harvard University Press, 1998.

Duncan, Isadora. *Art of the Dance*. New York: Theatre Arts, 1928.

——. *Isadora Speaks*. Ed. Franklin Rosemont. San Francisco: City Lights, 1981.

——. *My Life*. New York: Liveright, 1928.

Dunham, Katherine. *Dances of Haiti*. Los Angeles: University of California Center for Afro-American Studies, 1983.

Durkheim, Émile. *The Elementary Forms of Religious Life*. Trans. Karen E. Fields. New York: Free Press, 1995.

Ehrenreich, Barbara. *Dancing in the Streets: A History of Collective Joy*. New York: Holt, 2006.

Eliade, Mircea. *The Myth of Eternal Return, or Cosmos and History*. Trans. Willard R. Trask. Princeton: Princeton University Press, 1954.

Esposito, Gianluca et al. "Infant Calming Responses During Carrying in Humans and Mice," *Current Biology* 23, no. 9 (April 18, 2013): 739–45.

Fogel, Alan. *The Psychophysiology of Self-Awareness: Rediscovering the Lost Art of Body Sense*. New York: Norton, 2009.

Foster, Susan. *Choreographing Empathy: Kinaesthesia in Performance*. New York: Routledge, 2010.

——, ed. *Choreographing History*. Bloomington: Indiana University Press, 1997.

——. *Reading Dancing*. Berkeley: University of California Press, 1986.

Foucault, Michel. *Discipline and Punish: The Birth of the Prison*. Trans. Alan Sheridan. New York: Vintage, 1977.

——. *The Order of Things: An Archeology of the Human Sciences*. Trans. Alan Sheridan. New York: Vintage Books, Random House, 1970.

——. *Power/Knowledge: Selected Interviews and Other Writings, 1972–1977*. Ed. and trans. Colin Gordon. New York: Pantheon, 1980.

Fraleigh, Sondra Horton. *Dance and the Lived Body: A Descriptive Aesthetics*. Pittsburgh: University of Pittsburgh Press, 1987.

Freud, Sigmund. *Civilization and Its Discontents*. Trans. James Strachey. New York: Norton, 1961.

——. *The Future of an Illusion*. Trans. James Strachey. New York: Norton, 1961.

——. *Totem and Taboo*. Trans. James Strachey. New York: Norton, 1950.

Frymer-Kensky, Tikva. *In the Wake of the Goddesses: Woman, Culture, and the Biblical Transformation of Pagan Myth*. New York: Free Press, 1992.

Gardener, Howard. *Frames of Mind: Theories of Multiple Intelligence*. New York: Basic Books, 1983.

Garfinkel, Josef. *Dancing at the Dawn of Agriculture*. Austin: University of Austin Press, 2003.

Geertz, Clifford. *The Interpretation of Culture*. New York: Basic Books, 1973.

——. *Works and Lives: The Anthropologist as Author*. Stanford: Stanford University Press, 1988.

Gill, Sam. *Dancing Culture Religion*. Lanham, MD: Lexington, 2012.

Goleman, Daniel. *Social Intelligence: The Revolutionary New Science of Human Relationships*. New York: Bantam, 2006.

Gould, Rebecca. *At Home in Nature: Modern Homesteading and Spiritual Practice in America*. Berkeley: University of California Press, 2005.

Gould, Stephen Jay. *Punctuated Equilibrium*. Cambridge: Harvard University Press, 2007.

Graham, Martha. *Blood Memory*. New York: Doubleday, 1991.

——. *The Notebooks of Martha Graham*. New York: Harcourt, Brace and Jovanovich. 1973.

Gregg, Melissa and Gregory Seigworth, eds. *The Affect Theory Reader*. Durham: Duke University Press, 2010.

Griffith, R. Marie. *Born Again Bodies: Flesh and Spirit in American Christianity*. Berkeley: University of California Press, 2004.

Grimes, Ronald. *Deeply Into the Bone: Re-Inventing Rites of Passage*. Berkeley: University of California Press, 2000.

——, ed. *Readings in Ritual Studies*. Upper Saddle River, NJ: Prentice Hall, 1996.

Halmos, Paul. "The Decline of Choral Dancing." In *Man Alone: Alienation in Modern Society*. Ed. Eric and Mary Josephson. New York: Dell, 1962.

Halprin, Anna. *Dance as a Healing Art: Returning to Health Through Movement and Imagery*. Mendocino, CA: Life Rhythm, 2000.

Bibliography

Hanna, Judith Lynne. *Dance, Sex, and Gender: Signs of Identity, Dominance, Defiance, and Desire.* Chicago: University of Chicago Press, 1988.
———. *To Dance Is Human.* Chicago: University of Chicago Press, 1987.
Hanna, Thomas. *Somatics.* New York: Da Capo, 1988.
Haraway, Donna. *The Companion Species Manifesto: Dogs, People, and Significant Otherness.* Chicago: Prickly Paradigm, 2003.
Harmon, Katherine. "'Junk' DNA Holds Clues to Common Diseases," *Scientific American* 7, no. 1 (September 5, 2012).
Hartley, Linda. *Wisdom of the Body Moving: An Introduction to Body-Mind Centering.* Berkeley: North Atlantic, 1995.
Hayes, Shannon. *Radical Homemakers: Reclaiming Domesticity from a Consumer Culture.* New York: Left to Write, 2010.
Heckert, Justin. "Painless," *New York Times Magazine,* November 15, 2012.
Hegel, G. W. F. *Lectures on the Philosophy of Religion, 1827.* Ed. Peter Hodgson. Berkeley: University of California Press, 1988.
———. *Phenomenology of Spirit.* Trans. A. V. Miller. New York: Oxford University Press, 1977.
Heinrich, Bernd. *Why We Run: A Natural History.* New York: HarperCollins, 2001.
Heller-Roazen, Daniel. *The Inner Touch: Archeology of a Sensation.* Cambridge: Zone, 2007.
Helpern, Alice, ed. *Martha Graham. Choreography and Dance: An International Journal* 5, no. 2 (May 1999).
———. *The Technique of Martha Graham.* Dobbs Ferry, NY: Morgan and Morgan, 1994.
Horosko, Marian, ed. *Martha Graham: The Evolution of Her Dance Theory and Training.* Chicago: A Cappella, 1991.
Hrdy, Sarah Blaffer. *Mother Nature: Maternal Instincts and How They Shape the Human Species.* New York: Ballantine, 1999.
———. *Mothers and Others: The Evolutionary Origins of Mutual Understanding.* Cambridge: Belknap Press at Harvard University Press, 2009.
Irigaray, Luce. *This Sex Which Is Not One.* Trans. Catherine Porter and Carolyn Burke. New York: Cornell University Press, 1985.
Jantzen, Grace. *Becoming Divine: Toward a Feminist Philosophy of Religion.* Bloomington: Indiana University Press, 1999.
Jensen, Derek. *How Should I Live My Life? On Liberating the Earth from Civilization.* Oakland: PM, 2008.
Johnson, Don Hanlon, ed. *Bone, Breath, and Gesture: Practices of Embodiment.* Berkeley: North Altantic, 1995.
———. *Groundworks: Narratives of Embodiment.* Berkeley: North Atlantic, 1997.

Jones, David. "A Cardiac Conundrum," *Harvard Magazine*. 2013. http://harvard magazine.com/2013/03/a-cardiac-conundrum.

Kant, Immanuel. "An Answer to the Question: What Is Enlightenment? (1784)" and "Introduction to 'What Is Orientation in Thinking?' (1786)." In *Kant: Political Writings*. Trans. H. B. Nisbet. Cambridge: Cambridge University Press, 1991.

———. *Religion Within the Limits of Reason Alone*. Trans. Theodore Greene and Hoyt Hudson. New York: Harper Torchbooks, 1960.

Keeney, Bradford. *Aesthetics of Change*. New York: Guilford, 1983.

———. *Bushman Shaman*. Rochester, VT: Destiny, 2005.

———. *Shaking Medicine: The Healing Power of Ecstatic Movement*. Rochester, VT: Destiny, 2007.

Kehoe, Alice Beck. *The Ghost Dance: Ethnohistory and Revitalization*, 2d ed. Long Grove, IL: Waveland, 2006.

Kierkegaard, Søren. *Concluding Unscientific Postscript to "Philosophical Fragments."* Vols. 1 and 2. Ed. and trans. Howard Hong and Edna Hong. Princeton: Princeton University Press, 1992.

———. *Fear and Trembling/Repetition*. Trans. Howard Hong and Edna Hong. Princeton: Princeton University Press, 1983.

Knight, Chris. *Blood Relations: Menstruation and the Origins of Culture*. New Haven: Yale University Press, 1991.

Kristeva, Julia. *The Kristeva Reader*. Ed. Toril Moi. New York: Columbia University Press, 1986.

Kuhn, Thomas. *The Structure of Scientific Revolutions*. 3d ed. Chicago: University of Chicago Press, 1996.

Lakoff, George and Mark Johnson. *Philosophy in the Flesh: The Embodied Mind and Its Challenge to Western Thought*. New York: Basic, 1999.

LaMothe, Kimerer L. *Between Dancing and Writing: The Practice of Religious Studies*. New York: Fordham University Press, 2004.

———. "Can They Dance? Towards a Philosophy of Bodily Becoming." *Journal of Dance and Somatics* 4, no. 1 (2012): 93–107.

———. *Family Planting: A Farm-Fed Philosophy of Human Relations*. Ropley: Changemakers, 2011.

———. *Nietzsche's Dancers: Isadora Duncan, Martha Graham, and the Revaluation of Christian Values*. New York: Palgrave MacMillan, 2006.

———. "Passionate Madonna: The Christian Turn of American Dancer Ruth St. Denis." *Journal of the American Academy of Religion* 66, no 4 (Winter 1998): 747–69.

———. "Reason, Religion, and Sexual Difference: Resources for a Feminist Philosophy of Religion in Hegel's *Phenomenology of Spirit*." *Hypatia* 20, no. 1 (2005b): 120–49.

———. "Transformation: An Ecokinetic Approach to the Study of Ritual Dance." *Journal of Dance, Movement, and Spiritualities* 1, no. 1 (2014): 57–72.

Bibliography

———. *What a Body Knows: Finding Wisdom in Desire*. Ropley: Changemakers, 2009.

———. "What Bodies Know About Religion and the Study of It," *Journal for the American Academy of Religion* 76, no. 3 (2008): 573–601.

———. "Why Dance? Towards a Theory of Religion as Practice and Performance." *Method and Theory in the Study of Religion* 17, no. 2 (2005a): 101–33.

Langer, Ellen. *Counterclockwise: Mindful Health and the Power of Possibility*. New York: Ballantine, 2009.

Langer, Susanne K. *Feeling and Form*. New York: Scribner's, 1953.

Leopold, Aldo. *Sand County Almanac*. New York: Ballantine, 1949.

Lesho, Johanna and Sandra McMaster, eds. *Dancing on the Earth: Women's Stories of Healing Through Dance*. Findhorn: Findhorn, 2011.

Levin, David Michael. *The Body's Recollection of Being: Phenomenological Psychology and the Deconstruction of Nihilism*. New York: Routledge, 1985.

Levine, Peter. *Waking the Tiger: Healing Trauma: The Innate Capacity to Transform Overwhelming Experiences*. Berkeley: North Atlantic, 1996.

Lewis-Williams, David and David Pearce. *Inside the Neolithic Mind: Consciousness, Cosmos, and the Realm of the Gods*. London: Thames and Hudson, 2005.

Lieberman, Daniel E. *The Evolution of the Human Head*. Cambridge: Belknap Press at Harvard University Press, 2011.

Liedloff, Jean. *The Continuum Concept: In Search of Happiness Lost*. New York: Da Capo, 1986.

Llinás, Rodolfo R. *I of the Vortex: From Neurons to Self*. Cambridge: MIT Press, 2001.

Louv, Richard. *Last Child in the Woods: Saving our Children from Nature-Deficit Disorder*. Chapel Hill, NC: Algonquin, 2008.

Lovatt, Peter. "Dance and Thinking." TED talk, 2011.

MacAloon, John, ed. *Rite, Drama, Festival, Spectacle: Rehearsals Toward a Theory of Cultural Performance*. Philadelphia: Institute for the Study of Human Issues, 1984.

Manning, Erin. *Relationscapes: Movement, Art, and Photography*. Cambridge: MIT Press, 2009.

Massumi, Brian. *Parables of the Virtual: Movement, Affect, Sensation*. Durham: Duke University Press, 2002.

McDougall, Chris. *Born to Run: A Hidden Tribe, Superathletes, and the Greatest Race the World Has Never Seen*. New York: Random House, 2009.

McKibben, Bill. *The End of Nature*. New York: Random House, 1989.

McNeill, William H. *Keeping Together in Time: Dance and Drill in Human History*. ACLS POD, 1995.

Meltzoff, A. N. "Imitation as a Mechanism of Social Cognition: Origins of Empathy, Theory of Mind, and the Representation of Actions." In U. Goswami, ed., *Handbook of Childhood Cognitive Development*, 6–25. Oxford: Blackwell, 2002.

Bibliography

Merchant. Carolyn. *The Death of Nature: Women, Ecology, and the Scientific Revolution*. New York: HarperOne, 1980.

Merleau-Ponty, Maurice. *Phenomenology of Perception*. Trans. Colin Smith. London: Routledge, 1996.

——. *The Primacy of Perception*. Ed. James M. Edie. Chicago: Northwestern University, 1964.

Moore, Kathleen Dean. *Holdfast: At Home in the Natural World*. New York: Lyons, 1999.

Morgan, Barbara. *Martha Graham: Sixteen Dances*. Dobbs Ferry, NY: Morgan and Morgan, 1941.

Nietzsche, Friedrich. *Beyond Good and Evil*. Trans. Walter Kaufmann. New York: Random House, 1966.

——. *The Birth of Tragedy and the Case of Wagner*. Ed. and trans. Walter Kaufmann. New York: Vintage, 1967.

——. *The Gay Science with a Prelude in Rhymes and an Appendix of Songs*. Trans. Walter Kaufmann. New York: Vintage, 1974.

——. *Human, All Too Human: A Book for Free Spirits*. Trans. Marion Faber with Stephen Lehmann. Lincoln: University of Nebraska Press, 1984.

——. *On the Genealogy of Morals and Ecce Homo*. Ed. and trans. Walter Kaufmann. New York: Vintage, 1989.

——. "On Truth and Falsity in Their Ultramoral Sense." In *The Complete Works of Friedrich Nietzsche*. Vol. 2. Ed. Oscar Levy. New York: Macmillan, 1914.

——. *The Portable Nietzsche*. Ed. Walter Kaufmann. New York: Penguin, 1954.

Noland, Carrie. *Agency and Embodiment: Performing Gestures/Producing Culture*. Cambridge: Harvard University Press, 2009.

Nussbaum, Martha. *Not for Profit: Why Democracy Needs the Humanities*. Princeton: Princeton University Press, 2010.

Ochs, Peter. "Revised: Comparative Religious Traditions," *Journal of the American Academy of Religion* 74, no. 2 (2006): 483–94.

Oesterley, W. O. E. *The Sacred Dance*. New York: Cambridge University Press, 1923.

Olsen, Andrea. *Body and Earth: An Experiential Guide*. Hanover: University of New England Press, 2002.

Ong, Walter J. *Orality and Literacy: The Technologizing of the Word*. New York: Routledge, 1982.

O'Sullivan, Peter. www.bodyinmind.org/classification-based-cognitive-functional-therapy-for-back-pain/, 2013.

Otto, Rudolf. *The Idea of the Holy*. Trans. James Harvey. New York: Oxford University Press, 1958.

Ramachandran, V. K. *The Tell-Tale Brain: A Neuroscientist's Quest for What Makes Us Human*. New York: Norton, 2011.

Bibliography

Ratey, John J. with Eric Hagerman. *Spark: The Revolutionary New Science of Exercise and the Brain.* New York: Little, Brown, 2008.

Ray, Reginald. *Touching Enlightenment: Finding Realization in the Body.* Boulder: Sounds True, 2008.

Roszak, Theodore. *The Voice of the Earth: An Exploration of Ecopsychology.* Grand Rapids, MI: Phanes, 1992.

Sachs, Curt. *A World History of Dance.* Trans. Bessie Schonberg. New York: Norton, 1937.

St. Denis, Ruth. "Credo." *Dance News,* January, 1978.

——. *An Unfinished Life.* New York: Harper, 1939.

Schechner, Richard. *Between Theater and Anthropology.* Philadelphia: University of Pennsylvania, 1985.

Schechner, Richard and Willa Appel, eds. *By Means of Performance.* Cambridge: Cambridge University Press, 1991.

Schleiermacher, Friedrich. *On Religion: Speeches to its Cultured Despisers.* Trans. Richard Crouter. Cambridge: Cambridge University Press, 1996.

Serres, Michel. *The Five Senses: A Philosophy of Mingled Bodies.* Trans. Margaret Sankey and Peter Cowley. New York: Continuum International, 2008.

——. *Genesis.* Trans. Genevieve James and James Nielson. Ann Arbor: University of Michigan Press, 1995.

——. *Variations on the Body.* Trans. Randolph Burks. Minneapolis: Univocal, 2011.

Sheets-Johnstone, Maxine. *The Primacy of Movement.* Amsterdam: Johns Benjamin, 2011.

——. *The Roots of Power.* Chicago: Open Court, 1994.

——. *The Roots of Thinking.* Philadelphia: Temple University Press, 1990.

——, ed. *Giving the Body Its Due.* Albany: State University of New York Press, 1992.

Shlain, Leonard. *The Alphabet Versus the Goddess: The Conflict Between Word and Image.* New York: Penguin, 1998.

——. *Sex, Time, and Power: How Women's Sexuality Shaped Human Evolution.* New York: Penguin, 2003.

Shubin, Neil. *Your Inner Fish: A Journey Into the 35 Million-Year History of the Human Body.* New York: Vintage, 2008.

Siegel, Daniel. *The Developing Mind: How Relationships and the Brain Interact to Shape Who We Are.* New York: Guilford, 1999.

——. *The Mindful Brain: Reflection and Attunement in the Cultivation of Well-Being.* New York: Norton, 2007.

Smith, Jonathan Z. *Imagining Religion: From Babylon to Jonestown.* Chicago: University of Chicago Press, 1988.

——. *To Take Place: Toward Theory in Ritual.* Chicago: University of Chicago Press, 1987.

Smith, Linda B. "Movement Matters: The Contributions of Esther Thelan." *Biological Theory* 1, no. 1 (2006): 87–89.

Smith, Wilfred Cantwell. *The Meaning and End of Religion*. Minneapolis: Fortress, 1991.

Solnit, Rebecca. *Wanderlust: A History of Walking*. New York: Penguin, 2001.

Sparshott, Francis. *Off the Ground: First Steps to a Philosophical Consideration of the Dance*. Princeton: Princeton University Press, 1988.

Spinoza, Benedict de. *A Spinoza Reader: The Ethics and Other Works*. Ed. and trans. Edwin Curley. Princeton: Princeton University Press, 1994.

Taylor, Mark C. *About Religion: Economies of Faith in Virtual Culture*. Chicago: Chicago University Press, 1999.

——. *After God*. Chicago: University of Chicago, 2007.

——. *Altarity*. Chicago: University of Chicago Press, 1987.

——. *Disfiguring: Art, Architecture, Religion*. Chicago: University of Chicago Press, 1992.

——. *Erring*. Chicago: University of Chicago Press, 1985.

Thoreau, Henry. *Great Short Works of Henry David Thoreau*. New York: Harper and Row, 1982.

——. *Walden*. New Haven: Yale University Press, 2004.

Tillich, Paul. *The Courage to Be*. New Haven: Yale University Press, 2000.

——. *Systematic Theology*. Vol. 3. Chicago: University of Chicago Press, 1959.

Tomasello, Michael. *Why We Cooperate*. Cambridge: MIT Press, 2009.

——. "The Human Adaptation for Culture." *Annual Review of Anthropology* 28 (1999): 509–29.

Turner, Victor. *The Ritual Process: Structure and Anti-Structure*. New York: Aldine de Gruyter, 1995.

Van der Leeuw, Gerardus. *Religion in Essence and Manifestation*. Trans. J. E. Turner. Princeton: Princeton University Press, 1986.

——. *Sacred and Profane Beauty: The Holy in Art*. Trans. David Green. New York: Holt, 1963.

——. *Wegen en grenzen. Studie over de verhouding van religie en kunst*. Amsterdam, 1955 [1948].

Van Gennup, Arnold. *Rites of Passage*. Chicago: University of Chicago Press, 1975.

Vibe Fersum K., P. O'Sullivan, J. S. Skouen, A. Smith, and A. Kvåle. "Efficacy of Classification-Based Cognitive Functional Therapy in Patients with Non-specific Chronic Low Back Pain: A Randomized Controlled Trial." *European Journal of Pain*. PMID: 23208945 (2012).

Wade, Nicholas. *The Faith Instinct: How Religion Evolved and Why It Endures*. New York: Penguin, 2009.

Walter, Chip. *Thumbs, Toes, and Tears: And Other Traits That Make Us Human*. New York: Walker, 2006.

Bibliography

Warren, Karen J. *Ecofeminist Philosophy: A Western Perspective on What It Is and Why It Matters.* Lanham, MD: Rowman and Littlefield, 2000.

Whitehead, Alfred North. *Process and Reality.* Corrected ed. Ed. David Ray Griffin and Donald W. Sherburne. New York: Free Press, 1978.

Wilson, E. O. *Biophilia: The Human Bond with Other Species.* Cambridge: Harvard University Press, 1984.

——. *The Social Conquest of the Earth.* New York: Liveright, 2012.

Wolpert, Daniel. "The Real Reason for Brains." TED talk, 2011.

Wrangham, Richard. *Catching Fire: How Cooking Made Us Human.* New York: Basic Books, 2009.

Young, Iris Marion. *On Female Body Experience: "Throwing Like a Girl" and Other Essays.* New York: Oxford University Press, 2005.

Zukav, Gary. *The Dancing Wu Li Masters: An Overview of the New Physics.* New York: HarperOne, 2001.

Index

Index

Birth (*continued*)
as metaphor for beginnings, 85;
movement perspective on human,
94–98, 101, 132, 153; patterns of
sensation and response in, 95–96,
234n26; rebirth and, 85, 232n8; ritual
as, 167; as unique to each female,
231n3; Western fantasies related to,
106–7, 239nn57–58
Blacking, John, 242n17
Blakeslee, Matthew, 222n49, 235nn33–35,
243n25, 244n34, 250n29
Blakeslee, Sandra, 222n49, 235nn33–35,
243n25, 244n34, 250n29
Bodily becoming: attachment and, 117,
124–25; culture and, 178–79; dance
and, 7–9; healing as function of,
147; individuality replaced by, 117;
knowledge and, 65–66, 70–71;
philosophy of, 22, 217n16; rhythm of,
5, 28–29, 220n39; self-awareness
and, 233n16; terminology and dance
criteria, 4–6; *see also* Patterns of
sensation and response; Philosophy of
bodily becoming; Rhythm of bodily
becoming; Sensory Awareness
Bodily movement, *see* Movement, bodily
Bodily self, 29–34, 221n42; brain and,
99–101, 237nn42–43; earth and,
30–31, 171–72, 208; fetal development
and, 88–91, 232nn9–11; Hegel on
Spirit and, 219n34; infinity of, 78,
231n29; movement of, as source, 13,
214n17; revealed as movement, 17;
as rhythm of bodily becoming, 29;
science and, 10; sensory awareness
of, 21–22, 211n3; split from, 78–79,
231n30; *see also* Bodily becoming;
Rhythm of bodily becoming; Sensory
Awareness
Body: Abram's description of, 222n50;
extending consciousness into, 223n53,
239n55; language and, 228n4, 228n6;
lived body concept, 232n5; maps, 98,

235nn33–35, 250n29; mind over,
81–83, 140, 232nn4–5; Nietzsche on
delusion and, 222n52; in postmodern
theories, 228n6; Sheets-Johnstone on,
228n4; Shubin's definition of,
221nn42–44; Western culture denial
of, 228nn4–6
Body mandalas, 250n29
Books, in Western culture, 62–63, 228n3
Bottleneck, evolutionary, 92–93, 98
Bourdieu, Pierre, 137, 250n33
Bowlby, John, 240n6, 241n12
Braidotti, Rosi, 216n10, 216n14
Brain: bodily self and, 100, 236n40,
237n43; as closed system, 233n14,
239n56; dance and, 91, 97, 105,
234n30; difficult births and larger,
93–98; experience-dependent
development of, 95–96, 100–1,
114, 132, 236nn40–41; fetal
development of, 88–91, 233n12;
Fogel on, 237n44, 243n23; growth
of, outside womb, 234n23, 234n27;
hemispheric modes of, 259n44; as
internalization of movement, 24,
218n26, 236n36, 237n43; larger size
of hominid, 93–98, 227nn35–37,
240n2; Llinás on, 232n10, 233n14,
236n36, 237n43, 239n56; maps, 99,
235nn33–35, 257n30; in materialist
paradigm, 24, 82, 93; mirror neurons
of, 127–30; as movement-enabled,
95–105, 226n23, 230n18, 257n30;
plasticity of, 103–4, 238nn49–50;
purpose of as enabling movement,
24, 97–101, 218n27, 232n10; as
relational, 93, 100–1, 111, 237n43
Bramble, Dennis, 227n34
Breaths, cycle of, 80–81, 84–85, 144,
231n1
Brennan, Teresa, 237n46, 241n16; on
extending consciousness, 223n53,
239n55; on foundational fantasy,
213n11, 239n58

276

Index

Buell, Lawrence, 260*n*48
Bugs, 203–4, 209

Caregivers, 96–98, 114–15, 120–21,
227*n*37, 234*n*26, 234*n*29, 240*n*5,
243*n*24, 244*n*31, 249*n*26; relationship
to infant as dance, 124–27, 132–34; *see
also* Cooperative breeding; Infants
CB-CRT, *see* Classification-based
Cognitive Functional Therapy
Center, finding through dance, 66–68
Chamovitz, Daniel, 235*n*32, 248*n*20
Children, nurturing dance in, 207
Christianity, 12, 41, 204, 214*n*17, 238*n*48,
241*n*11, 256*n*26
Classification-based Cognitive Functional
Therapy (CB-CRT), 248*n*18
Collagen, evolution of, 221*n*43
Communal dancing, 224*n*8; in
agricultural societies, 240*n*10, 255*n*19,
258*n*40; in evolution, theories of, 43,
224*nn*8–9, 224*nn*11–15; in hunter-
gatherer societies, 240*n*10, 251*n*36,
256*n*26; idea of spirit emerging
through, 153, 249*n*28; McNeill
on, 234*n*31, 249*n*28; origins of,
133–35, 149–51; as religion, first
form of, 43–45, 140, 224*n*15,
225*n*16, 240*n*10, 241*n*13; as ritual,
140, 151–54, 183–86; social cohesion
through, 43–45, 115–17, 224*nn*11–13,
225*nn*16–17, 240*n*10; trance induced
by, 43, 164, 224*nn*9–10, 251*n*36;
see also Dance; Ritual; Ritual dance
Conception: bodily becoming,
perspective on, 85–91, 107, 118,
211*n*2; materialist perspective on,
81–82, 232*n*7
Conceptual self-awareness (CSA), 215*n*1,
230*n*26
Connection, *see* Impulse to connect
Consciousness: bodily becoming,
perspective on, 101–3, 146, 232*n*5,
233*n*13; dance as source of, 8, 10, 74,

149–50, 242*n*17, 249*n*23; ecological,
23, 218*n*22, 254*n*10; emerging and
dissolving of, 5–7, 237*n*44; in
experience of dancing, 17, 43, 66;
extended into body, 223*n*53, 239*n*55;
in materialist paradigm, 23–24,
218*n*24, 231*n*30; movement and,
218*n*28, 233*n*13; in newborn, 96, 124,
242*n*21; pain and, 146–47; ritual and,
249*n*23; in utero, 90; *see also*
Self-awareness
Consolidation, in cultural development,
188–89, 192–94
Contemporary culture, 197–202,
260*n*48; dance in, 11–12, 198–200,
204–5, 246*n*9, 260*n*50; pain in, 141–42,
197, 199; reading and writing
preoccupation of, 197, 260*n*48; shift
occurring in, 204–5; *see also* Western
culture
Cool-down, in ritual, 160–61, 184
Cooperative breeding, 55, 93–98, 227*n*37,
234*n*26, 245*n*41
CSA, *see* Conceptual self-awareness
Cultural autism, 260*n*51
Culture: birth of, 180–87, 255*nn*13–20,
256*nn*21–24; bodily becoming,
perspective on, 176–79, 182–84; dance
as enabling, 183–84, 234*n*31; demise
of dance in, 195–96; development of,
187–98, 255*n*16; five arcs of, 187–91;
of hunter-gatherers, 43, 133, 240*n*10,
251*n*36, 256*n*26; infant movement
patterns and, 120–21, 243*n*25; ironic
reversal in development of, 196; in
materialist paradigm, 173–74; nature
and, 173–74, 185, 253*n*2, 253*nn*4–5,
254*n*6, 256*n*22; as patterns of sensation
and response, 147–48, 176–79, 181–82,
191–97, 199, 207, 227*n*33; religion
in, 192–95, 257*n*31, 258*nn*34–39;
ritual dance as earthing, 177, 182–86,
255*n*19; *see also* Contemporary culture;
Western culture

Index

Dance, 3–11, 207–8, 211*n*1, 212*n*4; ancient imagery of, 9, 212*nn*7–8; in animals, 226*n*29; as biological necessity, 13–14, 83–84, 91–92, 98, 104–5, 107, 233*n*17; birth as, 81, 107; bodily becoming, perspective on as human, 57–58; consciousness and, 8, 10, 74, 149–50, 247*n*17, 249*n*23; contemporary culture and, 198–200, 204–5, 260*n*50; culture creation through, 182–83, 255*n*16; devaluation of, 82, 195–96, 259*n*41; in early humans, 130–36, 150–51, 249*nn*24–27; as ecological necessity, 13–14, 174–75, 178–79, 188, 200–1; empathy and, 126–27, 129–30, 244*n*33; as ethical necessity, 13–14, 110, 116–17, 127–30, 135, 244*nn*32–34, 244*n*36; evolution as, 48–53; experience shift and, 6, 16–17, 22, 26–27, 138, 201, 215*n*1; experiential frame on, 16–17, 22, 26–27, 36–38, 215*n*1; future projects on, 205–8; humanness and, 9, 45, 53, 226*n*29; as human universal, 9–10, 57, 212*n*5; infant-caregiver, 124–27, 132–33; language and, 72, 257*n*29, 257*n*32; materialist paradigm view of, 11, 20–21, 43–45, 64–66, 82–84, 115–18, 142–43, 173–74; matter and, 16–38; as metaphor, 20–21, 23–24, 64, 91, 219*n*30, 254*n*10; oppression and, 199–200, 261*n*53; in plants, 234*n*31; pleasure and, 2, 6, 35–36, 43–44, 49, 60–61, 73–74, 134–35, 150–52, 154, 172, 225*n*17, 230*n*27; prenatal movement as, 90–91; as problem-solving resource, 207; Reformation era and, 214*n*14; religion and, 191–95, 198–99, 214*n*14, 240*n*10, 256*n*26, 258*nn*37–40, 259*nn*41–43; ritual as, 149–54, 156–70; scholarly study of, 9–10, 20, 34–35; sensory education from, 74, 230*n*27; spirit and, 152–53;

as spiritual necessity, 13–14, 140, 152–54; tool use and, 183, 255*n*16; Western theories of, 115–17, 240*nn*9–10, 241*nn*11–15; writing and, 14, 65, 73–74, 229*n*12, 239*n*53; *see also* Bodily Becoming:Communal dancing; Culture; Healing; Knowledge; Patterns of Sensation and Response; Philosophy of Bodily Becoming; Ritual dance

Darwin, Charles, 41, 223*n*1

Dawkins, Richard, 223*n*3

Deacon, Terrence, 215*n*4, 215*n*7, 216*n*11, 218*n*25

De Certeau, Michel, 251*n*40

DeLanda, Manuel, 216*n*10

Derrida, Jacques, 230*n*25

Descartes, René, 29, 215*nn*5–6, 231*n*30, 232*nn*4–5

DNA, junk, 47, 226*n*22

Doidge, Norman, 238*nn*49–50

Donald, Merlin, 234*n*31, 248*n*22, 257*n*29

Dualism: Cartesian, 18–19, 215*nn*5–6, 231*n*30; between matter and meaning, 216*n*11; mind over matter, 18, 24–25, 81–82, 215*n*5

Dunbar, Robin, 234*n*24; on evolution, 223*n*1, 223*n*5, 227*n*36; on language as grooming practice, 223*n*5; on neocortex, 240*n*2; on sociality, 240*n*3

Duncan, Isadora, 35, 39, 180, 211*n*2, 223*n*54, 254*n*8; on children dancing, 238*n*52, 239*n*53; critique of ballet, 261*n*54; on Greek art, 212*n*8, 220*n*38

Dunham, Katherine, 252*n*48

Durkheim, Émile, 240*n*9, 241*n*14

Earth, 183–84; love for, 200–2, 208, 261*n*55; *see also* Nature

Earth within, sense of, 46–47, 56, 89, 178, 184–86; as guide for action, 191, 197, 260*n*52

Ecofeminism, 12, 254*n*11, 256*n*23, 261*n*55

Index

Ecokinetic knowledge, 8, 175–78,
184–86, 193, 197–99, 206, 260n52
Ecological consciousness, 23, 218n22,
254n10
Ehrenreich, Barbara, 224n11, 225n17,
261n53
Eland Dance, 9, 212n7
Eliade, Mircea, 251n34
Embodied self-awareness (ESA): CSA
distinguished from, 215n1, 230n26;
Fogel on, 237n45, 238n51, 252n47;
sensory awareness contrasted with,
211n3
Embodiment: Fraleigh on dance as,
229n13, 249n27; as function of
relational movement, 220n39, 231n28;
of knowledge, 214n18; Nietzsche and,
231n28, 232n5; Ray on, 252n44
Embryo, 85–87, 90, 232n9; see also Fetus
Emotions, 99–100, 113, 141, 145–47,
153, 165–66, 187, 220, 236n38; as
patterns of sensation and response, 95,
126, 145–47, 151–54, 215n1, 247n12,
249n26; religion and, 192–93; ritual
and, 151–54, 158–60, 165–66, 192,
234n31, 240n10; thinking and, 146–47,
247n13; see also Attachment; Sociality
Empathy, 55, 117, 126–30, 182, 205–6,
240n10, 244n35; dance and, 126–27,
129–30, 244n33
Endurance running (ER), 55, 58, 227n34
Epigenetics, 47–48, 100–101, 226n22
ER, see Endurance running
ESA, see Embodied self-awareness
Ethical necessity, dance as, 13–14, 110,
116–17, 135; mirror neurons as evidence
of, 127–30, 244nn32–34, 244n36
Ethical paradox, 112, 115, 118, 125–27,
134–36; dance and, 127, 130, 135–36
Evolution, theories of: bodily becoming,
perspective on, 45–48, 54–58; dance
and, 43–45, 48–53, 55–59; epigenetics
and, 47–48, 226n22; etymology, 50;
human, 52–58, 109–11, 228n38;

individual as unit of, 109–11, 223n1;
materialist paradigm and, 11, 41;
matter as unit of, 41–42; movement as
medium of, 45, 47–48, 50–53, 55–56;
mutations in, 42–43, 47, 62, 128,
224n7, 225n21; repurposing and, 55,
227nn33–37; scientific methods and,
41–43; selfish motive for, 41–42, 223n3,
224n6; senses and, 46, 225nn19–20
Experience-dependent development,
brain, 100–1, 236nn40–41
Experience shift, 6, 16–17, 22, 26–27,
138, 201, 215n1
Experiential frames, 14, 214nn18–20;
birth, 80–81, 84–85, 91–92, 105–6,
108–9, 231n3; dancing, 16–17, 22,
26–27, 36–38, 215n1; with newborn
infant (Leif), 108–9, 112–14, 125,
131–32, 136; pain, 137–38, 143–45,
154–55, 161–62, 170; pond, movement
in, 203–4, 209–10; teaching dance,
59–60, 74–76, 79; walking and/as
dancing, 39–41, 45–50, 171–72,
179–80, 186–87, 201–2
Eyes, 69, 225n19, 226n27

Feminism, see Ecofeminism
Fetus: brain of, 88–90, 232n10, 233n12;
movement in development of, 88–91,
232nn9–11, 233n12
First Nation Peoples, 254n11
Fogel, Alan, 247n11; on brain, 237n44;
on coregulating, 243n24, 244n31;
on embodied self-awareness (ESA),
211n3, 237n45, 238n51, 252n47; on
emotion, 247n12, 249n26; on ESA
and conceptual self-awareness (CSA),
215n1, 230n26; on expanding
self-awareness, 233n16, 244n36; on
infant awareness, 234n29, 237n44;
on mirror neurons, 244n36; on
movement, importance of, 222n46,
242n20, 253n51; on pain, 247n14,
247n16; on prenatal movements,

279

Index

Fogel, Alan (*continued*) 232*n*11, 233*n*12; on rerepresentation, 243*n*23
Foster, Susan, 212*n*4, 229*n*12, 229*n*14, 244*n*33
Foucault, Michel, 228*n*2, 229*n*7
Foundational fantasy, Brennan on, 213*n*11, 239*n*58
Four arcs, of ritual, 158–61
Fraleigh, Sondra Horton, 229*n*13, 249*n*27
Frymer-Kensky, Tikva, 255*n*18, 256*n*28 259*n*41

Garfinkel, Josef: on communal dancing, 240*n*10, 249*n*25, 251*n*36, 255*n*19, 258*n*40; on dance in agricultural societies, 212*n*8, 240*n*10, 255*n*19, 256*n*21, 258*n*40
Genetic expression: epigentics on, 47, 226*n*22; HOX genes, 224*n*7; as movement enabled, 48, 52, 100–101, 226*n*23, 226*n*27
Ghost Dance, 214*n*14, 258*n*38
Gods and Goddesses: belief in, 193–94, 206, 255*n*18, 259*n*44, 261*n*2; dancing as a, 164–65, 210, 252*n*50, 256*n*28; in ritual, 159, 184, 193–96, 259*n*41
Gould, Stephen Jay, 224*n*7
Graham, Martha, 1, 35, 59, 79–80, 229*n*8, 261*n*54; on communicating participation, 215*n*2; spirit defined by, 68, 230*n*17; technique of, 67–68, 186, 230*n*16; on truth of movement, 222*n*51
Greek art, 212*n*8, 220*n*38
Grimes, Ronald, 253*n*52, 260*n*49; ritual defined by, 246*n*3, 249*n*23, 250*n*30
Grosz, Elizabeth, 220*n*39, 248*n*21

Haraway, Donna, 241*n*16, 253*n*4
Healing: bodily becoming, perspective on, 145–49; as holistic, 147, 247*n*17; materialist view of, 139–43, 246*nn*9–10, 247*n*11; movement as path to, 147–48,

150–54, 253*n*51; origins of ritual dance and, 149–54; pain and, 139–43, 246*nn*4–7; pain as catalyst for, 145–47, 150–54, 163, 247*nn*15–16; as participation in rhythm of bodily becoming, 147–54; ritual and, 149–54, 166–70; *see also* Ritual; Ritual dance
Hegel, G. W. F., 12, 211*n*2, 219*n*34, 229*n*10, 236*n*38, 254*n*8
Heller-Roazen, Daniel, 227*n*30, 231*n*30, 232*n*4, 233*n*13
Homo erectus: cooking and, 227*n*35; cooperative breeding and, 227*n*37, 234*n*30; dancing and, 149, 234*n*31, 248*n*22; evolutionary bottleneck and, 92, 234*n*21; language development in, 100; mimetic skill in, 234*n*31, 248*n*22; running in, 227*n*35; tool use of, 248*n*22
Homo sapiens: dancing and, 105, 149–50, 234*n*31; earlier birth of, 93–94, 96–98, 234*n*21; evolution of, 54–55, 81–82, 92–98, 227*nn*35–37, 234*n*31; evolutionary bottleneck and, 93–94, 98
HOX genes, 224*n*7
Hrdy, Sarah Blaffer: on alloparent-infant bond, 234*nn*28–30, 240*n*3, 240*n*5; on Bowlby, 240*n*6, 241*n*12; on brain, 234*n*30, 242*n*22; on cooperative breeding, 227*n*37, 234*n*26, 245*n*41; on first social bonding, 245*n*40; on infants' need to connect, 234*n*29, 240*n*3, 241n15; on lactation and social intelligence, 240*n*5, 243*n*25; on mothering, 231*n*3
Human evolution, *see* Evolution, human
Humans: as completing own nature, 176, 191–92, 254*n*7; to dance is, 9–10, 45, 53, 57, 94–98, 105, 130–31, 135–36, 150–54, 212*n*5, 249*nn*24–27; distinguishing from animals, 9, 45, 47, 54–56, 96, 173, 180–82, 254*n*6; on overcoming themselves, 22–24, 47–51, 76, 170, 173–74, 217*n*16, 226*n*24; as rhythm of bodily becoming, 4–5, 15,

Index

29–34, 53, 83, 90, 121–25; as ultrasocial,
112; *see also* Dance; Homo sapiens;
specific topics, including Homo erectus
Hunter-gatherers, dancing of, 43–44,
133–35, 240*n*10, 251*n*36, 255*n*18,
256*n*26

Imitation, of intention, 182–83,
255*nn*13–14
Improvisation, 5–6, 74–76, 79, 162; in
ritual, 156, 159–60, 163–65, 168
Impulse to connect, 53–54, 109–36,
239*n*1, 241*n*15; blocked or ignored,
126; in infant development, 119–27
Individuality: attachment, theories of and,
114–17, 240*n*6, 241*n*12; bodily
becoming and, 111–12, 117–19,
124–25, 130–32, 135–36; in dance,
theories of, 115–17, 240*nn*9–10,
241*nn*11–15; evolution and, 47–48,
51–52; materialist paradigm on,
85–86, 109, 110–11; and pain.,
139–40; as patterns of relating,
51–52, 118, 130; relationality and,
118, 124–25, 134–35, 240*n*10,
241*n*16, 242*n*17, 245*n*42; in ritual
theory, 157, 160; *see also* Relationality;
Sociality
Industrialization, 10, 63, 213*n*9, 247*n*15,
261*n*53
Infants: attachment and, 114–15, 123–25;
caregivers and, 96–98, 117, 120–21,
124–27, 132–33, 227*n*37, 234*n*26,
234*n*29, 240*n*5, 243*n*24, 244*n*31,
248*n*22, 249*n*26; culturally specific
patterns learned by, 120–21;
dependence of, 93–96, 111–12, 117;
ethical paradox and, 125; experiential
frame on (Leif), 112–14, 125, 131–32;
as impulse to connect, 118–27,
241*n*15, 245*n*40; movement and
development of, 101–2, 119–27,
242*nn*20–21; movement-making as
key to survival of, 96–98, 101; pain

in, 96, 102, 119–25, 145–46, 240*n*5,
244*n*31; pleasure in, 96, 102, 119–25,
240*n*5, 244*n*31; rerepresentation and,
243*n*23; smiling in, 131–32, 136,
245*n*39; *see also* Birth
Infinity, of bodily self, 78, 231*n*29
Intention, imitation of, 182–83,
255*nn*13–14
Irigaray, Luce, 218*n*29

James, William, 222*n*47
Jones, David, 246*n*7
Junk DNA, 47, 226*n*22

Kant, Immanuel, 211*n*2, 236*n*38, 258*n*34
Keeney, Bradford, 246*n*5, 247*n*17, 248*n*19
Kierkegaard, Søren, 12, 171, 229*n*10,
236*n*38, 240*n*4
Kinetic images, *see* Patterns of Sensation
and Response
Knowledge: of bodily becoming, how to
participate consciously in, 76–79;
bodily becoming view of, 65–66,
70–71; dance as absolute, 59; dance as
enabling condition of all, 65–66,
72–73, 78–79; dance as unique,
67–68, 72–74, 76–79, 230*n*27;
ecokinetic, 8, 175–78, 184–86, 193,
197–99, 206, 260*n*52; materialist
perspectives on dance as, 64–66;
objective, 62–64; reading and writing
and, 62–65, 68–71; sensory education
required for, 73–74, 76–78, 214*n*20,
219*n*30, 231*n*28; *see also* Dance;
Reading and Writing; Sensory
Awareness
Kristeva, Julia, 239*n*58
Kuhn, Thomas, 215*n*3

Labor, upright walking and, 92–98;
see also Birth
Lactation, 112–13, 120, 233*n*12, 240*n*5,
242*n*22, 243*n*25
Langer, Ellen, 211*n*3, 246*n*6, 249*n*24

Langer, Suzanne, 225n18

Language: body and, 228n4, 228n6, 260n48; dance and, 44, 57, 98, 151, 185, 254n9, 257n32; evolution and, 55, 57, 223n5, 227nn36-37, 234n31, 257n29; movement and, 100; see also Reading and Writing; Writing

Lesho, Johanna, 229n15

Lewis-Williams, David, 257n33

Lieberman, Daniel, 227n34, 228n38

Lived body, 232n5

Llinás, Rodolfo: on brain as closed system, 233n14, 239n56; on brain as internalized movement, 212n26, 230n18, 232n10, 237n43; on evolution, 226n27, 236n36; on mindness, 218n26, 233n15, 237n44

Louv, Richard, 255n20, 256n24, 260nn51-52

Love: dancing as experiential source of, 1, 37-38, 60-61, 79, 117, 152-54, 162; for earth, 188, 200-2, 208-9, 261n55; as enabling condition of bodily becoming, 210; environmental ethics and, 261n55; as goal of dance forms, 134-35, 153-54, 201; for life, 214n17; as movement, 52-53, 200-1; of movement, 1, 102; origins of dance in, 133-34; for other humans, 109, 112-13, 135-36, 207, 239n1

Mandalas, body, see Body, maps

Manning, Erin, 243n26

Maps, see Body, maps

Marx, Karl, 16

Massumi, Brian, 214n19, 215n8, 219n31, 221n41, 253n5; on measurement, 216n13; on objects and movement patterns, 243n27, 244n29; on participation, 222n47; on proprioception, 220n36

Materialist paradigm: bodily becoming, philosophy of, emerging from, 22, 217n16; on culture vis-à-vis nature,

173-74; on dance, 11, 20-21, 43-45, 64-66, 82-84, 115-18, 142-43, 173-74; on evolution, 41-43; on healing, 140-42; history of, 10-12, 215n3; ideas comprising, 13-15; on individuality, 109-11; on knowledge, 61-64; on matter, 18-20; on mind over body, 81-82, 85; new materialists and, 12, 24, 213n12, 216n10, 217n21, 218n29; overcoming itself, 13, 21-26, 47, 68-71, 85-86, 111-12, 175-76, 204-8, 217n16

Matter: concept of as basis for materialist paradigm, 11-12, 17-22; dance and, 16-17, 20-21, 26-27, 34-38; dualism of mind and, 18, 24-25, 81-82, 215n5; meaning and, 216n11; as movement, 15, 21-34, 217n17; as resistant to change, 18, 22, 215n4; sensory perception of, as enabled by movement, 31-33, 222n48

Matter-based dance theory, see Materialist paradigm

Matter-based evolution theory, see Materialist paradigm

Matter-based knowledge theory, see Materialist paradigm

McKibben, Bill, 213nn9-10

McNeill, William: on community dancing, 224n8, 224n10, 224n12, 225n16; on dance and language, 257n32; on dancing in early humans, 234n31, 249n28, 255n16

Meaning: as function of movement, 69, 126, 195, 243n23; matter and, 216n11; pain and, 151

Measurement, of movement, 20, 216n13

Medical visit, as ritual, 167-68

Merchant, Carolyn, 213n13, 215n6, 216n9

Merleau-Ponty, Maurice: on the body, 228n6, 237n42, 238n47, 244n29; on psychogenesis and movement, 242n21, 243n28; on relationality, 108

Index

Index

Physics, 217nn18–19; classical, 215n6; conceptual prejudice in, 226n26; quantum, 216n12, 219n32
Pinker, Stephen, 224n14
Plants, 234n31; pain and, 248n20
Plasticity, brain, 103–4, 238nn49–50
Play, in ritual, 159–60, 184–86
Pleasure: from connecting with others, 113–14, 125, 131–33, 136, 240n5; dancing and, 2, 6, 35–36, 43–44, 49, 60–61, 73–74, 134–35, 150–52, 154, 172, 225n17, 230n27; as earthing culture, 184; as guide in bodily becoming, 5–6, 30, 56, 60, 73, 102, 104, 120–26, 150, 179; in infants, 96, 102, 119–25, 240n5, 244n31; of making new movements, 49, 53, 56, 102, 183; of participating in rhythm of bodily becoming, 56, 61, 122–24, 136, 154, 172; as pattern of movement-potential, 145; of reading and writing, 69; in ritual, 165–66, 169, 192; as source of wisdom, 34
Practice, 159, 168, 184
Preacceleration, 243n26
Prefrontal cortex, 99–100, 230n26, 236n37
Proprioception, 211n3, 215n1, 220n36
Psychogenesis, 242n21

Quantum physics, 19, 216n12, 219n32

Ramachandran, V. K., 244n32, 257n30
Ray, Reginald, 252nn44–45
Reading, 77
Reading and writing: alienation from natural world and, 54, 227n31; bodily becoming, perspective on, 69–73, 230n26; body denial in, 70, 228nn4–6; contemporary culture preoccupation with, 73, 197, 260n48; dance influenced by, 64–65, 239n53; knowledge and, 62–65, 69–71, 78; materialist paradigm and, 62–64, 228n4; as patterns of sensation and response, 65–66, 68–71,

230nn18–20; as practice of bodily becoming, 72–73; sensory education by means of, 69, 70–74, 104, 227n31, 239n53; word-world of, 70–71, 74, 230n25
Reason, Kant on, 236n38
Relationality, 32, 34–35, 51–53, 237n44; of brain, 100–1, 237n43; individuality and, 118, 124–27, 134–36, 241n16, 242n17, 245nn40–41; see also Sociality
Relationships, see Impulse to connect; Sociality
Religion: Christian view of dance, 241n11; in culture, 192–95, 257n31, 258nn34–39; dance and, 191–95, 198–99, 214n14, 240n10, 256n26, 258nn37–40, 259nn41–43; expulsion of dance from, 198–99; kinetic images and, 193; in modern Western culture, 11; origins in dance, 44, 57, 152, 192–93, 224n15, 225n16, 240n10, 257n33; as patterns of sensation and response, 192–93; split between science and, 11, 167, 198–99, 259n42; study of, 152, 174, 193, 198; see also Ritual; Ritual dance
Repetition, movement pattern of, 67, 116, 150–52, 237; in rituals, 43, 156, 162–63, 249n24, 251n43, 252n45; sense of spirit and, 152
Reproduction, as evolutionary motive, 41–42
Repurposing, 55, 227nn33–37
Rerepresentation, 243n23
Resistance: as attribute of matter, 18, 22, 25, 29–30, 33, 215n4; in infant movement patterns, 123; in womb, 87
Rhythm of bodily becoming, 4–5; conscious participation in, 8, 34, 53, 57, 90, 105, 129, 147, 169, 207–8; five senses and, 32–33; healing and, 147; human person as, 4–5, 29–34, 53, 83, 90, 121–25; infant as, 121–25; life forms and, 51, 226n25; plasticity and,

285

Rhythm of bodily becoming (*continued*)
103, 238*n*49; ritual and, 153, 157–68;
sensory awareness of, 5; *see also* Bodily
becoming; Philosophy of bodily
becoming; Sensory awareness
Ritual: birth as enabled by, 92, 98; bodily
becoming, as enabled by, 151–54, 161,
162–68; climactic moments of, 164;
communal dance as earliest form of,
140, 156–70; conflict in, 165;
consciousness and, 249*n*23;
cool-down, 160–61, 184; definitions
of, 156, 250*nn*30–33, 251*n*34;
dualistic structure of, 165; efficacy
of as dance, 166–70; four arcs model
for, 157–61; Grimes on, 246*n*3;
materialist approaches to study of,
157, 251*nn*40–41; medical profession
and, 167–68; pain and, 149–51,
163–64, 167–70, 249*nn*24–26,
252*n*45, 252*n*47; as participation in
rhythm of bodily becoming, 151–56,
158–70; patterns of sensation and
response catalyzed by, 154, 161,
166–69; play, 159–60; pleasure and,
165–66, 169, 192; rehearsal, 159, 168,
184; repetition of movement patterns
in, 43, 156, 162–63, 249*n*24, 251n43,
252n45; running as, 138; three-part
model of, 157; transformative power of,
151–54, 163–64, 166–67, 252*nn*44–46;
warm-up, 158–59, 168, 184
Ritual dance, 156–70; in agricultural
societies, 9, 240n10, 255n19, 258*n*40;
as birthing culture, 43–45, 140, 177,
224*n*15, 225*n*16, 240*n*10, 241*n*13,
246*n*3, 254n9; as communal, 140,
151–54, 183–86; as earthing culture,
183–86, 191–97; in hunter-gatherer
cultures, 240*n*10, 241*n*13, 251*n*36,
256*n*26; love and, 154; origins of,
149–54, 249*nn*24–25, 251*n*36;
religion and, 193–97, 240*n*10; sensory
awareness of nature through, 184,

191–92, 255*n*18, 256*n*27; social
cohesion through, 43–45, 115–17,
224*nn*11–13, 225*nn*16–17, 240*n*10;
see also Communal dance
Roszak, Theodore, 213*n*11, 246*n*9, 253*n*3;
on chance, 223*n*4, 225*n*21; on pain,
247*n*15; on survival, 261*n*3
Rouget, Gilbert, 224*n*9
Running, 138, 162; endurance, 227*n*34

San (Bushmen or !Kung) people, 9,
241*n*13, 248*n*19
Science, 10–11, 18–19, 41, 62–63,
98–100, 216*nn*11–12, 217*n*119; split
between religion and, 11, 167, 198–99,
259*n*42; *see also* Materialist paradigm
Scientific method, 11, 19, 41–42, 216*n*13
Self-awareness, 102–3; in animals, 102;
conceptual (CSA) distinguished from
embodied (ESA), 215*n*1, 230*n*26; as
emerging via experience of dancing,
16–17, 21–22, 26–27, 36–38, 149,
215*n*1; experience shift from dancing,
16–17, 22, 26–27, 215*n*1; Fogel on,
211*n*3, 233*n*12, 237*nn*44–45, 238*n*51,
252*n*47; Fogel on expansion of,
233*n*16, 238*n*51, 244*n*36, 249*n*26;
Merleau-Ponty on movement and,
238*n*47; pain as state of, 247*n*14;
as sensory-motor image, 233*n*15,
237*n*44
Selfishness, as driver of evolution, 41–42,
115–16, 223*n*3, 224*n*6
Self-who-did, 103
Sensation and response, movement as
both, 28, 220*n*37; *see also* Patterns of
sensation and response
Senses, five: alphabet and, 230*n*19; as
creative, 32; in dancing and writing,
73–74; evolution and, 46, 225*nn*19–20;
matter and, 11, 18, 32–33; nature and,
46, 256*n*22; as patterns of movement,
31–33, 46, 222*n*46; perception through,
31–33, 222*nn*48–49

Index

Sensory awareness, 5–6; birth and, 107; in children, 96, 104, 122, 238*n*52; deadening of, 8, 104, 126, 169, 200, 239*n*54; Duncan and, 220*n*38; of earth within, 178, 185; as educated by dance, 21, 61, 67, 72–75, 149, 151, 185, 214*n*20, 219*n*30, 230*n*27, 244*n*36; ESA and mindfulness contrasted with, 211*n*3; in fetus, 88–89, 233*n*12; as guide to participating in rhythm of bodily becoming, 5–6, 76–77, 90–91, 101, 107, 110, 126, 132, 135, 139–40, 161, 178, 237*nn*45–46; healing through cultivation of, 104–5, 147–48, 151, 239*n*55, 248*nn*18–19, 252*n*45; as knowledge requirement, 76–78, 231*n*28; lived body and, 231*n*28; Llinás on brain and, 230*n*18, 239*n*56; mirror neurons and, 128–29, 244*n*36; mobilization of, senses as, 32; of movement that is making me, 5, 21–22, 58, 76, 110, 126, 132, 135, 151, 211*n*3, 220*n*36, 254*n*8; of natural world, 184–85, 191–92, 256*n*27, 260*n*52; practice required for, 129, 206–8, 230*n*26, 245*n*37; prefrontal cortex and, 100; proprioception and, 220*n*36; in ritual, 158–63, 168–69, 178
Sensory-motor cortex, 99, 235*n*33
Serres, Michel, 219*n*30, 228*n*5
Sheets-Johnstone, Maxine, 215*n*6, 217*n*17, 218*n*28, 221*n*40, 228*n*4, 228*n*6, 253*n*2
Shlain, Leonard, 230*n*20, 259*nn*44–46
Shubin, Neil, 221*nn*42–44, 227*n*33, 232*n*9
Siegel, Daniel, 236*n*41
Skiing, 60, 61
Smiling, 113, 122, 131–32, 136, 172, 245*n*39
Smith, Jonathan Z., 251*n*34, 257*n*31
Social cohesion: communal dancing as means of, 44–45, 115–17, 134–36,

153–54, 164, 225*nn*16–17, 240*n*10; *see also* Sociality
Sociality, 111–12; dance and, 115–19, 126–27, 130, 132, 135–36, 240*n*9–10, 241*nn*11–15; Dunbar on, 240*n*3; ethical paradox of individuality and, 112, 118, 124–27, 130, 135; first dance and, 132, 245*n*40; individuality as created through, 118–19, 124–25, 134–35, 241*n*16; lactation and, 243*n*25; neocortex, evolution of and, 93, 111–12, 240*nn*2–3; *see also* Bodily becoming, Impulse to connect
Specialization, *see* Stratification/specialization, cultural development
Spinoza, Benedict, 222*n*48, 243*n*27
Spirit: communal dancing and, 153, 249*n*28; Graham's definition of, 68; Hegel on, 219*n*34, 254*n*8; idea of, as emerging through dance, 103, 152–53; in materialist paradigm, 85; patterns of movement and, 152; pleasure from becoming, 154
Spiritual knowledge, dance viewed as, 65, 229*n*15
Spiritual necessity, dance as, 140, 152–54
St. Denis, Ruth, 12, 252*n*50
Stratification/specialization, cultural development in, 189–90, 193–95
Survival, human, 10, 31, 47, 93, 116, 131, 179, 209, 261*n*3; dance and, 43–44, 96–98, 177–78
Synkinesia, 257*n*30

Taylor, Mark C., 215*n*5, 228*n*3, 229*n*9, 251*n*34
Technology, 35, 57, 206, 227*n*35
Tools, 94, 98, 176, 180–83, 188–90, 236*n*39, 255*n*16; books as, 197; movement patterns as, 159, 181–83, 248*n*22, 250*n*29, 257*n*30; movement patterns in use of, 56–57, 98–99, 177–78, 181, 185
Trance, 43, 164, 224*nn*9–10, 251*n*36

Index